Young People, Physical Activity and the Everyday
Living Physical Activity
Edited by Jan Wright and Doune Macdonald

Muslim Women and Sport
Edited by Tansin Benn, Gertrud Pfister and Haifaa Jawad

Inclusion and Exclusion Through Youth Sport
Edited by Symeon Dagkas and Kathleen Armour

Sport Education
International Perspectives
Edited by Peter Hastie

Cooperative Learning in Physical Education
An International Perspective
Edited by Ben Dyson and Ashley Casey

Equity and Difference in Physical Education, Youth Sport and Health
A Narrative Approach
Edited by Fiona Dowling, Hayley Fitzgerald and Anne Flintoff

Game Sense
Pedagogy for Performance, Participation and Enjoyment
Richard Light

Ethics in Youth Sport
Policy and Pedagogical Applications
Stephen Harvey and Richard Light

GAME SENSE

Pedagogy for performance, participation and enjoyment

Richard Light

Routledge
Taylor & Francis Group

LONDON AND NEW YORK

First published 2013
by Routledge
2 Park Square, Milton Park, Abingdon, Oxon OX14 4RN

Simultaneously published in the USA and Canada
by Routledge
711 Third Avenue, New York, NY 10017

Routledge is an imprint of the Taylor & Francis Group, an informa business

© 2013 Richard Light

British Library Cataloguing in Publication Data
A catalogue record for this book is available from the British Library

Library of Congress Cataloging-in-Publication Data
Light, Richard (Richard Lawrence)
  Game sense : pedagogy for performance, participation and enjoyment / Richard Light.
    p. cm. — (Routledge studies in physical education and youth sport)
  Includes bibliographical references and index.
  1. Physical education and training—Study and teaching. 2. Sports—Study and teaching.
  3. Sports for children—Study and teaching. 4. Coaching (Athletics) 5. Sports for
  children—Coaching. I. Title.
  GV361.L49 2013
  613.707--dc23
                                                                    2012003375

ISBN 13: 978-0-415-53287-7 hbk
ISBN 13: 978-0-415-53288-4 pbk
ISBN 13: 978-0-203-11464-3 ebook

Typeset in Bembo
by RefineCatch Limited, Bungay, Suffolk

CONTENTS

FIGURES

PREFACE

After six years of coaching rugby in Japan with three years at elite university level (Kansai A League) and three years coaching at high school level I returned to Australia in 1996 to undertake a PhD at the University of Queensland (UQ). Most of my teaching at UQ was in games teaching and soon after my arrival I was asked to attend a seminar conducted by Rod Thorpe. For the first thirty minutes at the seminar I was sceptical because what Rod was saying challenged a lifetime of experiences as a player and coach and the deeply embedded, unquestioned beliefs about good coaching and teaching arising from it. However, as the session unfolded to include participating in modified games, discussions with others at the seminar, reflection upon what we were doing in the games and Rod's calm, logical and smooth delivery, my resistance ebbed and I started to 'get it'.

I remember well what was going through my mind as I drove home after the seminar. I had been challenged, unsettled and stimulated to reflect critically and think deeply about how I had been coached and taught and how I had coached and taught up until that day. As I worked at UQ teaching TGfU, developing units of study and working through Rod's ideas about teaching and coaching, I was encouraged by my students' positive responses. My belief in this approach was later reinforced upon taking up an appointment at the University of Melbourne, where I initially taught pre-service, generalist, primary school teachers in a programme that emphasized physical education. Their responses as learners and their experiences of using this approach in schools made teaching a pleasure for me (see, for example, Light 2002; Light and Butler 2005). My attendance at the first International TGfU conference, convened by Dr Joy Butler in Plymouth, New Hampshire the next year (2001), and the enthusiasm that permeated that conference, boosted my passion for TGfU and my belief in it.

At this time Game Sense had been developed through collaboration between Rod Thorpe, local coaches and the Australian Sports Commission (ASC) and had attracted considerable attention in Australia. I initially used the term Game Sense for the approach I was taking but after attending the first international TGfU conference in Plymouth I saw the sense in using the same term, TGfU, across the globe to promote it. I did, however, tend to use Game Sense in relation to coaching to separate it from teaching in schools. Soon after the Plymouth conference I put my hand up to convene the second conference in Melbourne in 2003 and joined the TGfU Task Force formed at the 2002 AIESEP World Congress in La Coruña, Spain.

In 2003 I brought Rod Thorpe out to Melbourne as a keynote speaker and had many opportunities to talk with him informally. During discussions about TGfU he said to me that what was being developed was very good but perhaps it was not really TGfU as he had first proposed in the 1980s. This started me thinking about what I was doing and what the differences were, if any, between TGfU and Game Sense. Over the following few years I came to recognize that what I was doing was, in significant ways, different to the approach being promoted in the TGfU literature. The core ideas of learning through games and using questioning in a learner-centred, inquiry-based approach were the same but some of the details were different. I felt Game Sense was less structured and looser than TGfU. It seemed to be more like the original idea of TGfU proposed by Bunker and Thorpe, so I began using the term Game Sense. Also, as I developed a more sophisticated theoretical framework informed by constructivism, I found that there were some small, yet significant, tensions between this perspective on learning and some aspects of TGfU teaching as described in the literature.

As Dr Steve Mitchell suggested in his keynote speech at the 2005 TGfU conference in Hong Kong, the different versions of the same basic approach can be seen as different pathways up the same mountain. I agree with this analogy and am writing on one of those pathways. Although there is now a large literature on TGfU, there has been little specifically written on Game Sense. The terms are also often used interchangeably, with some confusion over any differences between them. My other motivation for writing this book is to emphasize the importance of establishing a dialectic between theories of learning and pedagogical practice. I came into academia comparatively late, with experience of teaching and coaching across a range of settings, but soon developed a strong interest in theories that could explain, enhance and make sense of learning. I have written on the theorization of learning in and through games and other movement but have developed my own deep understandings of it through being creative in trying it out in practice (see, for example, Light 2008a, 2009; Light and Wallian 2008). There is nothing more professionally satisfying for me than seeing theory working in practice and this is a prime goal of this book.

It is easy enough to talk of the importance of theory or of the mutually informing nature of practice and theory but it inevitably proves to be an insurmountable challenge, with teachers and coaches wary of theory and academics unable to show its relevance to practitioners. In writing this book I have built on the resources provided by the ASC in the late 1990s, including the handbook by Nicole den Duyn (1997), the game activity cards and the video featuring Rod Thorpe by drawing on relevant research conducted over the past two decades, contemporary learning theory and my own experiences of teaching and coaching using Game Sense. This is an attempt to link theory and practice to empower practitioners by providing a deep understanding of learning and the features of Game Sense pedagogy that shape and enhance it. It is an approach I have taken in my recent writing that, I feel, is essential for the development and implementation of Games Sense and any similar approaches.

ACKNOWLEDGEMENTS

First, I would like to thank my wife, Chiho, and my daughter, Amy, for putting up with my devotion to writing this book on something that has, at best, only fleeting relevance for them. I would also like to thank all the students in schools and universities, players in junior and senior teams, teachers and coaches around the world that I have taught using Game Sense. For me it has been an ongoing process of experimentation and reflective practice within which their actions and affective and articulated responses have been invaluable in developing and refining my approach. I also acknowledge the help of the colleagues with whom I have taught, talked about and conducted research on Game Sense, TGfU and other sports pedagogy. In particular, this includes colleagues in Australia, France, the UK and Japan, where, in each case, I have learnt through genuine dialogue and the sharing of ideas and experiences, and have drawn on ideas and ways of thinking that were both intellectually challenging and stimulating.

More specifically, I acknowledge the valuable assistance provided by Christina Curry, who acted as a practitioner sounding board, co-authored two sport-specific chapters in the book with me and organized some of the testimonials on the sport-specific chapters. I thank those teachers, academics, pre-service teachers and coaches who fieldtested the draft version of the book for me and provided such valuable and positive feedback. I also acknowledge the work of my daughter Amy in providing the digital line drawings for some of the activities in Part II despite her own demanding commitments to sport and study. Peter Robson at Carey Baptist Grammar was also very helpful in providing many of the photographs used in the book and getting permission to use them.

Finally, I would like to thank the positive and encouraging reviews by anonymous peers approached by the Routledge Studies in Physical Education and Youth Sport series editor Professor David Kirk, and the very helpful suggestions they made for improving the book.

ABBREVIATIONS

AFL	Australian Football League
AGQTP	Australian Government Quality Teacher Programme
AIESEP	Association Internationale des Ecoles Supérieures d'Education Physique
ANZ	Australia and New Zealand
ASC	Australian Sports Commission
CLT	complex learning theory
FIFA	Fédération Internationale de Football Association
FIT	Federation of International Touch
FMS	Fundamental Motor Skills
GCA	Games Concept Approach
GPAI	Game Performance Assessment Instrument
HPE	Health and Physical Education
IOC	International Olympic Committee
IRB	International Rugby Board
NBA	National Basketball Association
NESB	non-English-speaking background
NSW	New South Wales
PDHPE	Personal Development, Health and Physical Education
PE	physical education
PETE	Physical Education Teacher Education
QTF	Quality Teaching Framework
RFU	Rugby Football Union
SIG	Special Interest Group
TG	Tactical Games
TDLM	Tactical-Decision Learning Model

TGfU	Teaching Games for Understanding
TSAP	Team Sport Assessment Procedure
UQ	University of Queensland
VSF	Victoria Soccer Federation

PART I

1

INTRODUCTION

Bunker and Thorpe's (1982) modest publication proposing a model for teaching games in secondary schools that located learning within games put forward quite radical ideas about how games should be taught. It presented a challenge to the accepted focus on fundamental skills and was based upon their observations of how the focus on technique produced technically sound students who were not good games players. This publication and those that followed soon after stimulated a brief period of interest that was not sustained (Holt, Strean and Begoechea 2002). Bunker and Thorpe's concept of teaching games by teaching *in* and *through* games did not really begin to take off until a little over ten years ago. This has seen Teaching Games for Understanding (TGfU) and a range of variations and similar approaches develop into one of the main areas of research interest in the physical education literature.

The past decade or so has seen growing interest in similar student/player-centred, games-based approaches to coaching and teaching games and sport. The identification of constructivist theories of learning at the end of the 1990s as a means of understanding learning in and through games played a significant part in this revival of interest by triggering interest from researchers in the possibilities offered by TGfU and the growing number of variations and similar approaches (see, for example, Kirk and Macdonald 1998; Gréhaigne and Godbout 1998b). This interest was stimulated by the establishment of a regular series of international conferences beginning in Plymouth, New Hampshire in the USA in 2001 that further stimulated research interest while also developing practitioner interest. The first conference, convened by Dr Joy Butler, attracted a large number of international researchers interested in TGfU and a significant number of local teachers. This was a turning point in the revival of interest in TGfU, with the ensuing publication of the conference proceedings beginning a valuable and ongoing series of edited publications on TGfU. The response of those who

FIGURE 1.1   Practising hockey in small-sided games

attended was very positive and it was clear that this was a good idea that should be continued. I convened the second conference in 2003 at the University of Melbourne in Australia, which attracted an even larger number of academics, with more from Asia, including a large cohort of teachers from Singapore and some local sport coaches. The third conference was held in Hong Kong, where teacher interest continued, with the fourth held in Vancouver, Canada, featuring a large number of Canadian teachers. The fifth conference is to be convened in July 2012 where it all started, at Loughborough University in the UK.

TGfU variations developed from it, such as Game Sense (den Duyn 1997) in Australia, the Singaporean Games Concept Approach (GCA) and Tactical Games (Griffin, Mitchell and Oslin 1997) in the USA, and similar approaches such as Play Practice (Launder 2001) and the French Tactical-Decision Learning Model (Gréhaigne, Richard and Griffin 2005) form one of the more popular areas of research in the physical education literature. Play Practice shares much with TGfU but is not derived from it, as Launder emphasized at the Melbourne TGfU conference in 2003. In his keynote speech Rod Thorpe suggested TGfU and Play Practice were brothers, but in his invited address Alan Launder replied by emphasizing their differences, saying that, at best, they were distant cousins. There have been a number of edited books and conference proceedings devoted to TGfU that have been developed from the international conference series (see, for example, Butler *et al.* 2003; Light, Swabey and Brooker 2003; Liu, Li and Cruz 2006; Griffin and Butler 2005; Hopper, Butler and Storey 2009; Butler and Griffin 2010) and special issues of journals published on TGfU (Rink 1996; Light 2005a).

As well as stimulating interest from researchers and teachers, games-based coaching has caught the attention of sport coaching researchers and coaches. Alan Launder's (2001) book on Play Practice is perhaps the best known example but a range of other books on coaching suggesting a similar games-based approach to coaching have been published (for example see Breed and Spittle 2011; Harrison 2002; Slade 2010), with a special issue of the *Journal of Physical Education New Zealand* devoted to the games approach to coaching (Light 2006). There has, however, been little specifically written outlining the Game Sense approach since the publication of a slim handbook (den Duyn 1997) that formed part of the valuable Australian Sports Commission (ASC) Game Sense package produced in the late 1990s.

I wrote this book in response to this lack of writing specifically focused on Game Sense and a more general lack of authored books written on game-based, understanding approaches to teaching and coaching. This involves addressing what I see as a need to actually define or outline what Game Sense is and how it is different to TGfU and the other games-based approaches to coaching and teaching. As I outline in Chapter 2, TGfU has developed over three decades into something that is, in some ways, different to Bunker and Thorpe's original ideas (Thorpe and Bunker 2008; Almond and Launder 2010). Game Sense has also developed since 1997, but not as much, because it has received far less attention and what has been published specifically on Game Sense in physical education and coaching has been written by scholars in Australia (see, for example, Brooker, Kirk and Braiuka 2000; Brooker and Abbot 2001; Light and Georgakis 2005b; Light and Evans 2010). There are some practical publications available that offer useful ideas for taking up a Game Sense type of approach, with many very useful examples and training games that are both sport-specific and generic (see, for example, Pill 2007; Slade 2010; Breed and Spittle 2011). However, there is nothing that pays significant attention to pedagogy (how to do instead of just what to do), is strongly research informed, rigorously theorized with a sustained line of thinking that still offers practical ideas.

The idea for writing this book arose from the development of my teaching in collaboration with several colleagues in different universities (particularly at the University of Sydney with Dr Steve Georgakis) tied into my programme of research on pedagogy and learning. It was also motivated by my work with pre-service and in-service teachers and coaches in Game Sense workshops in Australia, Macau, Taiwan, Japan, France, Canada and the UK. In my teaching I have continually been pleased with student and teacher responses to the Game Sense approach and have developed teaching that balances the need for them to understand basic theory, read the research and experience it as both learners and teachers (or coaches). In my more recent work I have sought to establish a dialectic between theory and practice for them to become mutually informing that has involved grounding theory in practice (see, for example, Light 2008a; Light and Wallian 2008). My work with French colleagues, and with Professor Nathalie Wallian at the Université de Franche Comté in particular, has helped me work through this challenge. This dialectic between theory and practice and my attempt to facilitate a balance between theoretical and practical learning is reflected in the book. For readers to get the most from the book they need to move between the chapters in Part I and the practical chapters in Part II, think, and develop a stronger and deeper understanding of this pedagogy as they put the ideas to work.

One of the key features of Game Sense, TGfU and similar approaches is the understanding that learners develop about playing the game or sport rather than just being able to perform techniques isolated from the game. I take a similar approach to helping teachers and coaches learn to use Game Sense. I want teachers and coaches to have a basic understanding of how humans learn and how Game Sense pedagogy can enhance and shape this learning to empower them in their teaching and coaching to make decisions about how they teach and what they teach rather than relying on handouts. At the University of Sydney, where Game Sense formed a strong theme in the personal development, health and Physical Education Teacher Education (PETE) programme, I was very pleased to receive e-mails from some students on their practicum and a few who had recently graduated and taken up positions in schools outlining units or games they had developed and tested in their teaching. Many of these I then used in my teaching of pre-service teachers. This provides an example of the value of helping pre-service teachers develop deep understanding of what they are doing and how teaching Game Sense always involves learning for the teacher or coach. Drawing on Davis and Sumara (1997), this can be seen as the teacher/coach and students/players being partners in learning.

As busy professionals, teachers and coaches often look for practical ideas that they can immediately implement and can be disinclined to spend time reading theory because they don't see its relevance. Indeed, they can be quite averse to anything tagged as theory. The problem with this is that they can become too dependent upon 'experts' to provide quick-fix solutions to immediate problems and fail to build enough of an understanding of learning and pedagogy to become independent enquirers. From my experience of teaching undergraduate physical education and health teachers I have found that beginning with positive first-hand experiences of Game Sense, asking students to reflect upon and analyse this experience, then explaining it through understandable theory works well in producing thinking, independent games teachers. While I still get some students asking for ideas on teaching a particular sport during teaching experience or after graduation, I have also had some great ideas come in from them as I outlined in the previous paragraph. In this way they apply their knowledge and develop their own games and activities that, with colleagues, I have often taken up and taught to the next 'generation' of PETE students.

Taking this same approach in setting out this book means that it is necessary for those reading and using it to begin to take a Game Sense approach, or to further develop their Game Sense teaching, to read it all and not just pick out an odd game or activity to use at training or in class like picking items from the shelves of the supermarket. However, I have not in any way been prescriptive about precisely how to teach or what to teach. Some publications on TGfU have set out to clearly define and determine how it should be taught, step by step. I have taken a different approach that I feel sits better with the very notion of Game Sense developed by Rod Thorpe and the ASC. Instead of setting out 'how to teach Game Sense' I have, instead, set out a framework for Game Sense teaching and coaching within which practitioners can make decisions about how and what they teach by drawing on my own experiences of teaching to offer *examples* of a Game Sense approach to a range of major sports/games. Working within this framework provides more freedom and room to move for teachers and coaches but does then require them to read and think through the chapters in Part I and to make connections between this section (Chapter 5 in particular) and the chapters in Part II.

In the practical chapters I draw on my own experiences of using these units or activities but try to outline problems that have arisen for me or might arise in teaching or coaching. The exceptions to this are Chapters 9 and 16, where I asked Christina Curry, from the University of Western Sydney, to collaborate with me by drawing on her experience of teaching ultimate frisbee and oztag to undergraduate students and secondary school students. Every activity or modified game presented in this book has thus been tried and tested in the field. The most important thing for people using this book is to understand that it is the pedagogy that is important and to have an idea of how learning emerges or unfolds from it. Many teachers and coaches use modified games but don't get maximum value from them because they don't adopt a student/player-centred approach such as Game Sense (see, for example, Light and Evans 2010). The practical examples are just that. They are only *examples* from my teaching experience (and some from Christina Curry's experiences). They are drawn from experiences of teaching in pre-service teacher education programmes, coach education, primary school physical education, secondary school physical education, teacher and coach workshops and undergraduate and postgraduate workshops in Australia, Europe, Asia and North America.

I have set out the practical chapters as a unit of work beginning with a simple game and building in complexity as learning progresses to culminate in a full version of the game or a modified version of the game. This is intended to show how physical education teachers can structure and enhance learning by moving from simple to complex learning environments while building and scaffolding on previously generated knowledge. Generalist primary school teachers could, alternatively, just take one game and teach it for a single physical education lesson. Although a sound understanding of games is certainly very helpful it is not a prerequisite. Primary (elementary) school generalist teachers should not be intimidated by the challenge of teaching games due to any concern over a lack of specific experience or knowledge of the sport. Taking up a Game Sense approach means that their understanding of pedagogy and the student-centred nature of it is more important and that they will learn about tactics and skill as they teach by facilitating learning and, as Davis and Sumara (1997) suggest, becoming a partner in it (also see Light and Georgakis 2005a). On the other hand, coaches of youth teams would typically have a sound understanding of the sport they are coaching. They might still, however, just take one game, but it would be focused on a particular aspect of play that they want to specifically work on and adapt to their needs and to their players' ages, experience, dispositions and knowledge. While using the activities and modified games presented in the practical section (Part II) I want to repeat my suggestion that teachers and coaches go back and re-read sections of Part I when necessary to solve problems or just improve their Game Sense teaching/coaching. Teaching and coaching must always involve learning for the teachers and coaches as well as their students/ players.

The book

The first six chapters provide an understanding of the development of Game Sense, of how learning takes place through it, the differences between teaching games in physical education and coaching sport when adopting a Game Sense approach, an outline of its key pedagogical features and a chapter on assessment. These six chapters cover important issues and considerations for the adoption of a Game Sense approach that are linked to the following eleven chapters, focused on using a Game Sense approach for teaching/coaching specific sports. This is not a separation of theory and practice but, instead, an attempt to ground theory in practice to establish a dialectic between them. It is essential to understand and refer to Chapters 1–6 when implementing the units or particular activities presented in Chapters 7–17 or when adapting them to particular needs, learners and/or desired learning outcomes. In this way Chapter 5 is likely to be most useful in taking up the Game Sense pedagogy to get the most from the modified games and activities suggested in the sport-specific chapters.

Each of Chapters 7–11 is devoted to a particular team sport and with a strong emphasis on invasion games as these are the most common and arguably the best suited to a Game Sense approach. As I have suggested, moving between the sport-specific chapters and Chapters 1–6 will help enable teachers and coaches to successfully implement the examples and empower them to understand how to modify and adapt them and to build upon them in developing their own practical ideas. Just as the learners (students/players) should formulate ideas, test them and evaluate them, so teachers and coaches should be prepared to try out the ideas suggested in this book for teaching/coaching, reflect upon them, evaluate them, make changes and try again.

Chapters 1–6

There is now a range of student/player-centred, game-based approaches to teaching and coaching that are similar to TGfU, with many, like Game Sense, directly derived from it. There is also some confusion about what Game Sense is and how it is different to TGfU. I intentionally use capital letters to differentiate *Game Sense* as a distinct pedagogical approach from the idea of *game sense* as a broad concept of embodied, practical understanding of the game (a practical sense of the game or what Bourdieu [1986] calls *le sens pratique*). Indeed, the blurring of differences between the two uses of the term leads to misinterpretation of Game Sense and often to neglect of its pedagogy by teachers and coaches (see, for example, Light and Evans 2010). Chapter 2 traces the development of Game Sense as a variation of TGfU focused on sport coaching to highlight the differences and similarities between them while touching on some important issues in the use of Game Sense for teachers, coaches, students and academics. Among these are not only the influences that cultural and social contexts exert on the teaching or coaching of Game Sense and TGfU in local settings, but also the ways in which their development is influenced by larger social, cultural, economic and political contexts. Despite recognition in the literature of the importance of context for learning, there has been little attention in the TGfU literature paid to the larger cultural and social contexts or fields within which learning environments are constructed.

Game Sense was proposed by Bunker and Thorpe (1982) to meet practical needs in the development of tactically informed games players, but in 1998 researchers suggested that learning occurring through the use of approaches such as TGfU and Game Sense could be better understood or explained by drawing on constructivist perspectives on learning (Kirk and Macdonald 1998; Gréhaigne and Godbout 1998b). Chapter 3 looks at this theorization of the learning that occurs in and through Game Sense and which draws on constructivist perspectives on learning to enable us to *see* what is going on. This then allows coaches and teachers to understand, explain and enhance the learning that occurs when using Game Sense or TGfU (Light 2009). Such a theoretical understanding can empower them to maximize learning opportunities and critically reflect upon practice in an ongoing process of developing and refining their teaching and coaching. The theorization of learning that occurs when using Game Sense, TGfU or similar approaches by using constructivism also facilitates the alignment of good physical education pedagogy with good pedagogy in any subject area of the school curriculum, from outdoor education to mathematics and science.

While there is some overlap between games teaching in physical education and sport coaching, there are also very significant differences in aims, methods, cultures and measures of success. Physical education teachers have to deal with far more individual variation in skill, attitude and motivation in a typical class than coaches need to deal with in a sport team at any level. In most sport teams, because players choose to participate, they tend to be more motivated and more interested than many unwilling participants in PE classes. Sport teams are also organized, not only according to age, but also according to ability, meaning that there is less variation between skill levels than we typically find in a PE class.

Coaching contexts, aims and approaches also vary, from coaching five-year-old children to coaching the most elite and highly paid athletes in the world.

Chapter 4 looks at the differences between teaching and coaching in relation to adopting a Game Sense approach, with some suggestions about how this book might be used differently according to the context. Chapter 5 outlines what Game Sense is, its aims and its pedagogical features. It then examines some of the challenges involved for teachers and coaches in taking it up to offer ideas on adapting to this quite different approach. I intentionally avoid any prescription about how it must be done or setting up any step-by-step process or drawing on the TGfU model in its original form or modified forms suggested by some researchers (see, for example, Kirk and MacPhail 2002). Instead, I offer a framework for taking up a Game Sense approach with enough flexibility for teachers and coaches to adapt it to their own beliefs, the nature of their students or players and the particular circumstances within which they work. I do this in the hope that the ideas in this book on teaching and coaching team sports will have some positive influence on teaching and coaching in schools and sports clubs by allowing teachers and coaches to determine the degree to which they want to take up and use these ideas without feeling that it has to be all or nothing.

Chapter 6 completes Part I by looking at assessment. The holistic nature of the Game Sense approach makes it very different to traditional technical approaches that focus on the mastery of technique separate to the game and, therefore, it requires different methods of assessment in order to be authentic. In Chapter 6 I discuss the issue of authentic assessment for Game Sense teaching and briefly outline the Game Performance Assessment Instrument (GPAI) but focus more on the Team Sport Assessment Procedure (TSAP) as there has been far less written on it. This is clearly a significant issue for teachers taking up a Game Sense approach for both providing useful information on learning and making assessment part of the learning process.

Chapters 7–17 (sport-specific)

Each of Chapters 7–17 focuses on a particular team game and offers a progressively sequenced number of activities or modified games that might be used as a unit of work in a physical education programme. Each activity/game builds on the knowledge developed or constructed in the previous game in a scaffolding process moving the learners from simple to more complex games. Some of the activities are classic, small-sided, modified games, with the need for difficult skills reduced to allow for intellectual engagement and the development of tactical complexity. However, some other activities are more like traditional 'skill drills' but are contextualized to different degrees in physical environments that require and develop perceptual ability and low-level decision-making. This reflects the book's broad and inclusive approach to Game Sense to include a spectrum of activities from contextualized skill work to complex, small-sided games as content, yet retaining an emphasis on Game Sense pedagogy.

When using the chapter as a unit of work in physical education teachers should consider the knowledge, skills and inclinations of their students (Gréhaigne, Richard and Griffin 2005) and be prepared to modify the games to make them easier or more challenging, as outlined in Chapter 5. They should also be prepared to add or take out games to suit their specific situation. The modified games we use can also be easily adapted to other sports. For example, a 6 v. 6 game in which each team must complete six passes to score a point (tally ball), used in Chapter 12 on basketball, is used in the netball chapter (Chapter 13) by just changing the ball and in the Australian football chapter (Chapter 9) by changing the ball and making it a handball instead of a pass. There is also a possibility here to highlight the common tactical aspects of sports by having students play this game but letting them use different balls and techniques. The activities I use can be used across any games within the same game category (invasion, striking, net/wall and target games). For example, this is evident in the units on cricket (Chapter 14) and softball (Chapter 15), where I use the simple game of 'around the cone' that helps develop the same tactical knowledge while developing skills specific to the game. In the cricket unit the ball is placed on a batting tee just off the ground, to be struck by a cricket bat in a straight drive fashion, with the bat in a vertical position, but in the softball unit the ball sits on a T-ball tee and is struck with a lateral swing of the bat. Indeed the two units on cricket and softball provide a good example of how the same basic training game can be adapted to the specifics of the sport.

Primary school teachers looking for a fun game that helps students learn to play a particular sport as a one-off activity can just select a single modified game from the practical section. Over time, this approach will help the students learn a great deal about tactics in general across a game category, much like the idea of non-specific tactics and tactical concepts developed in the *Ballschule* approach (Memmert and Roth 2007) and used in Slade's (2010) book on transforming play. The social interaction involved in these games and the development of understanding makes them fun and motivating. On the other hand, primary school teachers can still take a unit approach, moving learners through games that increase in complexity and build on previous knowledge.

While a youth sport coach will likely value his/her players having fun, he/she will design training sessions to achieve specific outcomes typically related to preparation for upcoming matches or to the development of the team's perform- ance over the season. For this purpose coaches can take one specific modified game or activity from the practical section and adapt it to suit their purpose and the setting that they are working in. For those first experimenting with a Game Sense approach this might involve just including a Game Sense activity or two in their normal training session, but coaches using a predominantly games-based approach to coaching will work it into their normal regime of training to build on or lead into other game-based activities. While moving from a directive, 'command' style of teaching (Mosston 1972) to a student/player-centred teaching/coaching approach typically presents a challenge, beginning by introducing a few discrete games and seeing how they work could provide an easier way of taking up Game Sense. It also takes time for students/players to adapt to this style of teaching/coaching.

All but two of the practical chapters provide suggestions drawn from my experiences of teaching developed through reflective practice on my part and informed by relevant research and learning theory. This experience includes teaching and coaching across quite diverse settings ranging from coaching rugby in Japan for six years to teaching cricket in France and Australian football in Taiwan. In these settings I have learnt the importance of, and the need to account for, the specific nature of context that includes the age and experience of the learners, what knowledge and dispositions they bring with them and the socio-cultural context (see, for example, Light 1999). I have used these modified games and activities in most of my teaching with pre-service teachers (and some study-ing coaching) but I have also worked with coaches, in-service teachers, post-graduate students and primary school and secondary students. In these settings I have encountered challenges and problems in implementing Game Sense peda-gogy that required critical reflection, thinking and the development of an ability to manipulate the physical and socio-cultural environment to overcome these challenges. Certainly, the ability to be a critically reflective practitioner is central to being able to implement a Game Sense approach.

In 2007, when I was teaching masters students to play cricket in France, their complete lack of knowledge of cricket, or of any other striking game, presented a problem I had not faced before. This forced me to 'step back' a little from a Game Sense approach to do some technical work on batting and bowling before returning to modified games that I had to adjust to the students' knowledge and abilities. While this is programmed into the Tactical Games approach, it is only done when necessary in Game Sense. Beginning Game Sense teachers and coaches will invariably be confronted with similar challenges in making such a significant change and will need to have a reasonably good understanding of what they are trying to do and why. Through my own ongoing process of devel-oping my approach to Game Sense teaching and coaching I have learnt to adapt and sometimes compromise, but my faith in this approach to teaching and coaching is always reconfirmed and my enthusiasm for it enhanced. The two chapters on oztag (Chapter 8) and ultimate frisbee (Chapter 16) were written in collaboration with Christina Curry, who has recent experience as head of a PDHPE department in a large government secondary school in Sydney. She is now working as an academic and completing a PhD on implementing TGfU in an Australian secondary school (not the one she taught in). I have not had first-hand experience of teaching oztag and ultimate frisbee, so asked her to draw on her own experience of teaching these sports using a Game Sense approach and to write these two chapters in collaboration with me.

Once I had written the draft of the book I distributed copies of it to practi-tioners to test, evaluate and let me know what they thought of it. The feedback was all very positive, which pleased me and confirmed my belief that the book could contribute toward improving teaching and coaching and the experiences of students and players. The practitioners included primary (elementary) school generalist teachers, PDHPE (Personal Development, Health and Physical Education) secondary school teachers, university lecturers, coaches and sport development officers. Their comments on using the book are included as testimonials for the sport-specific chapters (Chapters 7–17).

Chapter discussion questions

1. Why does the author suggest that there is a need to differentiate between Game Sense, TGfU and other approaches, and what is your opinion? Are they significantly different and, if so, what aspects of Game Sense most differentiate it from TGfU?
2. Explain how the author aims to empower teachers and coaches in this book and why.
3. Explain and comment on the particular approach taken in this book to help teachers and coaches develop a Game Sense approach and suggest how it relates to the pedagogy that it expects teachers and coaches to adopt.

2

THE DEVELOPMENT OF GAME SENSE

While Bunker and Thorpe's (1982) proposition for games teaching made a radical break with traditional, technique-based approaches, it drew on ideas that can be traced back to the 1950s, if not earlier. For example, the use of games in coaching and physical education was evident during the 1960s and 1970s in the UK (Mauldon and Redfern 1969; Wade 1967) and in France (Mahlo 1974), occurring within the context of a rise of interest in child-centred approaches to education. The philosophy of John Dewey (see, for example, Dewey 1916/97), who is widely considered to be the most influential thinker on education of the twentieth century, had a profound influence upon thinking about education during this period that is reflected in the movement approaches of the 1960s. Elements of student-centred approaches to teaching are also evident in the physical education texts of the 1970s, such as at the more student-centred end of Mosston's spectrum of teaching styles published in 1972 (Rovegno and Kirk 1995).

In the latter half of the 1960s Wade (1967) advocated the use of simple, small-sided games in soccer coaching to develop tactical knowledge and skill-in-context by maximizing player contact with the ball and to make training fun and enjoyable (Evans 2011). Within the context of the child-centred approaches of the 1960s, he favoured taking a problem-solving approach in which the teacher (or coach) guides the learner toward finding solutions: 'Clearly the teacher (coach) who can set problems and also guide a child towards appropriate solutions has an advantage. But any teacher with imagination can set problems and guide a child towards possible answers' (Wade 1967: xiii). The four fundamental principles for coaching that Wade (1967) proposed align with the principles of TGfU and Game Sense. Wade's principles involve the coach (1) maintaining interest through maximum participation, (2) taking responsibility for players understanding the content of training, (3) stimulating players to reach their potential and (4) being able to explain the game within an environment that

FIGURE 2.1 A classic piggy-in-the-middle situation in a competition game

fosters integrity and fair play. During the same period Mauldon and Redfern (1969) suggested the use of games for developing skills in primary school children as an alternative to skill drills and, with the work of Wade, formed a significant influence on the thinking of Bunker and Thorpe.

Bunker and Thorpe developed TGfU in response to their concerns with traditional games teaching and the ways in which technical, directive approaches to teaching games produced players who were technically sound but who were not good games players (Bunker and Thorpe 1982, 1986). They suggested that an emphasis on teaching techniques out of the context of games resulted in poor decision-making, poor tactical awareness and an inability to reproduce technique learnt at training or in physical education classes in the game. They were also concerned with students' motivation when asked to stand in line to repeat techniques divorced from the game, captured in their asking, 'When do we get to play the game?' (Bunker and Thorpe 1982: 5). They also felt that this might have had something to do with the poor performance of senior national (British) teams at international level (Bunker and Thorpe 1982, 1986; Thorpe, Bunker and Almond 1986).

The development of TGfU has accelerated over the past decade, assisted by a regular series of international conferences beginning in 2001 and the publications that have flowed from it, as outlined in Chapter 1. A TGfU task force was also established at the 2002 AIESEP World Congress convened in Spain, comprised of researchers working with TGfU from around the world. This body worked at promoting research on TGfU and at expanding its implementation around the world, with the international TGfU conferences its major mechanism used to achieve this. Once the momentum had been established, the task force was later reformed as a Special Interest Group (SIG) operating within AIESEP, leading to the inclusion of TGfU symposia at the 2006 congress in Finland, the 2008 congress in Japan that I convened and the 2010 congress in Spain convened by a TGfU SIG committee. The TGfU SIG is now well established and respected within this global body. Each of the four conferences has produced conference proceedings and has offered a forum for debate on the development of TGfU that has seen it increasingly defined in structure and detail to make it easier to teach. Much of the drive for this process of development over this period has come from North American scholars and has been influenced by the Tactical Games (TG) approach developed by some of the leading US figures such as Linda Griffin, Judy Oslin and Steve Mitchell.

The TGfU approach

Bunker and Thorpe's (1982) solution to the problems they had identified in games teaching was comparatively simple. They focused on the game as a whole instead of breaking it up into fundamental skills or techniques. This gave relevance to what was learnt by locating learning within games that were modified to suit the learners' needs, skills, experience and inclinations and the teacher's desired learning outcomes. Instead of learning skills before being able to play the game, Bunker and Thorpe proposed that students learn skills in modified games while learning tactical knowledge and decision-making. In TGfU students learn skills in contexts that are tied into developing tactical knowledge and a growing sense of what the game is about (game awareness) at the same time. Bunker and Thorpe also emphasized questioning to stimulate thinking about the game on an individual and group basis, providing a conceptual model to guide teachers in implementing TGfU. Their notion of TGfU that they published in 1982 was very simple but has since been extensively refined and made more complex. For example, several researchers have suggested changes to the model Bunker and Thorpe offered to help conceptualize the ongoing, cyclical learning process involved in TGfU (see, for example, Kirk and MacPhail 2002).

As a pioneer in the early development of TGfU, Len Almond (Almond and Launder 2010) confirmed this development of TGfU over thirty years in his presentation with Alan Launder in the TGfU symposium at the 2010 AIESEP World Congress. He explained how TGfU was little more than a loose idea or concept when proposed by Bunker and Thorpe and how its current interpretation is now significantly removed from their original concept. He suggested that TGfU was designed to be a 'starting point' from which improvement in student learning in physical education could evolve. Bunker and Thorpe themselves addressed this very issue in their keynote address at the 2008 International TGfU Conference in Vancouver, Canada, where they recognized the need to develop TGfU but questioned whether or not the current form of TGfU had moved too far away from the original intent and principles to still be called TGfU. In conversation with me at the 2003 Melbourne conference Rod suggested as much by saying that current (2003) interpretations of TGfU were very good but perhaps were not TGfU as he had conceived it.

This section of the chapter briefly outlines the core ideas and features of TGfU rather than being drawn into detailed discussion of what TGfU now is and how it should be taught. In TGfU modified games are designed as learning environments by the teacher, by the students or through collaboration between students and teacher, depending upon the experience that the students or players have in this aspect of TGfU. Typically, TGfU starts with simple games or activities that progressively become more tactically complex, placing more demand on skill as they move the learners toward being able to play the full game or a modified form of it. For example, Chapter 7, on touch rugby, begins with small groups of three or four players running up and down a space at an easy pace passing the ball while several other groups do the same, with players needing to be aware of changes in the environment and make simple decisions about when to pass. The next activity involves pairs of players beating a defender who can only move laterally. This activity steps up in complexity, because there is more pressure on the person passing and on the receiver, but builds upon perceptual ability, skill and decision-making ability developed in the previous game. To adjust the pressure (increase in complexity) the teacher or coach can adjust the width of the playing space to get the right level of challenge and ability to succeed.

This is also very clear in the field hockey unit in Chapter 11 in Activity 2, stages 1 and 2. In this activity players first form pairs to practise dribbling, with the dribbler moving about the space and his/her partner following but occasionally moving to either side, with the dribbler responding by moving away. Once the dribblers have adjusted to this activity and the teacher/coach feels they are ready, the 'shadow' is then able to apply tackling pressure but can only tackle from directly in front and not from the side. The teacher or coach can then challenge players of adequate skill and confidence further by allowing a tackle from the side, working in a smaller space or with more pairs working in the same playing space. In this process of progressively increasing complexity students can 'scaffold' on previously constructed knowledge and skills as they improve their game play, but the teacher's or coach's ability to recognize when they are ready to step up a notch and how much more complexity they can handle is very important.

It is also important that they be kept engaged in the activity of the game and that they do not become bored because they have mastered the activity or game. After playing each modified game or game-like activity they are asked by the teacher to reflect upon particular aspects of it individually or in groups and to develop ways of solving the tactical problems that arise. They may also be asked about the skills they need for the game and how they can perform them to best play the game. In recent developments in TGfU, influenced by the Tactical Games approach in North America, students identify the skills needed for the game by playing a modified game, then practise them out of the game until they are good enough to play the game well enough to progress to a more complex form. This contextualizes skill and shows its relevance to the students, but does focus on skill and not the game as a whole.

Teacher (or coach) *questioning* is central to TGfU pedagogy and to making it student-centred. Questioning stimulates thinking, helps make students active learners and engages them intellectually in learning to play the game. Questioning is, therefore, a central strategy in TGfU for making learning student-centred and enquiry-based. It does, however, need to be open ended and generative, with the teacher or coach open to different responses in most instances instead of always looking for a predetermined answer. This has proven to be a challenge for teachers and coaches trying to adopt games-based, student-centred approaches (for example, see McNeill *et al.* 2008; Roberts 2011).

Language is very important in TGfU because it is used to bring experience up to a conscious level where it can be discussed, reflected upon and developed as articulated knowledge before being further developed as knowledge-in-action. For an in-depth discussion of this relationship between speech and action in TGfU, see Light and Fawns (2003). The role of language in TGfU and similar approaches has been emphasized particularly strongly in French research and writing (see, for example, Wallian and Chang 2007). Using language does not refer to the monologue of traditional games teaching where the teacher instructs the students. Instead, it refers to the productive dialogue between students and/ or between the students and the teacher that leads to the generation of understanding and the construction of new knowledge on both an individual and a collective basis, as emphasized in the social constructivism of Vygotsky (see, for example, Vygotsky 1978) and further developed by others such as Bruner (see, for example, Bruner 1966).

In TGfU skills are neither neglected nor seen as being unimportant but are learnt *within* modified games, along with tactical understanding, and improved as the demands and complexity of the games are increased. In the original version of TGfU proposed by Bunker and Thorpe skills were seen to be *enabling* skills that allow the (modified) game to be played and to progress, but more recent developments have embedded in them the practising of skills between games. This question of where skills are learnt is really about the relationship between skills, tactical understanding and decision-making and is an important issue for some of the following discussions.

The development of four *game categories* within which all games share the same tactical problems forms another core element of TGfU and is a distinctive feature of it (Bunker and Thorpe 1986; Griffin and Butler 2005). In TGfU and Game Sense games are categorized into (1) invasion games, (2) striking games, (3) net/wall games and (4) target games. There are few, if any, similarities in technique across different sports or games, but within each category there are common tactical demands and challenges, meaning that tactical learning and knowledge are transferable across games within categories. For example, the tactical knowledge developed within the soccer unit in Chapter 10 is clearly highly transferable to field hockey. The perceptual abilities and response to cues developed in the dribbling activities in the soccer and hockey chapters are also clearly transferable, as is the decision-making ability developed about running after striking the ball in Chapter 14, on cricket, and Chapter 15, on softball, between these two sports. Less obvious is the transfer of tactical knowledge from basketball to rugby or from Australian football to netball, yet this transfer is equally significant. They all involve manipulating a ball and striving to make space, put players in it and get the ball to them in attack, and reducing opposition space and time to make decisions and act. Playing the five versus three games in touch rugby and field hockey develops the same tactical knowledge about creating space to take advantage of a two-on-one situation in these sports and others such as netball or Australian football when carrying the ball.

For a physical education teacher this offers an ideal way of organizing the curriculum in games teaching. For example, this might involve using all of one term to do invasion games, with a large amount of time spent on one invasion game and the tactical learning being transferred to smaller samples of other games in the same category (Griffin and Patton 2005). This *sampling* forms a principle of TGfU and sits upon the notion that games within each of the four categories share common tactical considerations, and offers PE teachers a valuable and systematic way of structuring learning and organizing syllabi. The TGfU model has four *pedagogical principles* that underpin its application. They are sampling, representation, exaggeration and tactical complexity (Griffin and Patton 2005):

- *Sampling* provides opportunities for students to experience different games within a game category that allow learning to be transferred from one game to another. For example, a teacher may devote a semester or term to invasion games by focusing on soccer but provide briefer samplings of touch rugby, basketball or Australian football.
- *Representation* involves manipulation of the advanced or mature form of the game into a condensed version that has similar tactical requirements. This involves using a modified game to represent other forms of the game and teachers do not have to rely on one traditional game for teaching purposes.

- *Exaggeration* involves making changes to the game to emphasize a specific tactical goal or problem, for example in soccer using more attackers than defenders (for example 5 v. 3) to encourage scoring, or playing volleyball on a long but narrow court to encourage players to explore court depth with accuracy.
- *Tactical complexity* involves the game matching the capacity of players to play it in terms of its tactical demands. The complexity of the game is increased as players improve their understanding and are able to provide solutions to problems presented in the game.

Bunker and Thorpe provided a conceptual model of TGfU with six stages that learners pass through in a cyclical representation that might occur across a range of levels, from a single lesson or training session to a unit of work for the term in physical education. A number of suggestions have been put forward for modifying this model (see, for example, Kirk and MacPhail 2002) and it has since formed an important aspect of attempts to tighten up TGfU and to provide more detail on its implementation.

The development of Game Sense

Since the first publication on TGfU by Bunker and Thorpe in 1982 a number of variations and other approaches have been developed for teaching and coaching that are similar to it but which have been influenced to different degrees by local cultural or institutional contexts. After a decline in initial interest in TGfU over the 1980s (Holt, Strean and Bengoechea 2002), the 1990s saw a resurgence of interest, and particularly in the USA, that was characterized by lively debate over the relative importance of tactics and technique in games and often in the form of a 'technique versus tactics' argument. It also led to the emergence of an American version of TGfU labelled the Tactical Games approach (Griffin, Mitchell and Oslin 1997). This model dealt with the problematic relationship between skill and tactics by locating specific skills within game situations. It adopts a pattern of using modified games to highlight the place and importance of game skills within games followed by time spent out of the game to practise the skill before returning to the game or progressing to a more complex one. This follows a pattern of game–skill practise–game, with the games becoming more complex and moving students toward being able to play the final form of the game as the full form of the game or a slightly modified form of it.

Over the same period Rod Thorpe regularly visited Australia to work with Australian coaches and the ASC in the development of an Australian version of TGfU focused on sport coaching named Game Sense. Game Sense is less structured than either TGfU or the TG approach, with the term referring to coaching that bases learning within (modified) games and uses questioning to make it player-centred. Thorpe gave structure to the existing use of game-based training by many coaches but his most significant contribution was the emphasis he placed on questioning (Light 2004). Asking questions instead of telling players what they should do moved the focus of coaching from the coach to the players.

In 1997 the ASC published a set of resources that comprised a booklet (den Duyn 1997), a video and a set of activity cards that drew on coaching practice in Australia, showing a range of modified games for each of the four game categories. This package is a very useful resource for developing a Game Sense approach and it is still available on the ASC website. At approximately the same time, Allen Launder (2001) was developing Play Practice as a games-centred approach to teaching a range of sport skills, and the Americans who had developed TG were helping academics in Singapore develop a version of TG, called the Games Concept Approach (GCA), specifically for the Singapore context. GCA was endorsed by the Singapore Ministry of Education in 1999 as part of its Thinking Schools, Learning Nations policy (Rossi *et al.* 2007).

The core features of Game Sense are: (1) that most learning is shaped and contextualized within games or game-like activities that involve competition and decision-making, and (2) that the coach/teacher uses questions to stimulate thinking and intellectual engagement. Game Sense uses very similar pedagogy to TGfU but is less structured than TGfU has become, as is evident in the absence of a model for Game Sense in comparison to the six-step model in TGfU (Bunker and Thorpe 1982) and any reference to the four pedagogical principles of TGfU.

The ASC and local coaches wanted to avoid association with school-based physical education and being too prescriptive for coaches to encourage existing good practice while providing some structure for the development of Game Sense coaching and 'thinking players'. There is, therefore, no model as proposed by Bunker and Thorpe (1982) for TGfU and further developed and refined by researchers in the physical education field (see, for example, Griffin and Butler 2005; Kirk and MacPhail 2002). Games Sense is thus less prescriptive than TGfU and more open to different interpretations. From the first publication on Games Sense (den Duyn 1997) it has had an impact on coaching across a range of sports in Australia, the UK and some other countries (see, for example, Dixon 2010; Light and Evans 2010).

Not long after its introduction Game Sense was promoted by state and national sporting bodies, such as in touch football and soccer, through professional development and accreditation courses, but also had a significant influence in physical education teaching (Webb, Pearson and McKeen 2006). When taken up in schools, the differences between it and TGfU are often difficult to see, leading some researchers to suggest that there is no difference (see, for example, Kidman 2001). The two terms are often used to refer to the same approach to physical education teaching in Australia, but research and writing on Game Sense in sport coaching suggests significant differences and particularly in relation to the differences between sport coaching and teaching in school physical education (see, for example, Light 2004; Light and Evans 2010).

Despite Game Sense being very similar to TGfU there are some important differences. Its focus on sport coaching, the involvement of the ASC and

Australian coaches in its development, and its focus on coaches instead of teachers lead to a less prescriptive approach than TGfU, providing room for coaches to adopt it for part of their coaching while maintaining other existing practices. Even when applied in physical education classes, its looser, less prescriptive approach is appealing to many teachers, as is its leaning toward sport coaching. On the other hand, this can lead to a misunderstanding of Game Sense as being merely playing modified games and the neglect of its pedagogy. This is commonly an oversight on the part of governing sports bodies that just provide a series of training games under the heading 'Game Sense'.

Game Sense for sport coaching

When applied to sport coaching Game Sense is not used to introduce players to a game or show them how to play it, as it would be in schools. Instead, it is used to fit into a season of competition, whether for the local under-nine-years soccer team or a professional rugby team. Game Sense offers an ideal approach for developing young players who have deep knowledge and an inquiring mind who would respond well to the expectations of more senior sport, and this has been recognized by sporting bodies such as the Rugby Football Union (RFU) in England. However, it also offers much at the most elite levels. Evans' (2011) study on the use of Game Sense at the most elite levels of rugby in Australia and New Zealand shows the strong influence of Game Sense on the training approach of the 2011 Rugby World Cup winning All Blacks, as previously suggested by Kidman (2001).

At any level of coaching, rather than starting with a simple game and progressively increasing complexity the games used typically aim at improving or changing specific aspects of the team's play, which can be very tight in the case of older, more experienced players. This could involve tending to a weakness in play identified from analysis of the previous competition match (or matches) or working on an aspect of play designed to exploit a perceived weakness in the next opposition's playing style, or responding to an opposition strength. If Game Sense is used in this way, coaches might find one specific training game or activity, for example, to redress a team's deficiency in skill execution under pressure, to improve decision-making under pressure or to improve a tactical aspect of game play.

The basic ideas of using modified or specifically designed games, setting up problems to be solved, asking questions instead of telling players what to do and encouraging reflection and dialogue are the same as in TGfU but the focus is on a specific aspect of play rather than on learning how to play the game. As suggested in Chapter 5, this represents a big difference between physical education and club sport. It is also no coincidence that Game Sense was developed in a country with a very strong culture of club sport. Community-based club sport forms a distinctive feature of sport for young people in Australia and provides very different experiences of sport and games than games lessons in school-based physical education   (see Light 2008b). While some countries like the UK also have a strong club sport culture for young people, it is quite different to the sport available to them in countries such as the USA and Japan, where most sport is available through educational institutions such as schools, universities or colleges.

Game Sense for physical education

When Game Sense is used in physical education it is typically used to teach students how to play a game as part of many programmes' aims of exposing students to a wide range of games/sport and providing positive experiences of them. The main difference between Game Sense and TGfU arises from its 'looser' approach, which Thorpe suggests makes it similar to his and David Bunker's original ideas on TGfU (Kidman 2001). The relationship between skill and tactics is also different to the contemporary version of TGfU as influenced by TG. Writing on TGfU now typically suggests that modified games are used for students to understand the place of certain skills in the game through playing the game. The students then practise these skills before returning to the game or moving to a more complex game form. This has also been adopted in the GCA used in Singapore (for example, see Rossi *et al.* 2007). However, in Game Sense learning is located within games as much as is practicable and there is no prior identification of skills to be developed. If the skills are good enough for the game to progress (*enabling skills*), then they are adequate and are improved by raising the complexity and skill demands of the modified games used. They are thus learnt and developed within game contexts rather than being identified within, and practised for, game contexts. In Game Sense, where necessary a whole class, one group of students or even an individual student or two can be given some technical coaching outside the game, then return to it without stopping the game, as illustrated on the ASC Game Sense video. The conception of the game as a whole entity is stronger in the Game Sense approach than in TGfU.

Since the release of the ASC Game Sense resources in 1997 the terms TGfU and Game Sense have often been used interchangeably in publications, which has blurred the differences between them. As similar as they are, there is a difference between them, with Rod Thorpe suggesting that Game Sense bears more similarity to his original ideas about TGfU than to TGfU's more recent form (Kidman 2001). When asked about the difference between the two he said, 'I see Game Sense as incorporating more of the original teaching games for understanding' (Kidman 2001: 26). While this may at first seem a little confusing, it needs to be considered within the context of the growth and ongoing development of TGfU over the past three decades from Bunker and Thorpe's brief yet very influential article published in 1982. Over thirty years TGfU has undergone significant development from both a practical and theoretical perspective across a range of cultures that are different to the UK of the early 1980s. Given the comparative brevity of its description in 1982 and the extent to which it has been examined, analysed, theorized and had suggestions made for modification since then, it would be surprising if it had not changed. These changes, however, have moved it further away from Game Sense than was the case in 1997.

Chapter discussion questions

1. Outline the development of ideas about using games for learning/coaching that emerged in the 1960s and suggest how they may have shaped or influenced Bunker and Thorpe's ideas on TGfU.
2. Comment on the author's contention that TGfU has developed over three decades to a point where it is significantly different to Bunker and Thorpe's original ideas and how cultural contexts have shaped this development.
3. Suggest how a particular cultural and institutional setting has shaped the development of Game Sense as a variation of TGfU.
4. In the skills versus tactics debate they are given an oppositional relationship, with coaches having to focus on one or the other. Explain the relationship between them as suggested by the author and how it differs from the skill versus tactics view.
5. How is the conceptualization of where skill learning occurs in Game Sense different to TG and the contemporary development of TGfU?

3

THEORIZING LEARNING IN AND THROUGH GAME SENSE

TGfU and Game Sense were originally developed for very practical reasons and not from any theory about how people learn. David Bunker and Rod Thorpe's (1982) motivation for developing TGfU arose from concern with the fact that students who had developed good technique were not necessarily good games players. Likewise, Game Sense was developed to produce better (thinking) games players while providing more motivation for training across a range of levels. Suggestions for theorizing how learning occurs in games when using TGfU and Game Sense were made well after they had been developed and first published in 1982 (Bunker and Thorpe) and 1997 (den Duyn). It was not until 1998 that researchers first suggested that learning occurring through the use of TGfU could be understood by drawing on constructivist perspectives on learning (Kirk and Macdonald 1998; Gréhaigne and Godbout 1998b).

This theorization of learning has since been further developed to enhance learning, with Rovegno and Dolly (2006) suggesting that Light and Fawns' (2003) examination of the relationship between the mind expressed in speech and the body expressed in action provides the most thorough theorization of TGfU. Although a range of theories has been suggested to understand learning when using TGfU and Game Sense, since 1998 the constructivist perspective has become the dominant theory used. This includes variations that sit upon the same philosophical, ontological and epistemological assumptions, such as situated learning (Lave and Wenger 1991), complex learning theory (see Davis and Sumara 2003) and enactivism (see Varela, Thompson and Rosch 1991).

In discussing how theory should be used, Davis, Sumara and Luce-Kapler (2000) point out that the Greek word from which the word 'theory' derives literally means 'to see'. Looking at learning in TGfU from a constructivist perspective enables us to *see* what is going on. It allows us to understand, explain and enhance the learning that occurs when using Game Sense or TGfU (Light 2009). The focus of any teaching should be on learning and not teaching. Constructivism is a theory of learning and not teaching (Fosnot 1996). We need some way of understanding how people actually learn, to inform any teaching or coaching with attention to what teachers or coaches do considered in terms of the way in which it shapes learning. Teaching (and coaching) needs to focus on enhancing learning and providing the opportunity for learning to unfold or emerge from experience. As Heidegger (1968: 24) suggests, the teacher should not impose learning or close down thinking but, instead, 'let them learn' within a view of learning as a journey into the unknown. A theoretical understanding of how this learning occurs and how it can be enhanced can empower teachers and coaches. It can empower them to be able to understand learning and learners, maximize learning opportunities for them and critically reflect upon their own practice in an ongoing process of developing and refining their teaching and coaching. This is a core idea that informs this book.

Constructivism has become the dominant approach to teaching and learning in teacher education programmes over the past thirty to forty years in general education (Fox 2001). Over this period approaches have been developed in physical education, such as movement education, that are consistent with constructivism, but reference to constructivism has only emerged in the physical education literature over the past decade or so (Rink 2001; Light 2008a). The core ideas of constructivism were evident in the new teaching approaches of the 1960s, but contemporary constructivist approaches are far more rigorously theorized (Rink 2001; Light 2008a). Much of the impetus for this interest has been stimulated by researchers revisiting the TGfU approach (see, for example, Kirk and Macdonald 1998) and by the development of other student-centred approaches such as Sport

FIGURE 3.1 Decision-making under pressure in high school Australian football

Education (Siedentop 1994). While the term constructivism is now commonly used in the physical education literature, there is sometimes a little confusion over what it actually means, exacerbated by shallow understanding of it.

Broadly, constructivism refers to learning as a process in which learners draw on their own experiences and existing knowledge to make sense of new learning experiences and actively construct their own understandings and meanings. This implies that learning is a complex process that needs to involve active participation by the learner and that learning for anyone is a process of interpretation through which each learner 'constructs' unique understandings. It emphasizes the ways in which individual learners can construct different understandings according to their prior experience, knowledge and the inclinations through which they interpret the learning experience. This learning involves not adding to existing knowledge but change that involves constructing new knowledge. Despite the fact that learners may share a common culture and have similar life experiences, there will still be different ways in which they construct meaning and understanding shaped by their prior experiences. In an increasingly multicultural world this is clearly an important consideration.

Before outlining and discussing constructivism and complex learning theory, this chapter briefly examines what could be seen as the 'traditional' theory of learning, behaviourism, which still guides much teaching and many common-sense assumptions about learning.

Behaviourism

Behaviourism formed the dominant view of learning for much of the twentieth century and, despite being largely displaced by constructivism over the past few decades in most teacher education programmes, continues to have a strong influence in physical education. It is underpinned by a view of the learner as being isolated from the world and by a distinction made between mental activity and physical experience, leading to a range of dualisms that have particular significance for physical education. These include the separation of thought from action, self from others, knower from known and the subjective from the objective. As thinking is seen to be inaccessible, behaviourism focuses on the body in terms of observable, gross bodily behaviour to emphasize cause and effect in behaviour and the influence of environmental circumstances (Davis, Sumara and Luce-Kapler 2000). It is concerned with the effect of reward and punishment on behaviour and typically takes a 'training' approach to teaching, emphasizing the use of feedback and reward systems to change and modify learner behaviour. Behaviourism emphasizes the internalization of objective knowledge and requires a highly structured and technical pedagogical approach. It conceives of learning as being a mechanical process that needs to be reduced to its simplest components to be understood (Davis, Sumara and Luce-Kapler 2000). Despite the fact that behaviourism does focus on the body, it sees it as being separate from, and governed by, the mind.

Constructivism

Constructivism adopts a holistic conception of learning that extends beyond the individual mind as a separate entity to include the body and all its senses and others. Clearly this is an important consideration for physical education as a subject area that involves the body and its sensations. From a constructivist perspective, cognition does not occur only in the mind, but involves the whole person. Constructivism implies that knowledge is not merely that which can be expressed in speech and writing but also that which is enacted. Knowledge in games is expressed not only verbally in discussions about it but, more importantly, in playing the game as knowledge-in-action (Light and Fawns 2003). In much of the writing on TGfU this distinction is made by drawing on the notion of declarative and procedural knowledge from motor learning theory. Within this work knowledge about the game expressed in language is referred to as *declarative knowledge*, with the knowledge enacted in actually playing the game referred to as *procedural knowledge*. Alternatively, these two forms of knowledge can be seen as being knowledge-in-action or enacted knowledge (Varela, Thompson and Rosch 1991) and articulated knowledge. These are terms that sit better with a constructivist perspective on learning.

From a constructivist perspective, learning is a process of adapting to, and fitting into, a constantly changing world. This is helpful in thinking about how learning to play games or sport involves more than merely learning technique and is in many ways a process of adapting to the dynamic environment of games. Learning thus arises from the learner's engagement in the world through perception, motor action and bodily senses. The biological body is seen as being more than just a structure through which we learn. Instead, the body itself is seen to learn.

Although there is a diverse range of forms of constructivism that draw on different sources, they can be grouped into the two broad camps of psychological constructivism and social constructivism (Phillips 1997). Both camps of constructivism differ from traditional views of how people learn as involving a simple transmission of knowledge from teacher to learner and the internalization of pre-given knowledge. Psychological constructivism draws on the work of Piaget, later developed by others such as von Glasersfeld to focus on individual sense and meaning making. Social constructivism stresses the role played by social processes in learning and draws on the work of theorists such as Vygotsky, Bruner and Dewey. Social constructivism focuses on social dynamics such as that in the work of Lave and Wenger (1991) and Vygotsky (see, for example, Vygotsky 1978), and the social and cultural themes of Bruner (see, for example, Bruner 1966). Social constructivism is more useful in understanding and theorizing the learning that takes place in and through Game Sense due to its emphasis on learning as a social process, and how this can be applied to the social dimensions of games and the social interaction, collective thinking and collaborative problem solving that form features of Game Sense pedagogy.

Rather than learning being a process of adding on new knowledge, psychological constructivism sees it as a process in which the learner constructs unique knowledge through the interaction of his/her prior experience and knowledge and new experiences. It emphasizes learning as change and transformation. This assumes that knowledge is not merely something that is passed on or transmitted from teacher to learner as an object. Instead, knowledge is generated or constructed through interpretation by the learner and active exploration and discovery (McInerney and McInerney 1998). Psychological constructivism emphasizes the intra-personal dimensions of learning and personal meaning making. It sees the construction of knowledge as involving 'the activation and reorganization of existing knowledge to make a unique understanding of the world' (Chen and Rovegno 2000: 357). It also suggests that thinking and learning are not restricted to the individual mind but that they can be distributed among others and that they can extend to the body and its senses (Davis, Sumara and Luce-Kapler 2000)

Originating in the work of Vygotsky, social constructivism takes a more macro view of learning to see cognition occurring beyond the body and learning as being a social process. From a social constructivist perspective cognition is seen as a collective process spread across the individual's world. It rests upon an assumption that the understandings and capabilities that emerge from social interaction within a group are greater than those that are possible at an intra-personal level. Social constructivist approaches to teaching thus emphasize social interaction such as children working in groups to share ideas and solve mathematical problems collectively. Game Sense provides a good example of a social constructivist-informed approach. This is evident in the way in which it emphasizes collaborative problem solving on a whole-class basis and on a small-group basis in the development of team strategies in small-sided games. Social interaction in games extends beyond verbal interaction to include the embodied dialogue that is possible in games as an ongoing conversation between players/ students (Light and Fawns 2003).

Constructivist learning theory rejects objectivist views of knowledge. Some researchers in the physical education field have extended these ideas about learning and the challenge they present to the Cartesian division of mind and body that continues to shape thinking in education to argue that the body actually thinks (see, for example, Light and Fawns 2003). Such holistic conceptions of learning in physical education reflect a social constructivist view of knowledge as inseparable from the learner and of cognition as both embodied and distributed across groups of people rather than only occurring within an individual mind. This means that to 'know' something from a constructivist perspective is different to what it means from a behaviourist perspective. As Light and Fawns suggest, knowing something, whether it is knowing how to pass a ball in basketball or knowing the meaning of a word, means being able to enact it or use it in a meaningful way. Thus, knowledge is not an object but is, instead, inseparable from the knower and intimately tied into context. Work in enactivism emphasizes this view of knowledge as that which is enacted, suggesting a stronger challenge to the Cartesian separation of mind and body (see, for example, Varela, Thompson and Rosch 1991).

Complex learning theory

The term constructivism is now commonly used in the physical education literature but the diversity of constructivist approaches and the different sources they draw on can be confusing (Davis and Sumara 2003; Light 2008a). Davis and Sumara (2003) suggest circumventing this confusion by using the more general term complex learning theory (CLT). First applied to physical education only recently (Light 2008a), it has quickly stimulated interest in the TGfU literature (see, for example, Hopper, Butler and Storey 2009; Jess, Atencio and Thorburn 2011). Davis and Sumara suggest that all forms of constructivism meet around three common and inter-related and broad ideas. The three broad ideas are:

1   *Learning is active*: they are aligned more with a Neo-Darwinian notion of learning as an ongoing process of *adaptation* than with the Cartesian idea of linear cause and affect. Learning is seen to involve more than just the passive internalization of an external reality (Varela, Thompson and Rosch 1991). It is seen to involve the projection of the individual's life history of experience in a process of change and adaptation as an act of interpretation.
2   *Learning is social*: cognition is not only an intra-individual process but also a *social process* in which various cognizing agents/learners are inseparably intertwined. This perspective rejects the idea that cognition only takes place as an intra-individual process to locate 'the human mind and cognition in a larger framework comprising the socio-cultural and historical milieux in which human individuals live' (Saito 1996: 400). This view of cognition sees it as being an ongoing social process within which social interaction is pivotal to learning.
3   *Learning is a process of interpretation*: they all offer critiques of long-established, commonsense perspectives on learning that have dominated thinking about learning for the past three centuries in the West. They critique the idea that knowledge is an internalized representation of an external reality. Thus learning involves processes of interpretation in which there is no pre-given external reality.

CLT offers a more inclusive description of the basic ideas underpinning Game Sense that captures its core principles as suggested by Davis and Sumara (2003). The views on learning evident in CLT highlight how complex learning actually is and, more specifically, how it is socially, culturally and physically situated. Contrary to commonsense ideas based upon a mechanistic view of learning, CLT challenges the notion that learning is a simple, linear and easily quantifiable process that only takes place in schools. It highlights the ways in which learning emerges from people's sensory-perceptual and cognitive engagement in the social world. People learn outside formal settings such as schools and learning is part of social life. CLT recognizes and allows for accounting for the role of the body, its movements and its senses in learning by consistently emphasizing the role of experience in learning.

A range of work on learning that can be seen as emphasizing its complexity, from Dewey (see, for example, Dewey 1916/97), published almost a century ago, to contemporary writing such as that of Davis and Sumara (1997, 2003) and Varela, Thompson and Rosch (1991), emphasizes experience and the body's role in learning. It does not, however, makes any specific mention of physical education or sport. Given the ways in which physical education has traditionally been positioned outside the academic curriculum this is perhaps not so surprising (Light and Fawns 2003). However, when the learning that is possible through Game Sense is identified through the application of contemporary learning theory it points toward the possibilities for physical education to be repositioned in school curricula. Indeed, it suggests that it could even play a role in enhancing learning across the curriculum by assisting in engaging the body in learning (Light and Fawns 2003). At the very least, adopting a Game Sense approach in physical education, with its focus on physical modes of learning, reflection and the use of language in social settings, provides whole-person opportunities for learning not available in most other areas of the curriculum. However, this can only occur when we can look beyond the limitations of an exclusive focus on the physical dimensions of learning in physical education to recognize and enhance the wide range of affective, social and intellectual learning that is possible.

CLT makes a significant break from traditional views of learning founded on mechanical, cause and effect ways of explaining it that reduce things to their fundamental components or parts, which Davis and Sumara (2003) refer to as a complicated approach. In traditional games teaching, for example, this involves breaking the game down into what are seen as the 'fundamental skills' or core techniques needed to be able to play the game, and treating them as discrete components of the game. This approach assumes that these essential techniques or skills must be learnt before students can play the game, with classic technique-focused physical education teaching devoting most of a unit of work over five to six weeks to teaching technique first then allowing the class to put this technique to work in a game on the last lesson in the unit on the assumption that this will help them play the game better. The influence of this thinking on physical education in Australia is evident in the faith that is maintained in the Fundamental Motor Skills (FMS) programme as a means of increasing participation in sport. While there is a wealth of research showing how teaching the technical aspects of these skills improves performance of them, there is very little evidence of this having any positive influence on sport participation, which is not at all surprising.

As complex learning theory allows us to see, learning is a far more complex phenomenon than technique-focused teaching in physical education or the rationale for the FMS programme suggests. It allows us to see the possibilities for comprehensive and holistic learning that Game Sense offers. Instead of attempting to reduce learning in games to discrete, fundamental skills and techniques, Game Sense places learning in authentic contexts where they have meaning and relevance, to promote holistic learning. While traditional views of learning, such as behaviourism, see it as a mechanical process, approaches underpinned by CLT recognize it as being more spontaneous, more unpredictable and more alive.

Drawing on CLT allows for the identification of important pedagogical features of Game Sense and how they can facilitate learning. The following section explores the implications that CLT has for Game Sense by focusing on its three core themes as suggested by Davis, Sumara and Luce-Kapler (2000). These are that (1) learning is an ongoing process of adaptation, (2) learning is a social process and (3) CLT critiques the idea that knowledge is an internalized representation of an external reality to see learning as a process of interpretation. These themes are discussed below and linked to aspects of the practical chapters in the book.

Learning is an ongoing process of adaptation

Rather than being a process of simply adding to existing knowledge, learning is a multi-faceted process of continuous, ongoing change. Piaget's ideas on learning, developed from his work in biology, suggest that learning involves an experience that disturbs the learner's existing understandings, leading to the construction or formulation of knowing by restoring a state of cognitive equilibrium to their world of personal experience (Fosnot 1996). In Game Sense learning to play games or sport also requires providing challenges that unsettle the learner's prior understandings, requiring him or her to adapt to this challenge (individually and collectively) in ways that restore a state of cognitive balance. Each modified game or activity should then challenge students' cognition, whether operating at a non-conscious level while playing the game or at a conscious level when discussing tactical aspects of the game in team discussions and debate between games. For example, in Chapter 10, on soccer, in the game triangle soccer players do not stop after scoring but maintain possession and immediately attack another goal, with three goals set up in a triangular formation in which either team can score. This makes the game very different to a normal game of soccer, thus providing a cognitive challenge for all players/learners. Initially, learning occurs through embodied, non-conscious thinking but this learning is subsequently enhanced through reflection and dialogue in the Game Sense process, leading to restoration of a state of cognitive balance.

The challenges provided for students and the questions used to assist in meeting them using a Game Sense approach should not normally be designed to arrive at predetermined 'correct' answers but, instead, provide for a range of possible solutions because the process of learning is more important than the product of arriving at correct solutions. In Game Sense the questions asked by the teacher need to encourage group discussion, the development of possible solutions and open-ended explorations. To facilitate this the teacher needs to foster a socio-moral environment that is supportive and in which students are not worried about making mistakes or giving a 'wrong' answer (for example, see DeVries and Zan 1996). The teacher should also encourage students to raise their own questions, generating their own hypotheses and testing them because 'Learning requires invention and self organization on the part of the learner' (Fosnot 1996: 29).

The experience of learning how to learn in and through Game Sense has broad implications for the ongoing process of learning tied into human development emphasized in this book. This assists not only in students' general experiences of schooling but also in their broader learning that involves processes of personal transformation (Lave and Wenger 1991). Coaches working with children and young people and teachers using Game Sense must, therefore, be aware of the multi-faceted, complex nature of learning arising from games lessons, in which far more than just learning how to play a game is involved. They need to be able to link this to the growth of children and young people within the schooling process, to the process of learning how to learn and to their growing into citizens living in democratic societies. Given the alignment of Game Sense pedagogy with the principles of democracy and the powerful ways in which learning occurs through experience, it actually offers an ideal opportunity for young people to experience and learn democratic processes.

Learning is a social process

From a CLT perspective, learning is essentially a social process in which various learners are inseparably intertwined, with learning emerging, or unfolding, from social interaction. In any game there is constant social interaction, even without the use of language, as players engage in a conversation of movement (Light and Fawns 2003), perceiving and responding to the movement of the opposition in a non-verbal conversation. There is also always some verbal communication in team games, even without the structured debate and discussion between players used in Game Sense and the discussion that is essential for the collective development of ideas that is central to it. Learning arises from the verbal and non-verbal interactions that constitute games, but the structured verbal interaction used in Game Sense makes a very significant contribution to the learning process.

In the chapters in Part II suggestions for this verbal interaction (dialogue) tend to involve dialogue between the teacher/coach and the learners on a whole-class/team basis, and between teacher/coach and learners in smaller groups established for small-sided games in the early stages of each unit. The units then tend to suggest a movement into team talks at appropriate times during the game. The teacher could decide the appropriate moments, but as classes or teams develop an understanding of games and take up the opportunity to be more autonomous learners they will typically call for a time out when they recognize the need themselves. This is to be encouraged and is a marker of developing knowledge and autonomy as learners. For example, in Chapter 9, on Australian football, the first four activities (which include different stages of complexity within them) suggest dialogue between the teacher/coach and the class/team or smaller groups playing a small-sided game, but moves to team talks in the final game form of modified Australian football. As physical education classes or sport teams adapt to the expectations of a Game Sense approach, team talks could replace teacher/coach–class/team dialogue. Indeed classes or teams that have fully adjusted to a Game Sense approach will make these decisions themselves. While considerable time and effort are required to implement a Game Sense approach on the part of the teacher or coach, the investment pays off as classes or teams adjust to and adopt this approach to become truly independent, self-organizing learners.

Game Sense emphasizes dialogue between students and between students and the teacher as a core learning strategy. This can occur on a one-to-one basis during games but typically occurs in discussions as a whole class or in team talks during play in small-sided games. These provide opportunities for collective reflection and discussion and debate of ideas, which lead to the formulation of strategies and hypotheses that the class or team can then test in action. Once this is done the results are then discussed and collectively reflected upon. Such inter-action provides learners with opportunities to reflect upon experience to develop abstract ideas that they can generalize across situations (Fosnot 1996).

Game Sense teaching provides students with learning experiences within modified games designed for particular learning outcomes that are followed by immediate reflection and verbal interaction. This process typically involves the debate and formulation of ideas and the provision of opportunities to test and evaluate these ideas in the collective development of understanding and know-ledge. The dialogue stimulated within the class, as a community of learners, engenders collective thinking and the formulation of ideas as part of learning as an essentially social process. It also involves learning how to negotiate, deal with differences of opinion and arrive at outcomes that are the product of democratic processes.

Learning is a process of interpretation

Technical approaches to games teaching see knowledge as an external reality that is internalized by the learner. In games teaching the notion of having to learn 'fundamental skills' to be able to play sport provides one example of this approach. This reflects a view of techniques as being pre-given, external realities that need to be learnt before playing the game. Game Sense reflects a view of learning as an interpretative process within which the learner and what is learnt are inseparable. In Game Sense the learning of skill occurs within contexts that are dynamic, alive and often unpredictable. Whether or not a player can be considered skilful is dependent upon the particular situation within which the skill is performed. Learning within the context of games allows students to interpret and draw on their existing knowledge, skills and experiences to make sense of games and to construct knowledge. From a CLT perspective real learning thus occurs when knowledge is expressed or enacted in the game as knowledge-in-action.

Some of the chapters in Part II devote some time to focusing on learning technique or skill, with the difference being that skill is a technique performed within a game or game-like environment. Even when the focus is on skill (technique performed in context) there is no suggestion that there is one, non-negotiable, 'correct' way to perform it. For example, Chapter 10 (soccer) and Chapter 11 (field hockey) begin with practising dribbling, but within contexts that require perception and some decision-making while developing the skill of dribbling, thus giving it meaning and relevance. Likewise, the touch rugby unit (Chapter 7) begins with an activity for practising a lateral pass but in a context that gives it meaning and contextualizes the skill. When I have taught this in Victoria, a state in Australia where rugby is not popular, I have demonstrated the basic motion of the hands greeting the ball and moving it across the body to be released, but only as very basic instruction, leaving the players/students to learn the technique as practised in a context that requires thinking, decision-making, perception and the adjustment of technique to suit the specific demands of each occasion in which they pass. Rather than asking them to perform a 'textbook' pass, I am expecting them to interpret what I say and adapt it to their own knowledge and the specificities of the moments when they perform the skill.

Conclusion

CLT is not another new theory but more an attempt to identify broad common ideas shared by all forms of constructivism, informed by complexity theory. It provides a broad and inclusive means of looking at constructivism as a single approach. It encourages a broader conceptualization of the learning that occurs in and through Game Sense that goes beyond the mere acquisition of skill, the development of physical abilities, tactical knowledge and good games players. The examination of CLT, as applied to Game Sense teaching, in this chapter highlights the range of potentially rich learning experiences that can arise from games lessons when a Game Sense approach is adopted. The long-term development of Game Sense needs to be informed by (and to inform) the development of theory that helps understand the complexity of learning that occurs in and through games. This is not, however, merely a case of theory being 'applied' to practice, but a case of practice across different settings needing to inform the development of learning theory and pedagogy so that they become mutually informing to reflect the dialectic between theory and practice.

The expansion of research on TGfU and Game Sense over the past decade and the ongoing development of the two approaches arise from interest in constructivist learning theory as a means of understanding learning and of improving learning. The more recent development of CLT and its application to physical education (Light 2008a; Jess, Atencio and Thorburn 2011) offer further opportunities for highlighting the educational benefits of games taught using

Game Sense and of continuing to develop them (Light 2009). The understanding that emerges from using CLT to understand and enhance learning in and through Game Sense can also help to empower teachers and coaches to make important decisions about the strategies they adopt and to negotiate the range of challenges and problems that typically arise while teaching using this approach.

Chapter discussion questions

1. Explain the differences between psychological and social constructivism. Suggest which one might be more useful for understanding how learning occurs when using a Game Sense approach and why.
2. How is understanding of what it means to *know* something from a constructivist perspective different to a behaviourist perspective and what significance does this have when adopting a Game Sense approach to teaching or coaching? What does it then mean to know how to play a sport or game?
3. Drawing on CLT, suggest how a view of learning as a process of interpretation and adaptation challenges the idea of knowledge as an object that is transmitted from teacher or coach to student or player.
4. Suggest how the three core principles of CLT can be used to understand and enhance learning in and through games when using a Game Sense approach.
5. In reference to CLT and constructivism, suggest how learning through games, when Game Sense pedagogy is used, occurs in a way that is similar to how we learn to live in our world.

4

GAME SENSE FOR PHYSICAL EDUCATION AND SPORT COACHING

Although Bunker and Thorpe (1982) developed TGfU for physical education, the development of good games players is just as important for coaching children and young people in sport. TGfU has thus had an influence on sport coaching across a range of levels, from children's sport to elite-level sport, either directly or through the ideas underpinning it. The ideas about learning to play sport that underpin TGfU also inform other approaches such as Play Practice (Launder 2001) and Game Sense, as a variation of TGfU developed for coaching. They also inform more general suggestions for learner-centred coaching (see, for example, Harrison 2002; Martens 2004; Wein 2001). Some of the basic ideas of TGfU and Game Sense have also influenced coaching at a practical level in some countries. For example, in England they inform much of soccer (football) at all levels and the RFU's junior rugby coaching programme, as well as being introduced into coach education through coach certification in sports such as cricket (Roberts 2011). New Zealand's national rugby team, and 2011 World Champions, the All Blacks, follow an approach heavily influenced by Game Sense (Evans 2011; Kidman 2001). The All Blacks' former head coach and assistant coach for the 2011 Rugby World Cup, Wayne Smith, is an advocate of the Game Sense approach (Kidman 2001, 2005) and Ric Charlesworth, the highly successful coach of the Australian women's and men's (field) hockey teams, is a strong proponent of using modified games (designer games) for training (Charlesworth 1993). The Australian Football League (AFL) has recently adopted a Game Sense approach for its junior programmes and in Canada there has been widespread adoption of athlete-centred approaches to coaching.

One of the most significant ways in which the coaching literature differs from the physical education literature is that it pays significantly less attention to pedagogy, and this is a major factor contributing to the slow uptake of TGfU and its variations in coaching. The past five years or so have seen a growth in interest in pedagogy in sport coaching (see, for example, Jones 2006; Kirk 2010; Light and Evans 2010), but it remains dominated by the idea of coaching as teaching sports skills (Kirk 2010). In the context of considerable change in the place and practice of physical education, it was recognition of TGfU as being consistent with social constructivism and situated learning that kick-started the resurgence of interest in it over the past decade (Gréhaigne and Godbout 1998a; Kirk and Macdonald 1998; Kirk and MacPhail 2002). Up until quite recently the bulk of the main-stream coaching literature has, however, paid comparatively little attention to pedagogy and even less to theories of human learning. Instead, it tends to take a view of coaching as a non-problematic, linear process in which the coach imparts knowledge to the players. This is now being challenged by the emergence of a critical socio-cultural perspective on coaching (see, for example, Cassidy, Jones and Potrac 2004; Jones, Armour and Potrac 2004) and encouraging considera-tion of pedagogy (see, for example, Armour 2004; Light 2004).

Differences between teaching and coaching

While there is some overlap between the teaching of games and sport in physical education and sport coaching, there are also very significant differences in aims, methods, cultures and measures of success. Physical education teachers have to deal with far more individual variation in skill, attitude and motivation in a typical class than coaches need to in a sport team at any level. In most sport teams, because players choose to participate, they tend to be more motivated and more interested than many unwilling participants in PE classes. Sport teams are also organized, not only according to age but also according to ability, meaning that there is less variation between skill levels than we typically find in a PE class. On the other hand, coaching contexts vary from coaching five-year-old children to coaching the most elite professional athletes in the world. It is therefore difficult to speak of coaching in general terms due to the enormous variation in the physical and socio-cultural contexts in which it is practised. There are profound differences between the local community-based under-nine B soccer team, a highly competitive senior secondary school rugby or American football team and professional baseball or basketball played at the highest levels, where millions of dollars and coaches' careers can hang on the results of a single game. This means that the aims, the approaches adopted to achieve them and the criteria used to assess a coach's success in children's soccer on Sunday morning and in the final of the NBA or world cup in cricket can be profoundly different.

Coaching for human growth

Sport can, and should, form a valuable part of children's and young people's experiences of growing up, fitting into society and becoming responsible citi-zens. It is also important that children and young people enjoy sport and games.

Indeed, sport and games taught using a Game Sense approach can make a valuable contribution to achieving these outcomes.

The need for children and young people to develop a positive attitude toward sport and to have it make a positive contribution to their physical, social, moral and personal growth and development should be among the most important aims of junior-level coaches. Sport offers an ideal medium for encouraging important social and moral learning (for example, see Arnold 1986) if the coach adopts appropriate approaches. In sport children and young people need to make moral judgements about right and wrong and learn to get on with others, deal with success and failure, and experience a large range of learning arising from real experience. Sport can also provide valuable opportunities for learning about responsibility, democratic principles and citizenship through the ways in which it provides real experiences engaging the whole person socially, emotionally, intellectually and physically. Coaching sport for children and young people needs

FIGURE 4.1   High–performance youth basketball

to be seen as more than just developing skilful performers, even though this is an important aspect of coaching. It also needs to keep the stress on winning in perspective because the indirect social and moral learning that arises from sport is potentially more important than improving athletic performance.

For sport to engage all players and provide them all with positive experiences, coaching must be inclusive. This requires practices that provide opportunities for children to enjoy themselves, feel secure and set achievable goals. They need to have fun, enjoy the experience and want to come back for the next training session, and the next season. As so much research confirms, most children play sport, not to win trophies and develop skills, but to interact, socialize, be part of something and have fun (Australian Sports Commission 1991; Côté, Baker and Abernathy 2003; Weinberg *et al.* 2000). Indeed, fun and excitement in sports experiences from the age of six to thirteen are critical for children's continuing participation in sport (Côté, Baker and Abernathy 2003). For example, results of a study of children aged six to thirteen in Canadian ice hockey suggest that games and 'play activities' are essential to keep young players in the sport (Wall and Côté 2007). Thus junior coaching and physical education teaching have much in common. Coaches of children's and young people's teams, like teachers, will want to help their charges develop as better games players and better performers. This, however, is not the only aim of coaching in this context. They also need to emphasize coaching in ways that make training fun, inclusive and contribute to making sport enjoyable and a positive experience for all children in the team.

Inclusion and social interaction

Within the context of public and government panic over obesity and other life-style diseases, and the ways in which regular exercise can contribute to better health, participation needs to be a priority for junior sport organizations. However, participation in sport can contribute not only to good health in a medical sense, but also, more broadly, to participants' *wellbeing*, and this is probably a more relevant aim for sport and physical education than disease prevention. This allows us to take into account a wider range of benefits that young people can gain from playing sport and to consider the broader notion of our 'being'. This includes, for example, social and moral learning, making friends, the formation of identity and self-esteem, the joy of movement, experiencing a sense of belonging and achievement, and just having some fun. Any attempt to justify youth sport or physical education on the grounds of disease prevention excludes or neglects a far wider range of important benefits that contribute to wellbeing. Sports clubs are ideal settings for establishing meaningful communities for children and young people that can make a powerful contribution to improving their sense of wellbeing and developing skills, abilities and inclinations that can contribute to maintaining lifelong wellbeing (see, for example, Light 2006; Light and Curry 2009).

To contribute to developing wellbeing and maximizing participation, sports clubs or teams need organization and coaching that are inclusive and can accommodate a wide range of abilities, attitudes, inclinations and motivations. Kirk (2004) argues that the elitist model of sport is unsuitable for school PE. Neither is it suitable for junior sport due to its basic function of eliminating all but the best. Game Sense is inclusive in two basic ways. First, it is inclusive due to the ways in which it uses modified games designed to suit the developmental, emotional and social needs of the players. This modification includes changes in the numbers of players per side, the number of balls used, the size and shape of the area used and modifications of rules to encourage particular learning outcomes. The basic approach of Game Sense is to start with simple games in which the stress on technique is reduced to allow players to engage intellectually in the game. All the units presented in Part II thus begin with simple activities, such as running up and down a space passing in small groups while others do the same in touch rugby (Chapter 7), dribbling a soccer ball around a space while others do the same (Chapter 10) or hitting a ball from a batting tee to run around a cone in softball (Chapter 15).

As the players develop an understanding of tactics and strategy the complexity of the games is increased to build on previously developed knowledge in a progressive sequence. For example, in the field hockey unit (Chapter 11) players begin an activity dribbling a ball each in a small space while others do the same, then move to having a partner shadow them, moving up to either side and calling for the dribbling player to move away in control of the ball. This is then made more complex by allowing the shadowing player to attempt a tackle, but only from directly in front of the dribbling player, which makes it reasonably easy to evade. This progression increases complexity and pressure on the dribbling player, stage by stage. In this case the focus is on skill, but contextualized skill that includes developing perception and decision-making. Technique is thus developed within authentic game situations and hand in hand with understanding and tactical knowledge. This means that players learn not only how to perform a technique but also when, where and why.

The modified games used in coaching follow the same principles but, with the exception of young children, are usually not aimed at introducing players to the sport. Instead, coaches use games modified to attend to particular aspects of the team's game play that have been identified by the coach (and hopefully the players). They still, however, stress teamwork and reduce opportunities for the bigger and more skilful players to dominate. For example, the modified basketball game used in Chapter 12 limits the players to a three-bound dribble, which has a number of benefits, including being inclusive. In evenly matched games at any level, right up to and including the American National Basketball Association (NBA), there are few opportunities for one player to dribble the length of the court and shoot a basket on his/her own. Instead, players typically dribble for a short period, pass to another player and reposition themselves. This might be to take another reception or for other tactical reasons but is an important aspect of playing basketball as a team and not just as a collection of individuals. This simple modification brings in other players to include them in the game and help the team. It also pushes the better players to think about playing as a team and about movement off the ball. When using this simple modification it may be advisable to explain to all players that it is not punishing anyone for being a skilful player but, instead, is designed to improve all players' skills and capacities.

The second way in which Game Sense is inclusive is through the interaction that it fosters between all the players in the team. Discussions about strategy, tactics and technique are a feature of Game Sense pedagogy. They can occur at the beginning of a session or game/activity and during modified games as team talks where the players discuss tactics, develop ideas and test them. With the typically simple activities used at the beginning of each chapter in Part II the verbal interaction in discussions is usually between teacher/coach and students/players, but as the games or activities increase in complexity they provide more opportunity for team talks, or the debate of ideas (Gréhaigne, Richard and Griffin 2005), that lead to formulating solutions, testing and evaluating them. In some chapters the games used from the beginning mean that these team talks about tactics can begin quite early. For example, in the unit on netball (Chapter 13) the simple games used at the beginning, such as tag ball and keepings off, have enough tactical complexity to allow for team talks about tactics.

These meetings and the opportunities for discussion they provide are important not only for developing better games players but also for developing better relationships between players, better team harmony and the *esprit de corps* that all teams need. I conducted a study in an Australian primary school that enquired into the capacity for Game Sense pedagogy to make sport more enjoyable for children who were not fond of sport. The most prominent theme to emerge from this study was the ways in which the interaction between students fostered by Game Sense improved interpersonal relationships, empathy and understanding of other students in the class (Light 2008b). Over a school term I worked with the class teacher to teach cricket and used the progression of modified games presented in Chapter 14, finishing the term's work by teaching two lessons in softball (using games from Chapter 15) to evaluate the students' ability to transfer tactical knowledge.

The social interaction fostered by the Game Sense approach also provides valuable opportunities for the development of social skills and the principles of democracy and citizenship while developing better players. These group discussions focused on tactics, strategy and technique involve the same processes of collective purpose, negotiation, give and take and compromise required in all democracies. As I outlined in Chapter 3, meaningful and relevant learning arises from social interaction, with cognition being socially distributed. That is to say that we can learn more in interaction with others than we can on our own. The small-group tactical discussions in small-sided games and the larger whole-team discussions, therefore, form important modes of learning for developing as not only better players but also better people.

Game Sense for PE and sport coaching

43

Enjoyment and motivation

Fun and enjoyment should be central concerns of children's and youth sport coaching (Weiss 1995; Coakley 2001) and have received increasing research attention over the past few years (Bengoechea, Strean and Williams 2004; Jones 2002; Light 2003; Pope 2005). Research across a range of cultures confirms that having fun is one of the prime motivations for young people taking part in sport (for example, see Australian Sports Commission 1991; Weinberg *et al.* 2000). Common sense, and some research on Game Sense, also suggests that the positive emotional states of fun, joy and delight assist in learning to play sport (Light 2003; Pope 2005; Kretchmar 2005). Much of the enjoyment and fun experienced when learning to play sport through Game Sense arises from the social interaction it stimulates, from a sense of achievement and worth as a member of the team, and from actually understanding what the sport is about and what to do (Light 2002; Chen and Light 2006). This enjoyment is an important part of the learning process and the ways in which Game Sense emphasizes the social nature of team sports and games, the collective approach taken to problem solving in games and the need for real teamwork.

For the less skilled, being placed under the scrutiny of the coach and peers to perform techniques correctly can be stressful, demotivating and sometimes even humiliating (Ennis 1999). While traditional coaches may value their players having fun, it can prove difficult to fit this into their training as it is commonly seen by them as being separate from training and not a product of it. Coaches can often perceive a dichotomy between children learning to play a sport and having fun. For example, in their research on youth sport coaches in Canada, Bengoechea, Strean and Williams (2004) identified conflict between the idea of skill development and fun. The coaches in their study actually felt that they had to stop coaching to allow their players to have fun and felt they were losing valuable training time by doing this. Conversely, positive emotional states are a product of the learning and social interaction that are experienced in the Game Sense approach (Light 2003).

Players enjoy knowing what the game is actually about, knowing how they can contribute to the team effort, being empowered to make their own informed decisions as individuals and as a team, interacting with their teammates and enjoying the essentially social nature of team games. As one coach educator in a study I conducted on Game Sense coaches in Australia (Light 2004) argued, we have to give the game back to 'kids' and this is what Game Sense does. It does not, however, in any way compromise the development of skilful players. In fact, it produces players who can perform skill to suit the immediate demands of the situation at hand, understand the core concepts of the sport and teams, and play effectively as a team member to set a valuable foundation for their future development.

Coaching competitive sport for performance

The situation at the other end of the sport-coaching spectrum can be profoundly different. Coaches of baseball teams contesting the World Series or of national soccer teams competing in a FIFA World Cup final will obviously have a very different set of aims and methods to those of the coach of the local little league or junior soccer team. While good coaches do care about player welfare at the top levels (see, for example, Evans 2011), success is measured by wins and losses and not in terms of who enjoyed themselves. These two extremes of sport coaching thus seem to be worlds apart and to have very little in common. Indeed, this is a point that coaches of children's teams need to keep in mind so that they can make appropriate decisions and deal with negative manifestations of elite professional sport in the children's version that typically arise from an unhealthy emphasis on winning.

Many junior sport coaches and coaches of high school teams also operate at what can be seen as an elite level, and particularly in countries such as the United States of America and Japan, where school and university sport is so strong and so important for institutional status. High school American football or basketball games in the United States are major cultural events that can attract huge crowds of spectators and media interest. The annual national high school baseball, soccer and rugby championships in Japan are also major cultural events, and particularly the baseball championships at Koshien (see, for example, Moeran 1986). Even in Australia, where club sport is strong, some school sports events such as important rugby games in the Sydney Great Public Schools (the most exclusive group of elite independent schools) competition can attract up to 15,000 spectators to a game. Clearly these are examples of a form of elite-level sporting spectacle but, at the same time, they involve young people at school who are moving into the adult world and who need to learn more than just how to 'take out' an opposition player.

Adopting a Game Sense approach at this level can maintain some of the positive learning identified in this chapter while developing better players. Within this context, performance is clearly more important than at more junior levels, and I briefly outline areas where a Game Sense approach can produce better and more complete players while still making a positive contribution to their development as people.

Transfer from training to the game

One problem that often confronts coaches is the lack of transfer of performance from training to the game. Much of this arises from the differences between the environments in which players train during the week and compete on the weekend. Not only do players in all games need to know how to perform techniques but they also need to understand where these techniques performed as skills (technique performed in context) fit into the game, with their execution informed by tactical knowledge and game awareness. In Game Sense there is no separation between skill, tactical knowledge and decision-making as they all inform each other. As a holistic approach Game Sense coaching gives meaning to skills and encourages execution that adapts to the moment. This then contributes to the performance of 'intelligent action' (Light and Fawns 2001).

It can be frustrating for players and coaches to see little evidence of what appears to be good training during the week in improved game performance on the weekend, and this is because the practice environment does not resemble the competition environment well enough. A lack of transfer from training to the game is the result of not training athletes within contexts that are close enough to game conditions for transfer from training to competition. To be effective in improving game performance, training needs to replicate game conditions to some extent, including the pressure under which players must make decisions and execute skills. Game Sense can address this problem of a lack of transfer by placing learning and development within game-like environments that are structured by the coach to develop particular skills, tactical understanding and decision-making. For example, in Chapter 12, on basketball, extra pressure can be put on the attacking team in the half-court basketball by having five defenders but only four attackers, to duplicate the sort of pressure they might be under at critical times in a competition match. While the coach might start with a 5 v. 4 or 5 v. 3 advantage for the attacking team, he/she can build pressure as they improve and adapt.

Working off the ball

One of the most striking weaknesses in traditional technique-based approaches to coaching in terms of game performance is their inability to specifically develop the skills and knowledge needed to work off the ball. For example, in most invasion games only one player at a time is in contact with the ball yet training focuses on ball manipulation and the skills involved. During any invasion game most of the players in the attacking team, most of the time, do not have the ball yet need to be actively engaged in the game and contributing to the team's effort. This is a very obvious problem in children's soccer games, where the entire two teams are drawn to the ball like bees to a honey pot, no matter how much the coaches yell at them to 'spread out'. Coaches in invasion games need training approaches that can develop this play off the ball.

This was made very obvious by a soccer coach in a study I conducted on Game Sense coaches in Australia (Light 2004). He noted that in an analysis of youth soccer games in the UK in 2000 there was typically about sixty minutes of playing time, within which players were in contact with the ball for a maximum of only two to three minutes. He asked the rhetorical question: 'So what are they doing for the other fifty-eight minutes?' They are, of course, running and positioning themselves in tactically informed ways. As the coach in this study asked, if players in soccer are in possession of the ball for an average of less than three minutes in a game why do coaches continue to drill ball skills and overlook player movement off the ball? Games like keepings off (piggy in the middle) are examples of simple games used to develop off the ball movement and thinking. In Chapter 13, on netball, a 5 v. 3 game of keepings off is suggested. Often these games are quite static at the beginning, but, as coach questioning stimulates thinking, they become very dynamic, fast-moving games that develop decision-making off the ball, movement and passing/catching skill, anticipation, communication and agility.

Efficient coaching needs to address not only ball skills, but also perception, decision-making and movement off the ball, and this must involve using modified games. Player movement off the ball in attack, as players create and find space, is equally, if not more, important for the team's success than the manipulation of the ball by the player in possession. Research indicates that game-based approaches can achieve significant improvements in player movement off the ball (Mitchell, Oslin and Griffin 1995). Game Sense offers a means through which coaches can assist in the development of perceptual capacities and decision-making ability. While it is unlikely that such capacities and enacted understandings can be directly 'taught' by the coach, their development can be fostered by placing the player in appropriate contexts and by guiding learning through well-planned questioning.

Creating independent players

The All Blacks' assistant rugby coach for the 2011 Rugby World Cup winning team, Wayne Smith, argues that there is a need for player empowerment in rugby at the elite level and is a proponent of the Game Sense approach (Kidman 2001, 2005). In sports such as rugby, soccer and field hockey, where the coach has little opportunity to make decisions for players during the game, players must be independent decision-makers. In some sports, such as American football, this may be less important, but across most junior sport there is a need to 'give the game back' to children and young people by empowering them to make individual and collective decisions on the field independently of the coach. This is equally important in elite-level professional sport. Good coaching should produce players who, once on the field, do not need to look to the coach for advice. If a coach has to shout instructions from the sideline, then he or she has not empowered his or her players to make their own decisions. Players need to be empowered in training to be independent decision-makers on the field (Kidman 2001). Game Sense develops player autonomy by placing players in situations where they are required to make decisions independently of the coach at training. As a coach in my study of Game Sense coaches in Australia argues:

> At the grass roots level Game Sense is inclusive and helps make training fun for children. At the elite level it helps players to make quick decisions and promotes self-reliance. This means that players don't constantly need the coach to tell them what to do.
>
> *(Light 2004: 15)*

Conclusion

This chapter identifies two different areas of concern for coaches of children and young people and suggests how Game Sense can be applied to address them.

While concerns with using sport as a vehicle for social and moral development and a focus on competitive performance may seem to be poles apart, they need not be. Game Sense provides a very effective means of developing better athletes while developing better people, and this was a strong theme among the All Blacks' coaching staff in Evan's (2011) study on the influence of Game Sense in New Zealand and Australian rugby. Game Sense offers coaches a valuable way of developing better players and teams while making sport more enjoyable, increasing participation and contributing to the development of responsible and active future citizens with a working understanding of democratic processes. The appropriate use of Game Sense in children's and young people's sport, whether at grassroots community-based levels or at elite competitive levels, can make sport inclusive, rewarding and an important part of their physical, intellectual, social and moral development.

Chapter discussion questions

1. Identify the diversity of contexts, learners' experiences, capabilities and inclinations, coaching objectives and coaching approaches within the term 'coaching' and suggest how Game Sense can be adapted to these different contexts.
2. Suggest what the main differences between coaching sport outside schools and teaching physical education within schools are when working with secondary school-aged students and players, and how these differences shape the ways in which Game Sense is used.
3. Suggest what you feel would be the main differences between coaching children between the ages of five and twelve in sports clubs or schools and coaching senior players of age eighteen and above in a highly competitive league. Focus on learning aims and objectives, the nature of the learners and the application of the Game Sense approach.
4. What opportunities does a Game Sense approach offer for coaching team sports and the most competitive and elite professional levels that more traditional coach-centred approaches do not and in what specific areas of play can it redress the limitations of direct instruction?
5. Participation in sport and consumption of it as a media product can influence children's and young people's socio-moral development in negative and/or positive ways. The representation of sport at its most elite and competitive levels often emphasizes aspects of it that are accepted as being inappropriate for children and young people. Think about the learning processes used in Game Sense and suggest how they can make a positive contribution to participants' moral and social learning.

5

GAME SENSE PEDAGOGY

At its most basic level taking a Game Sense approach involves designing a game or sequence of games to achieve particular outcomes, asking questions to stimulate thinking and reflection, and ensuring that there are opportunities for group discussion, collaboration and the formulation of ideas/solutions that are tested and evaluated. While it might seem simple enough, it is typically very challenging for teachers and coaches who are used to traditional approaches, and it requires a considerable amount of work for it to begin to take shape and produce results (see, for example, Butler 2005). It involves more than just using games for learning. It involves a significant change in pedagogy and the role of the teacher or coach that has not been readily taken up by teachers and coaches (see, for example, Butler 1996; Light and Evans 2010; Roberts 2011).

The following section outlines the basic pedagogical features of Game Sense that provide a framework within which Game Sense pedagogy could be developed. It then examines some of the challenges for teachers and coaches involved in taking it up to offer some ideas on adapting to this quite different approach. I intentionally avoid any prescription about how it must be done by offering a framework for taking up a Game Sense approach with enough flexibility for teachers and coaches to adapt it to their own beliefs, the nature of their students or players and the particular circumstances within which they work. Game Sense pedagogy is game-based, involves indirect teaching/coaching and is learner-centred, and in this chapter I offer what I suggest are its four core pedagogical features, to offer a framework for its implementation. These features are that it involves: (1) designing the learning environment, (2) emphasizing questioning to generate dialogue, (3) providing opportunities for collaborative formulation of ideas/solutions that are tested and evaluated and (4) developing a supportive socio-moral environment.

FIGURE 5.1   All-class tactical discussion in primary school PE

Designing the learning environment

Game Sense pedagogy is based upon a holistic view of learning with a focus on the game itself rather than on distinct components of it such as skills, technique or tactics (den Duyn 1997). Drawing on CLT, this view implies that the game and the people playing it are one entity and that learning to play involves a process of adaptation to the game and its dynamics, with tactical knowledge, skill execution and decision-making all tied up together. Underpinned by constructivist or CLT perspectives on learning, this view contrasts sharply with the idea that games and sport can be learnt by mastering a predetermined number of 'fundamental' motor skills. In Game Sense most learning occurs within the context of modified games or game-like activities. As Dewey (1916/97) suggests, real learning occurs through engagement with the learning environment and not through direct instruction.

In Game Sense, even when the teaching or coaching focus is more on the development of skill, it is practised within a context requiring perception and decision-making. For example, instead of dribbling soccer or hockey balls around cones players can be asked to dribble a ball around an area in which other players are also dribbling, so that changing direction while dribbling is in response to a game-like environment in which perceptual ability is also developed (see Chapters 10 and 11). Instead of standing in lines waiting their turn to control and pass back to their partner, the same children or young people could work in a grid passing five metres to their partner then running five metres to another part of the grid to receive a pass, and so on, while other pairs are doing the same thing, as outlined in Activity 1, Chapter 10. This creates the need to find spaces, move into them and see free channels for passing. In this activity the better players can work on a 'one-touch' pass when appropriate. Players/students are still practising controlling and passing but in a dynamic context within which they develop perception and decision-making while developing skill execution *in context*. The game context also allows the better players to develop more demanding skills. Even when tightly focused on a demanding skill such as the dig in volleyball, practices such as that suggested in Chapter 17 locate it in a setting where perception and decision-making are also required and developed.

The design of the physical learning environment (usually a game or game-like activity) needs to suit the desired learning outcomes and the knowledge, abilities and inclinations/interests of the learners, and provide for modifications to make it more or less challenging on a class/team basis or on a small-group basis. The teacher or coach also needs to be able to identify when games need changing and be able to change them appropriately, and this is a skill that is developed with experience and reflective practice. Just as the students or players learn, so does the teacher or coach if he/she is open to learning. Over time learners should adapt to the Game Sense approach and take on more autonomy and responsibility for their learning while developing their knowledge base. This then allows the teacher or coach to encourage, or even expect, them to participate in game modification and to identify when a game needs changing. Early investment in learners by the Game Sense teacher/coach pays off over time as they become increasingly independent. In the beginning it can often be very challenging and time consuming, but it pays off over time (Light 2004). In a sports club or a physical education programme where all teachers or coaches take a Game Sense approach, students and players can develop over several years into independent learners with a well-developed sense of enquiry and a deep knowledge of games.

Designing the modified game(s) to be used is the first step in setting up a PE lesson or sport team training session. It is probably the most difficult aspect of a Game Sense approach and the most important. The Game Sense teacher or coach has typically done most of his/her work well before the lesson/session starts (Thorpe and Bunker 2008). My experiences of teaching Game Sense to undergraduate students at the University of Melbourne and the University of Sydney, and discussions with my colleagues there, led me to realize that, despite the obvious importance of questioning in Game Sense, the quality of the activities or modified games was more important in facilitating learning. Even when the teaching is poor, significant learning takes place purely by playing a well-designed game. This view was confirmed by Thorpe and Bunker's address at the 2008 TGfU International Conference in Vancouver, when they expressed the same idea in underlining the pivotal importance of 'getting the game right'.

Recognition of the learning that can emerge from just playing a well-designed game is evident in the Victorian Soccer Federation's (VSF) GoalKick junior development programme in Australia (now Football Federation Victoria). The VSF relies on parents running GoalKick programmes who invariably have little experience of playing soccer and even less of coaching. Instead of asking them to coach, the programme asks them to coordinate learning sessions where their role is to organize the playing of learning games and to encourage the young players. This is underpinned by the assumption that children will learn through playing the modified games. VSF coordinators' roles are seen to involve 'creating the right environment for learning to take place and letting the children play, offering encouragement along the way' (Greener n.d.: 3).

The traditional technical approach identifies core skills seen as fundamental to being able to play the game and then typically has students or players participate in skill drills separate from the game until they are considered good enough to put them together in a game. This means learning skills *before* playing the game, while in Game Sense skills are learnt *in* and *through* (modified) games. In physical education classes, designing a series of games that are progressively more complex and being able to modify them when a need is identified is a far more challenging task than correcting students or players standing in lines to practise technique. Likewise, designing appropriate training games that replicate game conditions and help players develop a particular aspect of play is also very challenging to begin with for coaches. Sometimes it might help to draw on the ideas of the players, and this is particularly the case with primary (elementary) classroom teachers, who have pedagogical knowledge but little specific game knowledge. The games in this book provide a starting point, but teachers and coaches need to get past putting their hands out for resources and be able to develop their own games. This requires some deep thinking about what is to be learnt and what environment will best enhance this learning.

Once the lesson or training session has begun, teachers and coaches should be able to modify, or have the learners modify, the games/activities that have been decided on for the lesson/session. It takes time and reflective practice to develop this skill, which is a marker of an experienced Game Sense teacher or coach. Most teachers and coaches will know their students/players well and be able to design games of appropriate difficulty that stretch them yet allow them to succeed. The right balance between challenge and success is critical in physical education and sport. However, until he or she is very skilful at Game Sense teaching, the teacher/coach needs to have ideas in mind or on paper for making the games easier or more challenging. This can simply involve changing the size and shape of the area used, the number of players, the number of balls or even adding a special challenge for the more skilful players. For example, in the modified cricket game called 'zone cricket' (Chapter 14), in which the aim is to hit the ball across as many zones as possible to gain points, if the game is played indoors with a soft ball, hitting the wall on the full can earn four points but the batter can be caught out and score no runs. To offer a challenge for the more skilful players the teacher/coach can place a bin in one corner of the space and give any batter who can hit the ball and land it in the bin ten points. This challenges not only the skilled batters but also the fielding/bowling team, who have to adapt their tactics accordingly.

Owing to the very significant differences between Game Sense and directive sport-skills teaching approaches, moving toward adopting Game Sense pedagogy takes time, not only for the teacher/coach, but also for the learners. However, once the class or team adjusts the students/players can be asked for suggestions about what modifications are needed, and when, to make the game better in terms of enjoyment and improving learning. In fact, classes or teams who have adapted to the Game Sense approach will not wait to be asked for input into modifying the game. One of my former students at the University of Melbourne who had great success in using Game Sense noted this, telling me that her students looked forward with enthusiasm to being able to modify every game she introduced and even offer their own games (Light and Butler 2005).

The game cards produced by the ASC are a valuable resource; however, coaches and teachers can also use many existing 'drills' across a range of sports but use them in a Game Sense way by asking for reflection upon experience, taking on a problem-solving approach, stimulating dialogue and asking players/ students to collectively formulate ideas and test them in games. Some of the games presented in this book may well be familiar to teachers and coaches because they have originally been taken from training manuals but transformed by using Game Sense pedagogy. Teachers and coaches can also call on students/ players to suggest modifications to games or completely new games that they make up or have used before in physical education or club sport. This has the added benefit of developing trust and a sense of collaboration between teacher and students or coach and players.

Emphasizing questioning to generate dialogue

Asking questions that generate learning can be difficult for teachers and coaches who are accustomed to telling students/players what to do (see, for example, Roberts 2011; McNeill *et al.* 2008). What sort of questions do I ask? When do I ask them? How many questions should I ask? Whom do I ask? Questioning is central to stimulating dialogue, reflection and the conscious processing of ideas about playing the game. Questions thus need to be open and generate dialogue, a sense of enquiry and the construction of new knowledge and understanding. From a constructivist perspective on learning, they need to generate possibilities and a range of answers rather than lead to predetermined answers. Wright and Forrest (2007) identify this problem through their criticism of the sequencing of questions suggested in some TGfU texts and the ways in which it limits the possible responses instead of expanding them. Questions are used to promote thinking and dialogue from which learning emerges, with Kidman (2005) suggesting that questions should ask 'What?', 'Where?', 'Why?' and 'How?'. Questions should stimulate thinking and discussion instead of simple yes or no answers. They should also stimulate further questioning by the students/players of each other and of the teacher/coach.

For teachers and coaches who are used to telling students/players what to do this can present a serious problem, as Roberts (2011) shows with his study on cricket coaches' attempts to introduce a TGfU approach into their coaching programmes. From my own experiences of teaching pre-service teachers and master's students in Australia, England, France, Taiwan, Japan and Macau I find that teachers and coaches often struggle to find the right balance between letting the students/players get on with learning by playing the game and stopping the action to ask questions. This is something learnt over time but is no different to any PE teacher's need to maintain the right 'pace' of the lesson. Too many stop-pages for teacher/coach questioning deprive students/players of the pleasure of playing the games and the time needed to understand by doing and for the body to think in action. It is better to ask too few questions than too many.

Questions can be asked 'on the run', at any time, of individuals or of the small groups of students/players playing in a single small-sided game, such as a 3 v. 3 or a 5 v. 3 set-up, while letting the rest of the team or class continue. A well-timed question can make a significant difference in learning even when not using a Game Sense or TGfU approach. At the end of the year in 2011 I was watching a year-nine physical education lesson on softball in a Melbourne school with a visiting colleague from overseas. In a girls versus boys game two boys in a row hit the ball over the heads of the fielders to complete home runs, but each time the fielders returned to the same positions. A freeze strategy (Turner 2005), asking a simple, open-ended question, would have stimulated the fielding side to think and respond, for example with 'They have scored two home runs by hitting well beyond the field you have set. What can you do about this problem?' If they pushed too many fielders back and the boys dropped the ball short into the space opened up and they did not respond to this, then another quick question might be needed, but once a class or team adjusts to a student/player-centred approach fewer of these questions are necessary.

The class can be stopped for questioning when the teacher/coach wants to change the game or modify it, and during the game to give teams the chance to discuss the problem(s) to be solved and develop a solution that they can test and evaluate. A teacher/coach might stop a game, pull the class/team in and ask some tactical questions in a whole-class/team situation but then send the different teams off to develop their own ideas and solutions. He/she would then walk around to the different groups encouraging and prodding to assist in the develop-ment of dialogue and to try to get all the students/players involved in discussions or 'debate'. It is also important to listen to the students/players, to really value their opinions and ideas and what they have to say, and be open to solutions and ideas that you may not have thought of. There are no right or wrong answers and students/players should be encouraged to be creative and to enjoy meeting the challenges involved.

At the completion of a class or training session the teacher/coach would typically ask questions about the class/session, both to assess how well the students/players had consciously understood and to reinforce the understandings developed. Again these need to generate deep thinking and reflection on the experiences of the session/class and not merely about whether or not the students/players enjoyed the class/session. Students and players who are not accustomed to being asked questions can be uncomfortable with being asked instead of being told, and need to understand why they are being asked. It might also be worthwhile taking time to introduce questioning to avoid the situation where a batter in Roberts' (2011: 43) study threw his bat on the ground and said to his coach: 'Please just tell me, its like being on Mastermind.' The same problem can emerge in physical education classes. When I was working at the University of Melbourne a pre-service teacher who was implementing a Game Sense approach encountered problems with students who were not accustomed to being asked questions and were more comfortable being told what to do. In response to a question she asked, a student replied: 'I dunno, you're the teacher, miss. You're getting paid to tell us what to do!'

Some of this learner frustration can come from the teacher/coach asking too many questions. Finding the balance between action and stopping for questions is a challenge in taking up a Game Sense approach, and I would suggest that too little questioning is better than too much as both teacher/coach and learners adapt. Most physical education teachers have a feel for the pace of any lesson and the need for things to keep moving along, and this should operate as a guide to when to intervene in action to ask questions. Other than this consideration, teachers/coaches need to be able to identify when there is something that is holding up the game and which warrants stopping to focus the learners' attention on it. Many of the games used in this book are also very physically demanding due to the continuity of play they generate, and when the class or team is tiring this might be a good time to take a break and ask some questions.

Providing opportunities for collaborative formulation, testing and evaluation of solutions

Once the students or players have played the game being used enough to get a practical sense of it, and have been prompted into thinking about what the problems are that face them and how they might solve them, they can be given time to discuss this as a group and to come up with some strategies that they feel might work. That is to say that this would typically follow the following order: (1) explain the game and ensure they understand; (2) let them play the game; (3) stop and ask a few questions to identify or confirm the problem(s) to be solved; (4) let them formulate a strategy or action plan through group dialogue; (5) let them implement the strategy or plan in the game; (6) stop and have them critically reflect upon how it went and suggest modifications or identify why it didn't work. This last step would be conducted within the team/group if they were going to have the chance to test it again. If not it would be conducted as a whole class/team in a collective reflection, evaluation and development of knowledge. This sequence is not at all prescriptive and should be open to change according to the learners and the situation at hand.

Once students adapt to this approach in physical education they can and should develop an enthusiasm for meeting the challenges presented by the teacher and look forward to being part of a collective effort that involves not only playing the game but also rich social interaction focused on a common goal. As is the case with a classroom teacher using a constructivist-informed approach, the teacher needs to move between the groups to ensure that there is a sharing of ideas and that all students are engaged in the process of problem solving. Some groups may not require any intervention by the teacher, while others may require some well-directed questions to engage the quieter students or reduce the dominance of a particular student. While the more confident and experienced sports people may initially dominate proceedings, the less experienced can often make very valuable contributions when encouraged. The important point here is that the students are learning not only about games and sport but also about how to draw on all of what members of the group have to offer and to listen to others.

When coaching sports team players, you will also initially need to encourage them to express opinions within a supportive environment and to be able to see that mistakes are part of learning and improving. The development of trust and dialogue between all team members will also make a significant contribution to a sense of being a team. It will assist in them developing the capacity and inclination to discuss and solve problems on the field or court during competition matches and at half-time and quarter-time breaks. Teams coached in this way should not need the coach to shout instructions from the sideline and should understand each other and care for each other as well. A sense of empathy and care for teammates is equally important in elite-level sport as in a physical education class, as Evans (2011) illustrates in his study on the culture of coaching within the 2011 Rugby World Cup winning team, the New Zealand All Blacks.

Developing a supportive environment

The culture and ambience of a Game Sense session or class are different to traditional directive classes due to the different sets of relationships it develops between students (or players) and between them and the teacher or coach. There are more equal relationships that are collaborative in nature and there is a sense that teachers/coaches and the students/players are what Davis and Sumara (1997) refer to as co-participants in learning. Students can 'hide' in a traditional class, where they are passive learners, and not engage or be noticed, but in a Game Sense class we ask them to speak up, come up with ideas and experiment, and we provide an environment where they are comfortable doing so.

In Game Sense we ask our students to take risks and in many ways open themselves up during discussions when they suggest ideas or tactics. To get students to be actively engaged, take risks and speak up freely, teachers and coaches have to build a supportive environment where learners feel secure enough to take these risks. As DeVries and Zan (1996) suggest with regard to constructivist-informed teaching, there needs to be a socio-moral environment that supports students (and players). Teachers and coaches also need to make it clear that students/players learn from mistakes and that they are an essential part of learning. This is not an easy task and takes time, just as it takes time for a class or team to adapt to the Game Sense approach. It is easy to speak of empowerment, but students who fear being embarrassed or humiliated if they make mistakes are unlikely to be interested in being empowered and happier to just do as they are told. These children and young people can avoid responsibility for their own learning and if anything goes wrong blame it on the teacher (or coach).

Challenges in implementing Game Sense

In the final section of this chapter I briefly discuss some of the challenges involved in taking on a Game Sense approach to coaching or teaching that I have not addressed in the previous section. The issues I look at are: (1) the aesthetics of training and other people's perceptions; (2) the repositioning of the coach/teacher; and (3) conflict with beliefs about learning and good teaching/coaching.

The aesthetics of training and other people's perceptions

In my study (Light 2004) on Australian coaches' experiences of using Game Sense a senior figure in a state soccer organization recommends that coaches who want to develop better players need to take a Game Sense approach but that when the committee comes to watch training they use nice neat drills. This is because drills look better to people than the sometimes chaotic appearance of a Game Sense session. This raises the important issue of what most people think a good training session or physical education class looks like and how this is actually nothing like the real game situation that players might be preparing for. Games, and particularly those played by children and young people, are typically chaotic, but they learn to make sense of this chaos (Light 2005b). Most people's idea of a good training session or games class is one that looks well organized and in which the coach/teacher directs proceedings with authority. The problem with this is that nice neat-looking drills are far removed from the chaos of real matches and this is one reason why they don't work.

Representations of elite-level coaches in the mass media also conflict with the ways in which a Game Sense coach relates to players and conducts himself/herself in training. The Game Sense coach does not yell at or abuse players, throw clipboards on the ground in a rage or take a 'my way or the highway' approach. Instead, he or she is calm and relates to players or students in a more equal and collegial way. Unfortunately this can be misinterpreted as lacking passion, not really caring or even not really teaching or coaching anything. To be proactive in addressing this potential problem teachers and coaches should think about letting significant people in their school or club community such as parents or committee members know what they are doing and why. For example, a first year out teacher who had worked with me at the University of Melbourne invited the parents of her students to take part in a couple of workshops on Game Sense in which they were taught as their children were. This proved to be very successful in getting them onside and in supporting the Game Sense approach.

The repositioning of the coach/teacher

Game Sense involves a repositioning of the coach/teacher in relation to his/her players/students. Typically, the traditional, technical coach or teacher is in charge of the class/team, telling the learners what, when and how to do skills and tactical moves. The coach in this approach is seen to hold knowledge that he or she transfers to his/her learners and which involves constant correction of technique by the coach/teacher (see, for example, Light and Evans 2010). On the other hand, Game Sense involves more equal power relationships and closer, more collegial relationships between coach/teacher and learners. Indeed, many suggest that instead of the coach/teacher passing on knowledge he/she should take on the role of a *co-participant* in learning (Davis and Sumara 1997). This obviously involves a radical change in the positioning of the coach/teacher and can often be a very difficult change to make.

I illustrate this with a quote from a coach in a study I conducted on Australian coaches' experiences of Game Sense that suggests the struggle that some experience in 'stepping off centre stage':

> I still have some problems. There are certain techniques that I feel have to be highlighted. I don't go into the heavily technique-driven program that I used to use but I still believe that players need to understand certain components of a technical movement. Then, sometimes I tell myself 'just back away and give them a little information and let them find out for themselves'.
>
> *(Light 2004: 10)*

Conflict between Game Sense and beliefs about learning and good teaching/coaching

In an examination of mathematics teachers' interpretation and use of constructivism, Davis and Sumara (2003) suggest that the teachers' unquestioned beliefs about learning present a core problem for them in implementing an authentic constructivist-informed approach. They suggest that pre-service programmes need to actually help pre-service teachers bring these unquestioned, deeply held beliefs about learning and teaching to the surface so that they can consider constructivism in relation to their own beliefs. Commonsense notions of knowledge as a pre-existing object and learning as involving the transfer of knowledge are at odds with a constructivist view of learning, as outlined in Chapter 3. While it is relatively easy to consider this at a conscious level, these beliefs about how we learn and what good teaching and/or coaching is operate at a deep, unconscious level to shape how teachers and coaches interpret or misinterpret Game Sense. This is a strong theme in Light and Evans' (2010) study of rugby coaches' interpretation and use of Game Sense, in which they used games but not Game Sense pedagogy. Butler's (1996) study of ten teachers' responses to TGfU highlights the same issue in PE teaching. Teachers, pre-service teachers and coaches reading this book might, therefore, think about what their beliefs are about what knowledge is, how humans learn and what actually is good teaching/ coaching, and look at how this sits in relation to the ideas about learning and notions of it outlined in Chapter 3.

Chapter discussion questions

1. Reflect upon your own experiences as a student in physical education and a player in sports teams at school or in sports clubs, with a focus on the pedagogy used by your teachers/coaches. Identify the key features of these approaches and compare them to the features suggested in this chapter for Game Sense, considering what and how you learnt.
2. Explain how the author's suggestion for using a framework comprising the features or characteristics of Game Sense pedagogy is different to more prescriptive approaches that have 'non-negotiable' aspects and provide a more tightly defined, step-by-step approach. Consider both approaches and suggest which would be more helpful for you, and discuss the relative benefits for teachers and coaches interested in taking up a Game Sense or similar approach.
3. Discuss the extent to which you think the framework offered in this chapter for games teaching and coaching team sports could offer a model for physical education pedagogy beyond games and team sports, or even beyond physical education, to be used in other practice-oriented subject areas in schools.
4. Summarize the main challenges facing teachers and coaches outlined in this chapter and suggest ways in which they can be redressed in teacher and coach education and professional development interventions. If you have had personal experience of dealing with these challenges when implementing a Game Sense or similar approach, include reflection upon this experience in your answer.
5. Drawing on any experience you have had in teaching games or coaching sport and of being taught and coached, suggest what you feel the biggest challenges are in taking up a Game Sense approach and what you feel they might be for either coaches or teachers more generally.

6
ASSESSING KNOWLEDGE-IN-ACTION IN TEAM GAMES

Expectations of contemporary policy developments in pedagogy at national and state (or equivalent) levels expose the limitations of traditional, directive, teacher-centred approaches to teaching physical education in many countries in the world. In a climate of increasing accountability across the globe expectations that teachers demonstrate high-quality teaching present a significant problem for physical education teachers (Curry and Light 2007). For example, in Australia these include the New South Wales (NSW) Quality Teaching Framework (QTF), the Victorian 'Professional Learning in Effective Schools' guiding principles and the South Australian 'Teaching for Effective Learning' (TfEL) at state level. At a national level this is evident in policy documents such as the 'Thinking Schools, Learning Nation' policy (see, for example, McNeill, Fry and Wright 2010; Wright, McNeill and Fry 2009) in Singapore and the Australian Government Quality Teacher Programme (AGQTP). It is also implied in the new Japanese national physical education curriculum, which mandates a tactical approach and group discussion to learning in and through small-sided games and was introduced in primary schools in 2011 and is due to be introduced in secondary schools in 2012. All these initiatives exert pressure on physical education teachers to demonstrate valuable intellectual learning and high-quality pedagogy.

In NSW, Australia, the QTF provides a valuable framework for the development of high-quality learning across the school curriculum but, in doing so, presents serious challenges for many, if not most, physical education teachers. For example, traditional practice in the teaching of sport and games that is based upon the mastery of discrete techniques and guided by the idea of learning as the transmission of knowledge as an object cannot meet the expectations of the NSW QTF (or similar documents in other states or countries). In games teaching this challenge can be met by taking up Game Sense pedagogy (Curry and Light

FIGURE 6.1   Low-key decision-making and ball manipulation

2007; Pearson, Webb and McKeen 2006). However, there is a range of significant challenges facing teachers in implementing it before the promises of this pedagogical approach can be realized. This has been very evident in Singapore, where despite the GCA being mandated by the Ministry of Education in 1999 traditional approaches have proved resistant to change (for example, see McNeill *et al.* 2004). It is also evident in China, where attempts to promote high-quality pedagogy in physical education have met resistance from physical education teachers (Jin 2011). I discussed some of these challenges in Chapter 5 and focus in this chapter on the challenge of using assessment that is both authentic and practical when teaching games using a Game Sense approach.

Pedagogy with a focus on different learning outcomes and objectives to 'traditional' technique-focused, teacher-centred teaching requires different methods of assessment that can provide authentic information on the achievement of the learning it aims to encourage. Good assessment methods should also make a contribution to the learning process. The Game Sense approach recognizes and can account for the complexity of learning in, about and through games as opposed to the technical approach that attempts to reduce this complexity to the mastery of discrete techniques. Directive, technical teaching that emphasizes the mastery of isolated techniques thus typically requires assessment of correctly executed techniques, and typically outside the game or a game-like situation. Owing to this focus on teaching 'correct' technique, the technical approach typically employs assessment that involves testing the execution of these techniques by gauging how close they come to an ideal form. For example, when the mastery of a set of core skills, such as in the Fundamental Motor Skills (FMS) approach to teaching sport, is seen as a necessary prerequisite for playing games it makes sense to test these 'fundamental' skills in isolation from the dynamics of game contexts. However, the problem with this approach is that it oversimplifies learning to play games, and while there is ample evidence showing how this makes significant improvement in technique or skill execution there is little convincing evidence suggesting that mastering these fundamental skills leads to better or more enjoyable game play.

Adopting a position based upon very different epistemology and ontology, Game Sense pedagogy is informed by a holistic view of games and of learning underpinned by very different assumptions about epistemology and human learning (Light 2008a). This starkly different set of assumptions about learning then requires a very different assessment procedure. When the focus of teaching is on students or players developing tactical understanding, decision-making and the performance of appropriate skills *within the game* new assessment approaches are clearly needed if they are to be authentic. This is even more important if we accept that knowing the game means being able to *enact* knowledge (Varela, Thompson and Rosch 1991) or demonstrate knowledge-in-action in games (Light and Fawns 2003).

Even when focused on the learning of tactical knowledge, decision-making ability and the flexible execution of skill, assessment that evaluates student knowledge *about* the game lacks authenticity as a measure of learning. While learning using a Game Sense approach begins with articulated knowledge about the game and what players or teams should do, this is only the first stage of learning when an enquiry-based learner-centred approach is adopted (Gréhaigne, Richard and Griffin 2005). From a constructivist perspective, to know the game does not mean having knowledge *about* the game as much as it means being able to enact knowledge *in* the game as knowledge-in-action. Game Sense assessment thus needs to provide information on learning performed within the context of games.

Two assessment instruments are commonly used to meet the challenges of providing authentic assessment of learning as enacted knowledge within the context of games. I outline them here only briefly but recommend further reading on them, including critiques of them and suggestions for improvement (see, for example, Memmert and Harvey 2008). The two assessment instruments are the Game Performance Assessment Instrument (GPAI) and the Team Sport Assessment Procedure (TSAP), with both being able to provide useful information about student/player learning. The development of the Tactical Games (TG) approach by North American researchers included the development of games-based assessment in the form of the GPAI, which has been widely taken up across the globe as the basic assessment instrument for game performance (for example, see Griffin, Mitchell and Oslin 1997). There is also a French-Canadian assessment instrument called TSAP that I have enjoyed using as a peer assessment approach when teaching undergraduate students and which is focused on team sports (Gréhaigne, Richard and Griffin 1997; Richard and Godbout 2000). I briefly outline the GPAI but pay a little more attention to the

TSAP as applied to team invasion games because it is less well known but very useful for assessing learning in team games.

Assessing knowledge-in-action

The long-running debate over the relationship between skills and tactical knowledge in games teaching reflects a misunderstanding of this relationship in criticism of Game Sense and similar approaches as neglecting skill development. This arose from debate in the 1990s that promoted the idea of having to choose between skill and tactical knowledge in a division of physical and intellectual learning (tactical versus technical). In Game Sense, skills are certainly not privileged but nor are they neglected, and this is evident in the practical chapters that follow (Part II). In Game Sense skills are seen as being part of the game developed in conjunction with tactical knowledge and decision-making within the game to give them meaning. The distinction between skills and technique is also important here, with skill being technique performed in context, but any debate about which is more important, skill or tactics, misses the core concept underpinning the approach, and that is that it focuses on *the game* (den Duyn 1997).

This focus on the game as a whole means that assessment has to be able to provide information about learning as a holistic process. Testing skills out of the context of a game is clearly not an authentic assessment approach for Game Sense but neither are tests of knowledge *about* the game. Well over a decade of research on TGfU and Game Sense shows how the ability to articulate tactical knowledge about the game develops well before the ability to enact this knowledge. Students and players learning through a Game Sense approach (and other similar approaches) can articulate what they should do well before they can actually do it. In the physical education pedagogy literature this is commonly referred to as 'declarative knowledge' (as knowledge about the rules and tactics of games) and 'procedural' knowledge (the enacting of knowledge in the game), but I use the terms articulating knowledge and enacting knowledge as they fit better with a constructivist, CLT and/or enactivist approach.

While learning in Game Sense can be seen as occurring through the mind (expressed in speech) and the body (expressed in action), the two are inter-related in an ongoing 'conversation' (Light and Fawns 2003). Knowing the game therefore means being able to play it intelligently and not merely being able to talk about it. The work of Varela, Thompson and Rosch (1991) draws on Eastern philosophical traditions to suggest that learning such as that which occurs in Game Sense involves a process of reducing the gap between the mind's intent (what we want to do) and the body's ability to enact it (what we can do). This view of learning sees a reduction of the gap between the conscious mind and the body, to the point at which they become one, with the performance becoming 'second nature'. From another perspective, this suggests that learning to play well involves bringing learning to consciousness through talking about it as part of the process of learning, but that complete learning is evident when the conscious mind is not in operation.

The following two instruments provide useful ways of assessing game performance and providing the authentic assessment I have argued for above.

The Game Performance Assessment Instrument

The GPAI was developed to measure game performance behaviours that demonstrate tactical understanding and the ability to solve tactical game problems by appropriately applying skills in the context of a game. It provides a means of analysing individual game performance and/or overall performance by breaking down performance into seven core components, and has been validated within the game categories of invasion games, net/wall games and striking games (Oslin, Mitchell and Griffin 1998). It can be used as a tool for measuring performance in games by the teacher or can be used as a peer assessment tool once the students are familiar with the instrument, and it is the most widely used instrument for measuring or gathering information on game performance. As with any model or pedagogical approach to teaching and learning, such as TGfU or Game Sense, it is something of an ongoing project that has been improved and adapted over time, with expected critiques of its perceived limitations and suggestions for its improvement (see, for example, Memmert and Harvey 2008).

The GPAI can measure on-the-ball and off-the-ball components of performance and game involvement. It provides seven identifiable components of performance and involvement in game play, from which the teacher chooses those that are most relevant and appropriate for the game and the focus of the teaching. The components are:

1. *base*: assessment of how well players return to a tactically sound 'base' position from which they can contribute to the team effort during play;
2. *decision-making*: this is a measure of the efficiency of the decisions on or off the ball made during play;
3. *skill execution*: this refers to the execution of a skill in the game but not just to its 'correctness' – it also refers to how appropriately it is executed in the context of the game;
4. *support*: this assesses how well the player(s) provides support for teammates;
5. *guard/mark*: this measure assesses the movement of the player in marking opposition players whether they are in possession of the ball or off the ball;
6. *cover*: this refers to the player's defensive cover or back-up provided in the game;
7. *adjust*: this assesses the player's ability to make adjustments in attack/offence or defence to the dynamics of the game and opposition players' movements.

A scoring rubric is used, with a five-point rating scale for each component chosen by the teacher to suit the particular sport or game. Assessment is typically undertaken in modified games such as 3 v. 3 volleyball, and once a class is familiar with the procedure it is easily used as a valid assessment of knowledge-in-action using a peer assessment approach as with TSAP. The reflection that this encourages for the student who is assessing his/her peers means that it can make a very valuable contribution to learning and form a significant part of the student's learning process. This reflection can be enhanced by students discussing their assessments in small groups and providing feedback to the player they are assessing.

The TSAP instrument

TSAP is an instrument used to evaluate performance in games as the integration of tactical understanding, decision-making and skill performance based upon the two basic notions of (1) how a player gains possession of the ball and (2) how he/she disposes of the ball. Players' behaviours are observed within a game and coded during game play on an observation grid. Two performance indexes and a performance score are then computed from the collected data. The assessment procedure is a form of peer assessment in which small-sided games are used for assessing performance, with students working in pairs where one is playing and the other coding behaviour. There are a number of versions of the instrument that can be adapted to the age and experience of the students. During this procedure the observation and recording of player behaviour focus the observer's attention on important aspects of play.

Observational variables

The aspects of play for which data is recorded are outlined in the following table.

Gaining possession of the ball	
Conquered ball (CB)	A player is recorded as having conquered the ball if he/she intercepted it, stole it from an opponent or recaptured it after an unsuccessful shot on goal or after a near loss to the other team
Received ball (RB)	The player receives the ball from a partner and does not immediately lose control of it
Disposing of the ball	
Lost ball (LB)	The player is recorded as having lost the ball when he/she loses possession of it without having scored a goal
Neutral ball (NB)	A routine pass to a partner that does not put any pressure on the other team
Pass (P)	A pass to a partner that contributes to the displacement of the ball towards the opposing team's goal
Successful shot on goal (SS)	A successful shot on goal (or try) is recorded when it scores or results in possession of the ball being retained

The computation of performance indexes and performance score is as follows:

Volume of play index = CB + RB

Efficiency index = $\dfrac{CB + P + SS}{10 + LB}$

Performance score = (volume of play ÷ 2) + (efficiency index × 10)

The TSAP provides information about student performance in games that quantifies an individual's overall offensive performance in selected invasion and net team sports, reflecting both technical and tactical aspects of game play (see Gréhaigne, Godbout and Bouthier 1997). The information provided by the individual variables, performance indexes and performance score is a reliable indicator of both technical and tactical performance related to successful game play (Gréhaigne, Godbout and Bouthier 1997). Gréhaigne, Godbout, Bouthier and Richard have verified the validity of the procedure in effectively measuring game play performance as a whole (Gréhaigne, Godbout and Bouthier 1997; Richard, Godbout and Gréhaigne 1998).

Observation items	Information collected
Received balls (RB)	Involvement of the player in play (availability, accessibility to receive a pass)
Conquered balls (CB)	The player's defensive capacities
Offensive balls (OB)	Player's capacity to make significant passes to his/her partners (offensive capacities)
Successful shots (SS)	Information related to the player's offensive capacities
Volume of play (PB = RB + CB)	General involvement of the player in the game
Lost balls (LB)	A small number reflects a good adaptation to the game

Using the TSAP

The full version can be difficult to use for the first time and this is likely to be more of a problem until students become accustomed to using it. To address this problem three versions of TSAP are available that are progressively more complex. The 1st Modified Version and the 2nd Modified Version can be used in situations where the teacher does not require as much information as the full version, and to make it more useable for the teacher or to adapt it to the age of the students and/or their inexperience in using the instrument. These simpler versions of TSAP have been developed and validated (Richard et al. 1999).

1st Modified Version

Volume of play (VP) = # of possessions (CB + RB)

Efficiency index (EI) = $\dfrac{VP}{10 + LB}$

Performance score = (VP ÷ 2) + (EI × 2)

In the simplest version of TSAP the number of observational variables is half that of the full version. There is no distinction made between CB or RB in the volume of play, with only the total number of possessions taken into consideration, along with the number of lost balls. This modification was a response to the difficulty that younger observers can have in differentiating between received and conquered possessions and the fact that the differences between these two variables were not seen to be as important for the learning of game concepts in lower grade levels such as at primary school.

The modifications in this version allow teachers to progressively familiarize students with the observation of game play behaviours and peer assessment. If students work with this approach to assessment from year six or seven, they should be very comfortable with it by the end of year eight and able to use the more complex version required for assessment from year nine. The variables retained in this first version still allow teachers and students to focus on important game play concepts, such as getting away from a defender (represented by the volume of play) and passing the ball while maintaining possession, for senior primary or junior secondary schools.

2nd Modified Version

Volume of play (VP) = # of possessions (CB + RB)

Efficiency index (EI) = $\dfrac{P + SS}{10 + LB}$

Performance score = (VP ÷ 2) + (EI × 2)

In the second version the efficiency index's numerator comprises the number of passes and successful shots on goal, with an emphasis in the efficiency index put on what the teacher might want the student to do when he/she gets possession of the ball (pass or shoot on goal). This increases the number of observational variables to four as an intermediate version between the simplest version and the full version of the TSAP. Both teachers and students unfamiliar with the TSAP can begin with the simplest version and move up to the others if there is a need for more complexity, for example in older classes in secondary school.

Discussion

Possibilities

Good assessment should form part of the learning process. The nature of the TSAP and the GPAI as peer assessment approaches assists learning by encouraging student reflection. Constructivist-informed teaching emphasizes the role of reflection in learning (see, for example, Fosnot 1996; Dewey 1916/97), with reflection upon action/experience central to the Game Sense approach. The TSAP and GPAI both provide another opportunity for students to reflect upon the aspects of game play as elements of an assessment process that emphasizes learning as part of assessment. The Game Sense learning process, which involves tactical discussions, game analysis and reflection, should help prepare students to take on the role of observer and learn from it as well as fostering relationships between students through discussions about assessment. The observers reflect upon the games they are observing and use this to arrive at an evaluation of the quality of the play, helping them make connections across their experiences of playing games and assessment (Gréhaigne and Godbout 1995), making the assessment a valuable learning experience.

Game Sense involves students and players collaboratively arriving at solutions for problems that arise in game play that may not necessarily lead to the discovery of 'correct answers' predetermined by the teacher. The teacher may well have some specific tactical solutions in mind in providing students with problems to be solved in TGfU/Game Sense and be adopting a discovery teaching style (Mosston and Ashworth 1986) that leads the learner to discover something predetermined by the teacher. However, the teacher needs to be open to the idea that there is not always only one 'correct answer' and to realize the importance of the process of learning, not just the product of it. For example, the first activity in Chapter 16, on ultimate frisbee, is focused on familiarization with the disc and the skills of throwing and catching it in three quite simple sub-activities. The teacher may, therefore, have a clear expectation of how the skills of throwing and catching should be performed, but be prepared to accept variations that work for that specific task.

As suggested in previous chapters, the teacher also needs to allow students to make mistakes because they are a valuable part of the learning process as constructive errors (DeVries and Zan 1996). The 'correct' answer or solution to tactical problems is also best judged upon how well it works in the game. This then encourages critical evaluation of some assessment methods used to assess tactical understanding in team games that, for example, show video clips of sections of play in real competition games and ask students to choose 'the correct' response (A, B or C). Such methods are at odds with the reality of game play and lack authenticity, whereas instruments like the TSAP and GPAI provide an authentic assessment of game knowledge in action without setting any 'correct' answers. They assess knowledge-in-action instead of consciously articulated knowledge about action.

Limitations

The main limitation with TSAP lies in its focus on what the player does with the ball in attack/offence and its lack of specific attention to movement off the ball. Time on, or with, the ball is limited in any invasion game, from rugby to basketball and soccer. In the TSAP off-the-ball movements and decisions made are not directly measured, but the observer and player can infer these movements. Instruments that can accurately and authentically measure individual player behaviour off the ball are far more complicated to design and administer, and would likely be impractical for teachers and youth sport coaches. While this is a limitation of the TSAP, as Richard, Godbout and Gréhaigne (2000) argue, it does provide indirect information on player movement off the ball. Inferring behaviours based on the observation of other behaviours also has a constructivist connotation as it forces the observer and player to discuss and reflect on what actually happened (product) and what could have caused this to happen (process) (Gréhaigne and Godbout 1998a).

The GPAI does allow for measurement of decision-making off the ball and adjustment to changing game conditions, but one of its strengths is also a weakness, or a limitation. The GPAI offers flexibility in what the teacher wants to assess and is easier than the TSAP for students and teachers to conduct due to the simple grading from 1 to 5 of a small number of components of the game, including off-the-ball movement in attack/offence and defence. However, dividing game play into seven discrete components detracts a little from the holistic notion of the inseparability of decision-making, tactical understanding and skill execution. This then suggests that while the TSAP does not provide for specific information on movement off the ball it may provide a more complete assessment of game performance than the GPAI. That is to say that a limitation of both approaches is, at the same time, one of their strengths.

Both the GPAI and the TSAP provide authentic forms of assessment for game performance that can form part of the learning process when focused on playing the game. We might, however, not limit our attention to the learning *product* of games teaching. The *process* of learning through a Game Sense approach involves learning how to learn and a range of implicit, positive social and moral learning that can unfold from the pedagogy used (see, for example, Light and Kentel 2010). Given that this learning is implicit, it is difficult to assess and even more difficult to measure, but this could possibly be addressed through the teacher's subjective assessment. For example, if we value student effort, social skills, caring for others and a sense of fair play, could we not include some assessment of them? This would not only add to the information we have on student learning but also flag that these are aspects of learning and engagement in game that are valued. For example, a simple set of these aspects of learning could be listed and scored, with the total used to augment the game performance scores in a ratio that reflects the relative importance placed upon game performance and socio-moral learning. This would likely be given more weight for primary school students and would help redress the problems associated with the less capable students consistently getting poor performance scores. I offer the following example of what this assessment might look like, with 'other' learning listed and scored subjectively by the teacher. A score of 1 is very poor and a score of 5 is outstanding.

	Learning	Score (1–5)
1	Effort	
2	Cooperation	
3	Social interaction	
4	Support and care for others	
5	Fair play	
	TOTAL	/25

The total for this rubric could then be used in conjunction with the GPAI or TSAP score for a total assessment of learning in and through games for the unit or term. This socio-moral learning would likely vary according to the situation, for example according to the age of the learners and the stress in the school or class placed on this other learning.

Authentic assessment and learning

For assessment to be authentic it requires the active participation of students in the assessment process as it is integrated into the teaching–learning process (Wiggins 1993; Zessoules and Gardner 1991). While the peer assessment in the TSAP would be too difficult for junior primary school students, research suggests it can be used by students as young as ten years of age (Gréhaigne, Godbout and Bouthier 1997; Richard, Godbout and Gréhaigne 1998, 2000; Richard et al. 1999). Adequate reliability has also been established with older students (14–18 years) in soccer and volleyball (Gréhaigne, Godbout and Bouthier 1997), but students need to be taught how to use the instrument and be given time to develop the required observational skills. The same applies to use of the GPAI as a peer assessment tool because the students have to learn how to do the assessment for it to be effective in providing useful information on performance in games and to become a valuable part of the learning process. Time used for students to learn how to use the TSAP or GPAI might be seen as time that might otherwise be used for physical activity, but learning to use the instrument promotes learning about game play and forms part of the learning process.

Using the TSAP and GPAI focuses students' attention on the tactical aspects of games and encourages them to make tactical connections across games within the four game categories. While there is little skill transfer across different games (and sometimes it can be negative), there is a strong tactical transfer when a Game Sense approach is used. The TSAP also provides students with opportunities to reflect upon the performance of others and of themselves, and to learn about themselves as games players. It also contributes to them believing in the authenticity of the information provided on performance, which, in turn, makes it more likely that they will use the feedback produced from assessment to improve their game play. While the GPAI and TSAP focus on performance in games, this knowledge-in-action is developed through an integration of the body expressed in action and the mind expressed in speech (Light and Fawns 2003). The reflection involved in assessing peers represents an intellectual dimension in the Game Sense learning process that can make a valuable contribution to learning.

Chapter discussion questions

1. What is meant by authentic assessment, and to be authentic what does assessment in games teaching when using a Game Sense approach have to focus on, and why?
2. After reading beyond this chapter, compare and contrast the GPAI and the TSAP in terms of authentic assessment, ease of use and how likely you think it is that teachers will use either one or both of them.
3. Explain and discuss the features of these two assessment instruments that enable them to form a valuable part of the learning process.
4. If you have used either one of these instruments please comment on your experience in terms of how useful the information generated was, how difficult it was to use and how you feel about using it/them.
5. Identify an initiative in your country or state that has been developed to encourage the development of high-quality teaching or coaching. Then briefly discuss to what extent Game Sense pedagogy addresses the core concerns or ideas in the document and how either the GPAI or TSAP can be used to assess student learning in these areas.

PART II

7

TOUCH RUGBY

Introduction

Rugby union football is played in over 100 countries in the world, with the Rugby World Cup being the third biggest sports event in the world, after the FIFA World Cup and the Olympic Games. The recent decision made by the IOC to include sevens rugby in the 2016 Olympic programme has already had a very significant impact on the interest paid to rugby by governments, major sporting bodies and the public across the globe, with strength in performance in this version of rugby already evident across a host of countries outside the traditionally dominant countries in the fifteen-a-side game. In countries such as the United States of America and Russia where rugby has not figured on the sporting landscape, sevens rugby is already gaining in popularity and receiving increased support from the government and major sporting bodies, as well as gaining the attention of multi-national commercial giants in sport. Given that there will be medals to be contested by women as well as men, this will have a major impact upon the development of women's sevens rugby, with major growth in women's sevens rugby expected.

As a heavy contact game rugby is not really suitable for most schools unless modified to reduce contact. In countries like Australia, New Zealand and England independent schools typically promote rugby among boys, where it forms a major part of the school extra-curricular programme (see, for example, Light and Kirk 2000). In the same countries it is also offered in government schools but is not really suitable for physical education classes and even less suitable for primary (elementary) schools. Sevens rugby has far less head-on, heavy contact than the traditional fifteen-a-side game but still involves contact that is likely to be too dangerous for most schools, and particularly for primary (elementary) schools, without significant modifications. On the other hand, touch rugby removes the contact yet maintains most of the running and passing skills and the tactical knowledge of the fifteen- or seven-a-side forms to provide a fast-moving invasion game that can be played by both sexes across a very wide range of ages. At the same time, touch rugby is often used as a warm-up game, or for situations where coaches want to avoid contact but develop passing, running and thinking skills at the highest levels of professional rugby union and rugby league.

More commonly known as touch football, touch footy or just touch in Australia, and sometimes referred to as 'six down' elsewhere, touch rugby is governed globally by the Federation of International Touch (FIT) and the International Rugby Board (IRB). Touch rugby is widely played in Australia and New Zealand, is expanding to many other countries and stages its own World Cup. It originated from rugby league in Australia in the 1960s, with the tackle being replaced with a touch, thus making it a limited contact sport. The first official game of touch rugby was played in Sydney in 1968; it involves many of the skills of rugby union and rugby league but requires only minimal equipment and can be played without fear of injury from contact. In Australia it is played across a very wide range of ages, from lower primary school-aged children to over-fifties competitions, and is widely played in schools and by mixed-gender teams.

The activities suggested in this unit range from contextualized skill development through to complex modified games, and show the variety of ways in which coaches and teachers can take on a Game Sense approach, from a focus on skill or technique to a focus on tactics, but never excluding either of these components of game play. Some of the activities suggested in the chapter can also be used for rugby or rugby league and sevens rugby.

How to play touch rugby

Teams of six players play touch rugby, but sometimes teams of seven are allowed. Positions are divided into (1) two wings, (2) two centres and (3) two middle players and a central link with teams of seven. Teams of up to fourteen players are allowed, with no limit on the number of changes. It is played over two forty-minute halves on a 70×50 metre grass field and kicking is not allowed in any form. The most distinctive feature of the various forms of rugby such as touch rugby is the backward pass rule. It is also the most problematic aspect of learning the game for people raised on other invasion games such as football (soccer), basketball, netball, grass hockey and Australian football. Passes must not travel forward in touch rugby and typically need to travel backwards, yet the aim of the game is to take the ball forward and over the opposition try line. In settings where learners have not had significant exposure to either of the rugby codes this typically presents a conceptual problem.

Possession is maintained for six touches, after which the ball must be turned over to the opposition. It is also surrendered when the dummy half (player receiving the roll ball) is touched in possession; the ball is intercepted; the ball is dropped; there is a forward pass or a player in possession goes out of play. Play begins at the start of the game and is restarted by the side scored against, at the halfway line, with a tap kick (just touching the ball with the foot) after every try that is scored. At this time defending players must be back at least ten metres from the point of the tap. During play the defensive players must be at least five metres back from the point of touch during play until the dummy half touches the ball. Any defensive players inside this five metres are deemed to be offside and will be penalized by having to retreat ten metres and giving the attacking team a restart, with the touch count beginning again from zero. Play is always restarted with a tap kick; this occurs after scoring, at the halfway line, and after any infringement of the rules that results in a turnover, or after six touches.

Unit plan

Activity 1	*Passing in traffic*
Focus	Basic pass and catch while developing perception and low-level decision-making
Activity 2	*Beating a defender*
Focus	Maintaining and using space in attack, pass timing and technique, pass/run decision-making
Activity 2.1	*Beat the defender extension*
Focus	Tactics of passing to move the ball away from defence, movement off the ball, more complexity in decision-making
Activity 3	*5 v. 3 touch rugby*
Focus	Taking advantage of a 2 v. 1 situation in game play
Activity 4	*Quick-thinking attack*
Focus	Decision-making, quick alignment for attack, perception and creativity
Activity 5	*Beach touch rugby*
Focus	To apply skills and tactical understanding developed in a touch rugby game of 7 v. 6
Activity 6	*Touch rugby*
Focus	To play touch rugby with even teams, drawing on knowledge and skills developed in the unit

Activity 1: passing in traffic

This activity may seem similar to a 'skill-drill' for passing but it is performed within an environment that requires the use and development of perceptual ability and some decision-making. It provides a good example of how traditional 'skill-drills' can be contextualized within an environment that has aspects of game conditions for the development of perceptual abilities and decision-making. It is also something that is commonly used by many coaches who would not see themselves as being Game Sense coaches.

Players form small groups of three to five, passing as they run. This could just be a simple flat pass 'through the hands' and back, with players ensuring that they accelerate onto the ball for a few paces to put them in front of the possible receivers. The space needed and numbers of players in the space would depend upon their experience of this type of training and skill level, with less skilful players needing more space. First the players perform this passing routine a few times by running and passing to the end of the space, waiting for the other groups to arrive and then repeating. Then the coach can split the groups evenly to have them facing each other from opposite ends, running directly at each other, with players maintaining the same fluency while avoiding the other groups and the ball they are using. As performance improves and the coach wants to apply a little more pressure on the players he/she can reduce the space used or increase the number of players in the grid.

Sample questions

What have you got to look out for when doing this activity? How can you ensure you maintain pace and fluency in a crowded space? If you have to keep your eye on the ball when passing or catching it, how can you look for interference from other teams? How do you have to adjust your passing and catching to adapt to other players and/or balls?

Playing area/set-up

Set up the class in groups of three to five with one ball per group. The size of the grid depends upon the number of players and their experience, but teachers or coaches might start using half of the quarter between the try line and twenty-two metre line, with four groups of five (twenty players) in this area, meaning that each group has to negotiate two other groups each 'lap'.

FIGURE 7.1 Passing in traffic

Equipment

- One rugby ball for each group

Players

Three to five players per passing team.

Aim/intent

To negotiate the other teams while maintaining fluency, accuracy and timing.

Playing rules

Teams try to maintain efficiency, accuracy and pace while negotiating the other oncoming teams without any errors such as forward passes and dropped balls. Each lap completed without error and on time earns a point.

Modifications

- *More challenging*:
  1. Decrease the space or increase the number of teams.
  2. Use more complex passing drills such as turning the ball inside (returning the ball in the direction it came from without crossing the centre line of the body) or a pattern like a cut-out pass (cut out one player) and inside pass and another cut-out pass (group of five).

- *Less challenging*: use a larger space or fewer teams.

Activity 2: beating a defender

Attacking teams form pairs, with a ball for each pair, and attempt to beat stationary single defenders in a long narrow alley approximately ten metres wide and thirty metres long. Place two, single defenders in the alley about ten metres apart, with each of them only allowed to move laterally. The attacking pairs start at the bottom end of the alley, jogging and passing between themselves outside the alley at an easy pace until they round the top end marker to enter the alley; then they attempt to beat the touch of the defender by either passing or running. The attacking players must complete a clean run to score a point by avoiding being touched with the ball, dropping it, running out with the ball or making a forward pass.

This activity develops passing and catching skills, decision-making and evasive skills, but the focus is on maximizing the use of available space and manipulating the defender. Basically, the attacking ball carrier needs to stay close to the touchline to commit the defender and to provide enough space for the receiver, while using a pass that is flat and quick enough to give the receiver enough time to get through the gap. This two-on-one situation is very common in invasion games and it is important to develop this knowledge in action and the appropriately executed skills. There are, however, other possibilities that the attackers should be allowed to explore and test.

Sample questions

To attackers: *how can you give the receiver as much space as possible? How can you stop the defender drifting onto your receiver? If the defender continues to drift onto your receiver what options do you have? What type of pass do you need to throw in this situation and why? When should you pass? What can you do to prevent the defender being in a position to cover both attackers? If the receiver is overrunning the ball, what is the problem and how can you correct it?*

To defenders: *which attacker should you pressure? Where should you position yourself? How can you force the ball carrier to pass early?*

Playing area/set-up

Set up groups of eight to ten players, with two defending and the others in pairs rotating the defending pair. Use an alley about thirty metres long and ten metres wide, with cones at the mouth of the alley. The attacking teams start at the end of the alley and jog up to the mouth of the alley to attack after rounding the marker cone. Pairs should practise entering from both sides.

FIGURE 7.2   Beating a defender

Equipment

- Marker cones
- A rugby ball for each attacking pair

Players

Players form pairs.

Aim/intent

To complete as many clean runs as possible, scoring a point for each one.

Playing rules

In attack: pairs must avoid being touched in possession or making any touch rugby infringements such as dropping the ball, running out in possession and throwing a forward pass.

In defence: the defenders can only move laterally. They cannot move forward or chase the attacking pair at any time.

Modifications

- *More challenging*: make the alley narrower or place an extra defender in it.
- *Less challenging*: widen the alley and/or make a two-handed touch rule.

Activity 2.1: beat the defenders extension

This activity builds on beat the defender by increasing the size of the attacking teams, the space used and the number of defenders. The coach or teacher should be prepared to modify the size of the playing space to find the optimum level of difficulty for the attacking team that provides a significant challenge yet offers a reasonable opportunity for success.

Use either a three-person or five-person attacking team and widen the alley to a 15 × 30 metre space. This activity should retain the two defenders spaced about ten metres (longitudinally) apart and still limited to only lateral movement. If the space is too wide the defenders cannot put enough pressure on the attacking team, so the coach/teacher needs to adjust the width to suit the skill levels of the players. In this activity the aim is still to make a clear run to score a point but the team must stop if touched in possession or if an infringement (as outlined in Activity 2) is committed, and must move to one side to rejoin the teams moving through to enter the mouth of the playing space.

Modifications

- *More challenging*: place an extra defender in each of the two defensive lines.
- *Less challenging*: widen the playing space.

Activity 3: 5 v. 3

This activity builds on the skills and tactical knowledge developed in the previous activities by moving tactical thinking, skill execution and decision-making into the more complex environment of a game. Exaggeration is commonly used in TGfU and Game Sense to facilitate learning, with using uneven team numbers probably the most common way of doing so. This typically provides more space and opportunity in attack and reduces the defensive pressure on the attacking team while the players are learning and developing their abilities. Giving the attacking team a two–player advantage in this game provides more opportunity to score tries but this is dependent upon the space available and the knowledge/ skills developed up to this stage. I suggest beginning this game in a narrow, long space that significantly reduces the opportunity to take advantage of the extra numbers in attack. This then provides a problem to be solved by the players through discussion and debate between them and with the teacher/coach, while highlighting the core importance of space. The teacher/coach should then increase the width of the space to allow the attacking team to better take advantage of their numbers, with the appropriate time given for discussion about this.

The aim in this game is for the attacking side to score as many tries as possible in a given time and I suggest that this might be two minutes or so. In this game there is initially no limit on the number of touches the attacking team has, but if there is any infringement such as a dropped ball the team must return to the start line of the playing space. If the players have the skill to maintain possession over long periods of time the teacher/coach should introduce a limit on the number of touches the team has before having to stop and return to the start line. This game also introduces the roll ball and the dummy half. After each touch the ball carrier must return to the point at which he/she was touched and roll the ball between his/her legs to a 'dummy half' who distributes the ball. If the dummy half is touched in possession the ball is turned over to the opposition. At each play-the-ball the defensive players must be at least five metres back when the ball is touched by the dummy half. The roll ball is a simple skill that should not require any special practice out of the game, but the speed of the roll ball is an important tactical weapon that can be used to catch opposition players offside with short quick attacks.

In this game the teacher/coach needs to introduce the skill of rolling the ball after each touch and the rules about marking and the 'dummy half'. This can be briefly done prior to starting the game, with the teacher/coach teaching 'on the run', but if it requires a little more attention the players can break briefly from the game to receive some instruction; however, the skill only needs to be good enough to enable the game to be played. This game also introduces the offside rule, where the defensive team has to be ten metres behind the person playing the ball. When there is no touch limit this means that the defensive players caught offside cannot touch the attacking players. When a limit to the number of touches is introduced, the defence is penalized by allowing the attacking team to restart the tackle count.

Sample questions

When using narrow space: *why can't you score when you have extra players? What can you draw on from what you learnt in some of the previous activities about using space in a 2 v. 1 situation? How can you move the defence to where you want them to be? How can you draw the defensive players in close to play the ball to create space out wide? If you create space out wide how can you move the ball quickly to that area? How can you catch the defence offside?*

Playing area/set-up

Use a playing space about twenty metres long and fifteen metres wide.

FIGURE 7.3   5 v. 3

Equipment

- Marker cones
- A rugby ball for the attacking team of players
- Two sets of coloured bibs

Players

An attacking team of five players and a defending team of three, totalling eight players per game, changing the defending team regularly so that all players experience defence and attack.

Aim/intent

To score as many tries as possible within the set time period.

Playing rules

- The attacking team score by touching the ball over the try line.
- For any infringement such as going out in possession, forward pass or a dropped ball the team returns to the start.
- If a limit on the number of touches is introduced and this is reached before scoring, the attacking team returns to the start.
- There is never any handing over of possession to the defensive team.
- Defenders must be no closer than five metres at each play-the-ball and the ball must be rolled back to the dummy half after each touch.

Modifications

- *More challenging*: keep the playing space narrow.
- *Less challenging*: widen the playing space and/or make a two-handed touch rule.

Activity 4: quick-thinking plays

This activity places attacking teams under pressure to make instant responses to the defensive situation facing them. Teams of five players face forward in a playing space of about 30–50 metres long and 15–25 metres wide, with three defensive players fifteen metres behind them. (Playing cross field in between the try line and the twenty-two metre line of a rugby field would be ideal.) The attacking team begins to jog down field, passing the ball between them, followed by the defensive players, who remain fifteen metres behind them. When the teacher/coach or another player blows the whistle, the attacking team must quickly face the opposition and attack and score a try. If the team fails to score it starts again. The defensive players should be rotated through the attacking team. The teacher/coach can ask the defensive team to provide particular opportunities for attack that the team in possession can take advantage of.

Sample questions

What are you looking for when you first turn and face the defence? What should the ball carrier do immediately after he/she turns? Once the ball carrier attacks or moves, what can the supporting players do?

Playing area/set-up

Use a playing space 30–50 metres long and 15–20 metres wide, for example playing across a rugby field between the twenty-two metre line and the try line.

Equipment

- One rugby ball per game

FIGURE 7.4 Quick-thinking plays

Players

Eight players for each game, with five in attack and three in defence; players should be rotated to experience being in attack and defence.

Aim/intent

For the attacking team to score a try for each play.

Playing rules

- Play stops when any infringement is committed, for example going out in possession, a forward pass, a knock on (ball dropped forward) or a player in the attacking team obstructing the defenders.
- The defending team must not be any closer than fifteen metres to the attacking team while jogging behind them.
- If the player in possession of the ball is tagged, play stops and the game must be restarted.

Modifications

The coach or teacher can begin with five defensive players, three on the field and two spares. He/she can then decide how many to drop out of or add to the defensive line before each round, but should direct these changes silently while the attacking team cannot see. He/she can also decide formations or distribution of defensive lines to provide specific opportunities or challenges.

For example, start with five attacking players, as above, but also five defenders available, with a designated number on the field that can be quickly changed by dropping players or drawing on 'bench' players to increase the number of defenders. Changes to the number and position of defenders should be made without the team in possession knowing so that they must respond to different circumstances every time they turn around to attack. This could mean the attacking team suddenly facing only one defender, four defenders but all in one section of the field, five defenders spread across the field or three defenders up in a line with a late extra defender coming in from the end of the field. There are endless possibilities here to challenge the attacking team and the defending team.

Activity 5: beach touch rugby

Play a game of beach touch rugby with one team having one player fewer. Play with a team of seven versus a team of six players over a forty-minute period divided into two halves of twenty minutes each. When in possession the team must hand over possession to the opposition after six touches have been completed or when any infringement of the rules occurs, such as being offside, running out of the field in possession or dropping the ball. Tries are scored by placing the ball over the opposition's try line. The team with the most tries at the end of the game is the winning team. The team in possession must return to the point where touched and roll the ball while facing in the direction of the opposition try line, and the defensive team must retreat at least five metres from the point of touch. A dummy half picks up and distributes the roll ball and can run with the ball, but if touched before passing loses possession to the opposition. See the section 'How to play touch rugby' (pp. 74–75) for more details on the rules.

During this game the teacher/coach should provide opportunities for teams to discuss and formulate tactics and try swapping one player for the second half so that both teams can experience having one fewer and one extra player. While the coach can use similar questions to those used in previous activities and games to stimulate thinking, players should be provided with opportunities for self-directed debate and discussion about tactics and strategies in their collective effort. If dialogue is progressing the teacher/coach does not need to intervene, but if it is limited or being dominated by one or two players he/she needs to facilitate productive dialogue. While skills and knowledge should have developed by now, interaction and relationships should also have developed among the players.

Playing area/set-up

Half a rugby field (70 × 50 metres).

Players

One team has seven players and the other has six, with three to five reserve players on each team.

Equipment

- A set of coloured bibs for each team
- Marker cones
- A rugby ball for each game

Aim/intent

To score more tries (points) than the opposing team.

Playing rules

- After six touches the team in possession must turn over the ball to the opposition.
- Any infringement, such as a forward pass, a dropped ball, going out in possession, results in a turnover.
- The defence must retreat five metres from play-the-ball.
- If the defence is offside they must retreat ten metres, with the opposition touch count going back to zero.

Activity 6: touch rugby

This game is played in the same space and uses the same rules as beach touch rugby does but has even teams and is played over two forty-minute halves. Alternatively the teacher/coach could organize a mini-gala contested between a number of teams in games conducted over two ten-minute halves on a round robin basis, with the teams not playing watching those playing to analyse their performances and develop tactics to take advantage of identified weaknesses. In a school setting this provides the celebratory ending suggested for the Sport Education (Siedentop 1994) model in physical education and should help make the unit a positive and enjoyable experience.

8

OZTAG

With Christina Curry

Introduction

Oztag is one of the newest and fastest-growing sports in Australia and has also become very popular in a number of other countries such as New Zealand, the Pacific Islands, Ireland, the United Kingdom, South Africa, the United States and Japan. These countries are all embracing the sport and are at the developmental stage called tag rugby, with Australia leading the way in this innovative and fast-paced game. Oztag is used in training in rugby league and rugby union to develop players' speed, passing and decision-making, as they are able to practise tactical plays and train for speed and agility without risking incurring the injuries that are caused by tackling.

Oztag was first played in the early 1990s; a number of associations are now in existence and there has been an explosion in the number of competitions and player festivals. The introduction of junior oztag a few years ago has been a welcome addition as it provides children with a great opportunity to learn the skills of rugby league and rugby union without the physical contact of the tackle. Oztag has become the preferred game over touch football as it offers children a greater challenge in skill as they have to make a tag. This allows the attackers more opportunity to find space and gives real incentive for defenders to defend. There is less chance for dispute or arguments because when a tag is made it is clearly visible and the point at which play is to resume is clear for all to see. Players can also easily officiate in their own games. In Australia it has been introduced as a competitive school sport, both in the physical education syllabus and sports afternoons, as well as the many gala days taking place throughout the country. Most importantly, it is a fast-paced exciting sport that can be enjoyed by male, female and mixed teams of all athletic abilities from the age of six onwards.

Oztag is a non-tackling invasion game, with the rules specifically designed to encourage the development of skill through the non-tackling rule. The object of the game is to score tries. Defenders prevent this by tagging the ball carrier (removing the tag from the shorts or belt). Players wear official oztag shorts with a Velcro patch on each side or specially designed Velcro belts and a 'tag' (a strip of cloth is attached to the Velcro). Tagging instead of tackling offers players of all skill levels, sizes and weights the opportunity to compete evenly.

Many of the activities used in touch rugby (Chapter 7) can be used in oztag. Therefore this chapter focuses more on the tagging aspect, which is unique to oztag, and kicking. The games are situated in contexts that require evasion skills, perception, decision-making and good communication among players. Each game increases with complexity, ensuring that players are able to apply the skills within a game of oztag.

How to play oztag

Oztag is played over two halves of twenty minutes each, with a break of five minutes between them. Eight players from each team are on the field at one time. It is played on a 70 × 50 metre field (half a soccer/rugby field), but times and field size may be varied to suit the age group and conditions. In oztag the attacking team has six plays or tags to try and score a try or to move the ball down the field as close to their try line as possible. A try is awarded to the attacking team when they ground the ball on or over the try line. There are no dead ball lines and all players may score a try.

The game is exciting as successfully tagging a player requires great skill and is never guaranteed! The invention of the tag also prevents 'phantom calls', resulting in more fair play.

Unit plan

Activity 1	*Zooloo ball*
Focus	Warm-up game that involves kicking and passing
Activity 2	*Kick tennis*
Focus	Kicking technique and ball positioning, quick play to improve reaction time
Activity 3	*Tag me!*
Focus	Tagging technique, developing spins and stepping to avoid being tagged
Activity 4	*Tag bullrush*
Focus	Maintaining and using space in attack, evasive running skills, tagging technique in defence
Activity 5	*3 v. 2 pass tag*
Focus	Maintaining and using space in attack, tagging technique in defence, pass timing and technique, pass/run decision-making, scoring
Activity 6	*Five-a-side round robin*
Focus	To apply skills and tactical understanding to a small-sided game
Activity 7	*Oztag*
Focus	Applying all skills and understanding in the full game

The unit moves through a series of games which focus on the three main skills of oztag, which are passing, tagging and kicking. The first four tend to emphasize developing skills in context, while the last three are more complex, building up to the full game.

Activity 1: zooloo ball

In this game there are two teams, batting (kicking) and fielding. The field is set up like a softball field. The batting team take turns to kick the ball and then run around as many bases as possible, while the fielding team must pass and/or kick the ball back to the middle person (standing at the pitcher's plate) before the batter gets around all bases and back to home base to score a point for their team. Every player has a kick and then teams are changed over. The fielding team gets a player out by either catching the kick on the full or by getting the ball back to the middle person before the kicker gets to a base.

Sample questions

To attackers: *how can you get enough time to get to home base? Where is the best place to kick the ball? Why? In what ways do you have to work together to get more home runs?*

To defenders: *where should you position yourself? What do you need to do to stop the other team getting home runs? What is the best way to communicate with your team? How can you avoid over-throws?*

Playing area/set-up

This is best played in an open space and set up like a softball pitch.

Equipment

- Four bases
- One pitcher plate
- One oztag ball

Players

Two even teams with approximately ten players in each team.

Aim/intent

To make the most home runs.

Playing rules

Batters may stop on any base except home base. Once they get back to home base they get a point and may continue to go around until they get out. There is no limit to the amount of players on a base.

Modifications

- *More challenging*:
    1. Only low kicks (grubber kicks) are allowed.
    2. The ball must be passed through a certain number of fielders before it is passed back to the middle player.

- *Less challenging*: use a soft ball.

Activity 2: kick tennis

This is a fast-paced kicking game that allows players to further develop their kicking skills. It is played in a square or rectangle, which is divided in half, and contested by two equal teams. This game is played quickly to try and catch the other team off guard. The game begins with a player from one team kicking the ball above waist height, but not higher than head height, to the other side of the court/field, trying to get the ball to hit the ground for a point on the opposition side of the court. The other team must catch the ball to prevent it touching the ground inside their half of the court, unless it is going out, in which case they have the choice of letting it go out. After any player has caught the ball inside their half of the court he/she attacks by trying to kick it back and score by having the ball land inside the opposition half of the court (like a return in tennis). He/she also has the option of passing to a teammate in a better position to kick, but no forward passes are allowed and if the ball is dropped there is a turnover of possession. The first kick (serve) is delivered from one corner, as in tennis, and whichever team scores, serves. When service is maintained it is delivered alternately between left and right corners.

Sample questions

To attackers: *what are you looking for when kicking the ball (space)? What different types of kicks can you use and when would you use them? How can you catch the other team off guard?*

To defenders: *is there any way you can anticipate where the opposition will kick the ball? How do you decide where you need to position yourself? What is the best way to communicate as a team? How can you support your teammates when they are attempting to catch a kick?*

Playing area/set-up

Set up a square or rectangle with a halfway line. The size and dimensions of it will depend upon skill levels, confidence and the type of kicks the teacher/coach wants the players to practise. For example, twenty players could work 10 v. 10 cross-field in the area between the goal line and the twenty-two metre line on a rugby pitch, which provides the opportunity to explore depth and vary distances significantly. If the players are skilful enough, height provides time to catch the ball, so the kicking side will have to use flat kicks to land the ball before it can be caught. If, in the same space, catching skills are not good enough,

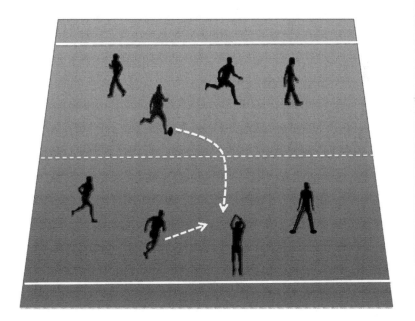

FIGURE 8.1   Kick tennis

more players can be used to close up the gaps. Alternatively, half this field could be used for a number of 5 v. 5 games. In modifications that involve more players or less space, questioning should focus on the difference this makes.

Equipment

- Cones to mark the designated area
- Three oztag balls

Players

Adjust the number of players to suit skill level, experience and the space available.

Aim/intent

To kick the ball so it hits the ground before the other team can catch it.

Playing rules

If a team member drops the ball or misses it and it hits the ground when kicked, the other team gets a point and gains possession to restart with a 'serve' from the rear corner of the court or field. This can also be played as elimination. So if a player drops the ball he/she is eliminated, and if it hits the ground untouched the closest player is eliminated. This gets really exciting towards the end, but teachers and coaches need to be able to deal with the inherent problem associated with elimination games, where the less skilled are eliminated early and deprived of game time to improve.

Modifications

- *More challenging*:
    1. Add more oztag balls.
    2. Increase the playing area.
    3. Use more grids with smaller numbers of players.
- *Less challenging*:
    1. Decrease the playing area.
    2. Use a large soft or foam ball.

Activity 3: tag me

This is a good warm-up game to introduce the skill of tagging. Players have tags on and are spread out in a designated square. On the whistle, players move around trying to 'steal' as many tags as possible. Players are not allowed to fend off players or hold their tags in a way that prevents their tags being taken and must stay inside the marked area. When a player has lost both tags he/she can still steal others' tags but must replace the two tags lost from the belt as soon as he/she steals them. The players should be given an appropriate time in which to steal as many tags as possible. For example, this might be thirty seconds or a minute. The skills focus should be on using spins and stepping to avoid being tagged. At the end of the decided time period the teacher/coach blows the whistle to stop the game and the players(s) with the most tags wins. This is then repeated any number of times, and pairs or groups can be added as a variation.

Sample questions

What do you have to look out for when doing this activity? What is the best way to tag others? How can you avoid being tagged? What is the best way to move around the area? Should you focus on moving to avoid having your tags stolen or on stealing tags yourself?

Playing area/set-up

A designated square on either the oval or the basketball court (the size will depend on the number of players).

Equipment

- Tags and belts for each player
- Cones to mark the designated area

Players

The number of players depends upon the class size and the skill level of the group. The teacher/coach has control over the level of difficulty. The more crowded the field of play, the more difficult it is to find space and to avoid being tagged.

Aim/intent

The aim of the game is to get as many tags as possible.

Playing rules

All players should avoid making contact with others yet maintain continuous movement and cover as much of the designated area as possible. Players must not protect their tags or fend off attackers.

Modifications

Making this activity more or less challenging is achieved by manipulating the size of the space and/or the number of players working in the space. Create pairs/groups to work together.

Activity 4: tag bullrush

This is a simple game that is easy to play and which involves the skills of evasion running and change of pace as well as defensive skills and tactical understanding. A small number of taggers begin in the middle of the grid, with runners attempting to beat them by running from one side of the grid to the other without being tagged. When the runners are tagged (by the tagger removing at least one tag, calling and holding it up in the air) they have their tag returned and become a tagger, with the size of the tagging team growing as the number of runners decreases, until there are none left.

Sample questions

To attackers: *what do you need to look for? How can you avoid being tagged? Do you have any ideas for getting to the other side without being tagged? Should you run individually or all at once and why? How could/can you take advantage of other runners creating gaps for you? What individual running skills can you use to beat the tag?*

　To defenders: *which attacker should you pressure? Where should you position yourself? How do you make a successful tag?*

Playing area/set-up

Use a playing space 30–40 × 30–40 metres but this can be altered depending on the number of players.

Equipment

- Tags and belts for each player
- Cones to mark the designated area
- Oztag balls (optional)

Players

This game can be played with any number of players.

Aim/intent

Try to get to the other side without getting tagged. The defenders try to tag as many players as they can. If tagged they become a helper.

Playing rules

- Players cannot run out of bounds (outside the grid).
- When there are too many defenders they are all asked to freeze and tag from a stationary position. Only the original defender can continue to run.

Modifications

- *More challenging*:

  1. Increase the space.
  2. Set a time limit to get to the other side.
  3. Students who get tagged are stuck in the spot where they were tagged but can still tag.
  4. Allow attackers to practise running with balls.

Activity 5: 3 v. 2 pass tag

The focus of this game is to allow players to practise their attacking and passing skills while still building on their defending skills. Students are put into two even teams – an attacking team and a defending team (teams will rotate). Teams stand on opposing sidelines of an oztag field on the halfway mark. On the whistle three players from the attacking team (carrying a ball) must run to their right, go around the corner post on their corresponding sideline, then enter the field and attempt to score a try on the far try line. At the same time two players from the defensive team run to their right around the corner post then enter the field and attempt to tag the attacking team to prevent a try from being scored.

Sample questions

To attackers: *what do you need to take advantage of an extra player (space)? How can you create and/or maintain space for the extra player to go through? If the defenders are drifting across onto the receivers, how can you stop them (run straight with the ball)? What do you do as a ball carrier if the two defenders drift wide onto your receivers too early?*

   To defenders: *which attacker should you pressure? Where should you position yourself? How can you force the ball carrier to pass early? How can you possibly cover two attackers (drift)?*

FIGURE 8.2   3 v. 2 pass tag

Playing area/set-up

Set up a field smaller and narrower than a normal oztag field.

Equipment

* Tags and belts for each player
* Cones to mark the designated area
* Five oztag balls

Players

Form two even teams. Attackers move in threes and defenders move in pairs.

Aim/intent

Attackers try to use the extra player they have to score, while defenders try to prevent them from scoring.

Playing rules

The attacking team may pass the ball between themselves but once they are tagged that round stops and the defensive team gets a point. If they score a try they get a point. Keep going through until everyone has had a turn. Then swap the defence to attack and vice versa. At the end the team with the most points wins. No forward passes are allowed and normal oztag rules are to be used.

Modifications

* *More challenging*:
    1. Add time limits.
    2. Make the playing space narrow and long.
    3. Add another defender.
    4. Include a kick and recover.

* *Less challenging*: make the playing space wider and shorter or play 4 v. 2 if there is enough space.

Activity 6: five-a-side round robin

Players are divided into teams of five players playing on a field approximately
30 × 40 metres. The size is determined by the space available and the conditions
the teacher/coach wants to maximize learning. All regular oztag rules apply.

Sample questions

To attackers: *how can you give the receiver as much space as possible? When
should you pass? What is the best way to get the ball to the other end? When
should you kick/pass/run?*

   To defenders: *how can you stop the other team from making ground (take
their space)? How can you stop them from scoring? Where does your team need to
be positioned? How can you reduce their time?*

Playing area/set-up

Play on a small field (30 × 40 metres).

Equipment

- Tags for each player
- Cones to mark the designated area
- One oztag ball per game

Players

Two teams of five players for each game.

Aim/intent

To score more tries than the opposing team.

Playing rules

- The game commences with 'tap off' (kick).
- No marker is allowed.

- The dummy half may run but if he/she is tagged, a turnover will occur.
- The dummy half cannot score.
- The defence must retreat five metres from the play-the-ball.
- The defensive line cannot move until the first receiver touches the ball or the dummy half runs.
- After six tags the team in possession must turn over the ball to the opposition.

Modifications

- *More challenging*:
  1. Reduce the field size.
  2. Increase the number of players.

- *Less challenging*:
  1. Increase the field size.
  2. Use fewer players.

Activity 7: oztag

This is the culmination of the unit where the students/players play the full game of oztag. If the game is played in a physical education class we suggest dividing the class into three teams of eight, with any extra students rotated through the team. This organization allows two teams to play while one rests and watches the other teams, during which they should be encouraged to discuss strategies and tactics. The normal twenty minutes over which oztag is played is too long to organize teams in this way so we suggest playing ten–minute games but on half a normal-sized rugby/soccer field. The lesson/session could be organized as a round robin competition, with a final as a type of celebration at the end of the unit.

Sample questions

Use the range of questions asked over this unit and in the touch rugby unit where appropriate. Teachers/coaches should also encourage team talks at half-time and after the completion of each game for the students/players to reflect on the team performance and improve it. Teachers or coaches can also stop games at tactically critical points in the second half to identify significant tactical issues and provide a minute for a quick team discussion. At the end of the lesson/session the teacher/coach should ask questions of the entire group to link aspects of the full game to the previous games and to reinforce learning in this game and over the unit.

Playing area/set-up

Play on half a rugby/soccer field.

Equipment

*   Tags for each player
*   Three sets of differently coloured bibs (not sashes)
*   Cones to mark the designated area if lines are not already marked
*   One oztag ball

Players

Two even teams of eight per game, with extras rotated from the bench into the team.

Aim/intent

To score more tries than the opposing team.

Playing rules

*   The defender must remove one or both tags to stop the attacker's progress. He/she then holds up the tag and drops it to the ground marking where the play-the-ball should occur.
*   There is a marker in the play-the-ball.
*   The defence must be back seven metres.
*   The defensive line can move forward only when the dummy half (the person first playing the ball from the play-the-ball) touches the ball. The dummy half can run and be tagged with the ball.
*   Six tags/plays are allowed before a changeover.
*   An attacker must stop and play the ball if he/she is in possession with only one tag on.
*   The only persons able to promote the ball with one tag on are the dummy half and the player taking the tap (as long as they do not take more than one step with the ball).

- After a knock-back, players should play on, and if the ball is knocked forward (knock-on) the advantage rule applies, which allows for the non-offending side to take advantage of the infringement. This is the same as rugby league and requires the referee to delay a decision to stop play if the non-offending side is in possession.
- This is a non-contact game. The attacker cannot deliberately bump into a defender. A defender cannot change direction and move into the attacker's path. Whoever initiates contact will be penalized. The onus is on the attacking player to avoid the defender.
- The ball carrier is not allowed to protect his tag or fend off defenders.
- A try is awarded to the attacking team when they ground the ball on or over the try line.
- After a simultaneous tag, players should play on. (If the referee is unable to decide, the pass is allowed – play on. The advantage goes to the attacking team.)
- An attacker may pass the ball over his/her try line to a teammate, who may run the ball out. If the ball is dropped, the ball is deemed dead. A player in possession may run behind his try line and back out into the field of play.
- Players can dive to score a try; however, if a player touches the ground with knees or arms before the try line or slides across the line and a defender is within tagging distance, the try is disallowed and a tag is counted.
- A player can go down on their knees to score a try over the try line.

Kicking

- A team may kick the ball before the first tag is made. (For example, a team that picks up the ball in general play from a kick-off, knock-on, loose ball, etc. may kick the ball before being tagged.) Once a tag has been made, the ball may not be kicked again until after the fourth tag.
- Kicks in general play cannot be above the shoulder height of the referee. The attacking team cannot dive on a kicked ball in any situation, but can kick it on.
- Kick-offs and line dropouts: if the ball lands in the field of play and then rolls across the try line, whether touched or not, a line drop out occurs. The try line becomes the dead ball line for all kicks.
- If the ball is kicked or passed to the referee, the referee will order a changeover where he was struck.

Modifications

None suggested.

9

AUSTRALIAN FOOTBALL

Introduction

Australian football is an excellent invasion game for children and young people of all ages when modified to remove heavy contact, and is well suited to teaching using the Game Sense approach. When teaching Australian football in physical education, using it as a warm-up game for other youth sports or coaching young children, contact should be removed, but this will not detract from the dynamic nature of the game. I have taught Australian football using a Game Sense approach in France, Canada, Taiwan and China, where the students had no previous knowledge of, or exposure to, the sport yet quickly picked it up and enjoyed it. This is largely due to the tactical transfer that is possible across invasion games and the relatively low demands on skills needed to just get a game going.

With regard to the skills needed, most students in any setting have had some previous exposure to the basic techniques of catching the ball, the punt kick, evasive running and contesting the ball in the air in other games. The distinctive 'handball' is not too difficult to become proficient at within the right game context, but the requirement of bouncing the ball every ten metres when running can be a little more challenging due to the oval shape of the ball. However, this skill does not need to be introduced until the later stages of the unit and players can bend down to touch the ball to the ground without bouncing it if a lack of skill in bouncing the ball is holding up the game. Little specific skill teaching is required for beginners to be involved in modified games from the first lesson, apart from showing the basics of punting and handballing. If available, authentic Australian footballs should be used, but if not a standard rugby ball can be used or even soccer balls as are used in 'international rules', which is a hybrid game contested between Ireland and Australia.

This unit begins with a focus on developing some basic skills within the context of games, building the complexity of the game contexts used, leading up to playing a game of modified Australian football. As is the case with the other units, time and opportunity should be provided for reflection and collaborative problem solving. As the modified games used increase in complexity the teacher should provide more opportunities for students to discuss, develop and test strategies and tactics as an essential part of the learning process.

How to play modified Australian football

Australian football is played by eighteen players on each team on large oval-shaped fields without any formal size requirements. Reducing the number to between ten and fifteen a side and playing on a normal rugby/soccer-sized field would provide an open, high-paced game with full engagement by all players, but team numbers and the size of the field could be determined according to the number of students in the class and the space available.

The aim of the game is to kick the ball between two posts at the end of the field the team is attacking. There is no height at which the ball must pass between the posts and it can even dribble between the posts, but if it is touched at all by anyone from the attacking team or defending team it is not a goal. A goal scores six points. There are also two posts either side of the main posts and if the ball misses the main goal yet passes between the two posts to the outside it scores a 'behind', worth one point. The ball can only be kicked to score a goal or a behind.

The referee starts play by tossing the ball up (like basketball) in the centre for two players to contest. In possession the team moves the ball down field by running with it, handballing it or kicking it to teammates. Players can run with the ball but it must touch the ground every ten metres (you might make it five metres in a smaller space). Usually players bounce the ball, but if this is too diffi-cult they can touch the ball to the ground while they are holding the ball in their hands to keep the game going, and possibly do a little practice on this out of the game if necessary. The ball can only be passed by handballing (holding it in one hand and hitting it with the top of a clenched fist). The opposition can win possession by intercepting, picking up a loose ball or taking the ball from the player in possession but can only grab the ball and not the player's arms. The defensive team can also 'tackle' the player in possession by holding him/her around the waist and calling 'Held'. When the ball carrier is held around the waist he/she must stop running and pass or kick the ball. If the defender prevents the ball carrier from releasing the ball, play stops and there is a turnover.

If the ball goes out of bounds (run out, passed, kicked, etc.) the non-offending team restarts from the point at which the ball went out, with an overhand throw (like soccer). When the ball is punted ten metres or more and is caught before touching the ground, the player catching it is awarded a 'mark'. Play then stops and all opposition players must move at least ten metres away from the point at which the mark was taken to allow the player taking the mark a 'free kick', including a kick for goal. When a goal is scored play is restarted from the centre, but if you are using a small space this can be changed to a restart from in front of the goal.

Unit plan

Activity 1	*Unopposed marking and kicking*
Focus	Accurate kicking, catching (taking a mark unopposed) and off-the-ball movement
Activity 1.1	*Kicking and marking under pressure*
Focus	Receivers finding space under pressure, evasion, kicking into space, communication
Activity 2	*Handball goal tally*
Focus	Developing perceptual ability, decision-making, communication, accurate handballing
Activity 2.1	*Handball pass tally*
Focus	Off-the-ball decision-making, handball skill, communication, anticipation and perception
Activity 3	*Four handball kick game*
Focus	Finding space off the ball, making effective passes, dribbling, using available space
Activity 3.1	*Handball kick for goal game*
Focus	Handballing to move the ball toward goal to set up a shot at goal
Activity 4	*Modified Australian football*
Focus	To apply skills and tactical understanding developed in a modified game

This unit moves through a series of three sequenced modified games with activities designed to increase complexity within each major activity (comprising seven activities), leading to playing a modified version of Australian football. In this unit activities focus on learning basic skills within the context of games or game-like activities that increase in complexity, culminating in a modified game of Australian football. Each of these activities involves tactically informed decision-making and focused perception.

Activity 1: unopposed marking and kicking

This lesson focuses on punt kicking and taking a mark within a game-like activity. It begins with a simple activity focused on developing an accurate punt kick and making a clean catch to take a 'mark'. This is performed within the context of movement and some anticipation but without any direct pressure on the marker or the kicker.

Form groups of six players with three at either end of a long, narrow space of about 20–25 metres in length and 5–10 metres in width. The space used is narrow to place importance on accuracy, to create the need for players to develop perceptual ability and find a space in which they can take a mark. The teacher begins by briefly explaining and demonstrating the drop punt, with the ball gripped laces up, fingers spread across the ball and thumbs near the laces at the top of the ball, and the ball tilted slightly forward. He/she should walk a few steps forward before dropping the ball onto the foot, kicking it so that it spins backwards, making it easier to catch. He/she should keep his/her eyes on the ball and try to kick it accurately to the catcher.

Next, have students work with partners and practise kicking so that the partner can make a clean catch. Each pair should then see how many 'marks' they can make within the space they are working. They should change partners regularly and count the number of marks they make in a time period determined by the teacher (for example, thirty seconds or one minute). The teacher should stop the class from time to time and ask questions about how the students can improve their scores, focusing on kicking and catching technique as well as perception, looking for space and placing the ball where the catcher is going, if they are moving. The players can only take a mark on their side of a halfway line and kickers cannot cross a line five metres in from the beginning of the space.

Sample questions

To kickers: *where is the space? How can you get your receiver out of the traffic? How can you lead the receiver into space? How can you make it as easy as possible for your partner to make a clean catch? If your partner is running, where should you try to place the ball?*

To receivers: *how can you let the kicker know where you want the ball? If you are running into space where do you want the ball placed? Where is the space? When you are catching a short, flat kick, how can the kicker make it easier for you to catch?*

Playing area/set-up

Set up the class in groups of six per game, each in a long narrow space of 20–25 × 8–10 metres with a five metre line at either end and a halfway line. The game can be played indoors but there needs to be enough height for high kicks.

Equipment

- Marker cones
- Sets of coloured bibs
- One Australian football per pair (three balls)

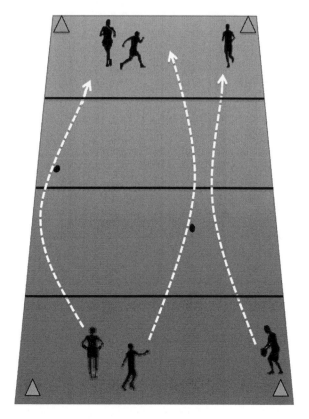

FIGURE 9.1   Unopposed marking and kicking

Players

Six players for each team, with extras rotated through the team.

Aim/intent

To gain as many marks as possible within a set period (typically 30–60 seconds).

Playing rules

- The ball must travel at least ten metres.
- The ball must be caught on the full (no bounce) and within the designated area to score a 'mark'.

- If a receiver takes a mark close to the kicker, he/she must take the next mark at the back of the space.

Modifications

Vary the size of the field. Making it bigger offers possibilities to create more space for receivers.

Activity 1.1: kicking and marking under pressure

In the same space and with the same students/players, have one student/player stand at one end of the space as the kicker who kicks to any one of three receivers, with the other two students becoming defenders in a 2 v. 3 situation. Use the same rules as in the previous activity, with the defenders able to intercept the kick or knock the ball away to prevent a mark. Coloured bibs should be used to help the kicker pick up cues to distinguish defenders from receivers. Play for a minute, count how many marks were taken and then rotate players, stopping groups one at a time to discuss tactics and the use of space. It may be necessary to widen the space if kicking skills are not good enough, to enable the game to be played with an adequate degree of success. The receivers should be encouraged to use as much space as possible to spread the defenders, but by using questions that stimulate problem-solving solutions instead of telling them.

Sample questions

To receivers: *how can you best use the space available to ensure one receiver finds space? How does the shape of the space available influence movement to find space?*
   To the kicker: *when a receiver is running into space, where should you place the ball?*
   To defenders: *how can you best position yourself to cover two receivers?*

Playing area/set-up

The same as for the previous activity.

Equipment

- Marker cones
- Sets of coloured bibs
- One Australian football per game

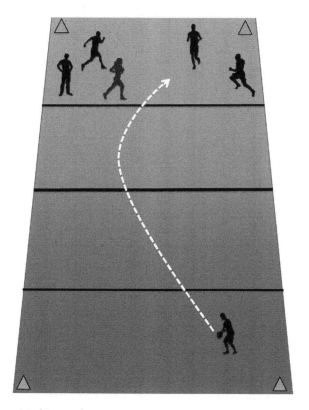

FIGURE 9.2 Marking under pressure

Players

Six players for each team, with extras rotated through the team.

Aim/intent

To score as many marks as possible in two minutes.

Playing rules

- No contact.
- The kicker must not cross the line at the kicking end.
- The ball must travel at least ten metres.
- Receivers cannot cross the ten-metre line at the kicking end of the space.

- The ball must be caught on the full (no bounce) and within the designated area to score a 'mark'.
- Defensive players may punch or strike the ball to prevent a mark but cannot make contact with the catcher.

Modifications

- *More challenging*: reduce the size of the area or increase the number of defenders (for example, 2 v. 2).
- *Less challenging*: begin with a 4 v. 1 set-up and move to 3 v. 2 as they develop their skills.

Activity 2: handball goal tally

Briefly demonstrate the handball technique. The ball is held on the palm of the upturned non-dominant hand and struck with the thumb end of a closed fist while moving the support hand forward. The ball should spin backwards to make it easier to catch. This is achieved by striking in a slightly downward motion.

Working in pairs, with a ball for each pair, one player runs to stand inside a hoop and receive a handball pass that travels at least three metres to score a point. They then run to another hoop to repeat this, with the aim being to score as many points as possible within thirty seconds. There is one fewer hoop than pairs of players and only one player can be in a hoop; if the ball is dropped the pair does not get a point and must move on to a new hoop.

Sample questions

What strategies did you use to get a high score? What technique did you use to ensure the ball was easy to catch? What do you have to be aware of and think about while playing this game?

Playing area/set-up

Form five or six pairs, with one ball and one hoop fewer than the number of pairs. Place hoops in an ad hoc manner in a space of about 15 × 15 metres.

FIGURE 9.3   Handball goal tally

Equipment

- Marker cones
- One ball per pair of players
- Coloured bibs – one per player, with the same colour for each pair
- One hoop per pair of players

Players

A total of 10–12 players formed into five or six pairs.

Aim/intent

Pairs score by having the receiving partner make a clean catch of the ball when standing inside a hoop from a handball delivered from at least five metres away. The handballer then runs to another hoop to act as receiver, but must be aware of all the other pairs working in the grid. The aim is to score as many times as possible in thirty seconds. Receivers in the hoop stand with their hands out to provide a target for the handballer.

Playing rules

- No contact.
- The handball must travel at least three metres.
- You cannot pass to a hoop next to the one just used.
- The receiver cannot enter a hoop that is already occupied.
- If the receiver drops the ball there is no score and he/she must move to another hoop.

Activity 2.1: handball pass tally

Form two teams of six players (6 v. 6) in an area of about 20×20 metres, with one ball per game. The aim is to complete four handballs without the ball hitting the ground, to score a point, after which the ball is turned over to the opposite team. The defending team may intercept but not attack the ball when in possession, and the ball carrier can run with the ball up to five metres.

Sample questions

To receivers: *how can you find space and communicate this to the ball carrier? Where do you want the ball when you call? How can you make space as a team?*

To the ball carrier: *how can you help your receivers find space and deliver a good handball?*

To defenders: *what do you have to do to intercept? Who should you pressure – the ball carrier or receivers – and why?*

Playing area/set-up

Set up the class in groups of twelve, working in a space about the size of half a basketball court.

Equipment

- Marker cones
- Two sets of coloured bibs
- One Australian football per game

Players

Six players for each team (6 v. 6), with extras rotated through the team.

Aim/intent

The aim is to score more points than the opposing team does. Points are scored when a team completes four handballs in succession without the ball being intercepted, being knocked down, being taken out or touching the ground.

Playing rules

- No contact.
- The ball must not touch the ground and the players in possession must not go out of the court/area.
- Defensive players cannot contest the ball in possession but may intercept.
- When the ball is intercepted, goes out or is taken out, or touches the ground, the team hands possession to the defensive team as a turnover.
- When six consecutive handballs are completed, the team in possession scores a point and hands over possession to the defensive team.

Modifications

- *More challenging*: increase pressure on receivers and kickers by allowing the defensive team to attack possession and strike the ball in the air to prevent a catch.
- *Less challenging*:
    1. Provide the team in possession with an extra player, for example 6 v. 5.
    2. Require fewer handballs to score a point.

Activity 3: four handball kick game

This game is played in a larger area, with teams of six competing against each other to perform four handballs, as in the previous game, after which they can try to kick to score a mark. Four completed handballs score one point, after which a successful mark scores another five points. The team in possession may perform more handballs if they choose to but will not earn any more points. The defensive team can intercept but cannot tackle. If the ball is intercepted, touches the ground, is taken out or goes out, possession is turned over.

Sample questions

How should you distribute your players in this space for this game and why? When defending, should you focus on disrupting the four handballs or on preventing the mark? What limits the space you can use in handballing and when kicking for a mark? What strategies did you use and how did they work?

Playing area/set-up

Play across a quarter of a soccer/rugby field or use approximately a 50 × 20 metre space.

Equipment

- One ball per game (twelve players)
- Cones to mark playing spaces if not already marked
- Two sets of coloured bibs

Players

Two teams of six players each (6 v. 6).

Aim/intent

The aim is to complete as many marks as possible. Points are scored by completing a mark, but four handballs must be completed beforehand. There is no limit on the number of handballs executed before kicking, but if the mark is unsuccessful the ball is turned over.

Playing rules

- The kicker may run with the ball but must touch it to the ground every five metres.
- The ball must be caught on the full (no bounce) and kept under control to score a 'mark'.
- The ball must travel at least ten metres from a kick before being caught for a 'mark'.

- There is no limit on how many times the ball can be handballed, but the
  , ball cannot be kicked until at least four handballs have been completed.
- When a mark is scored the ball is then turned over to the opposing team.
- Defenders 'tackle' the ball carrier with a two-handed hold or touch around
  the waist or hips, calling 'Tag' after which they have three seconds to
  unload the ball.
- When the ball carrier fails to unload the ball within three seconds when
  tagged or a player goes out of bounds with the ball, it is turned over.

Modifications

- *More challenging*: allow the defence to hit the ball away from the team in
  possession.
- *Less challenging*: reduce the number of handballs needed before kicking.

Activity 3.1: handball kick for goal game

This activity builds on the previous activity, moving toward the final modified
game by introducing a direction of attack and a kick at goal. After first completing
three handballs, the team in possession can choose to kick or handball to move
toward the goal they are attacking for a shot at goal. Once the initial three handballs have been completed there is no limit to the number of handballs or kicks.
The goal is kept narrow so as to make the attacking team get close enough to be
accurate and to discourage shots at goal from too far out.

Sample questions

In attack: *now that the game has direction, how does this change tactics? How
does the unlimited number of kicks change tactics from the previous game? What
are the consequences of kicking for goal from a long way out? How close should
you get the ball to the goal before kicking for it? When might you take the risk of
kicking for goal from a long way out?*

   In defence: *how does having a direction of attack and defence change
defensive tactics?*

Playing area/set-up

This game requires an area of approximately 20 × 30 metres to provide enough
space for kicking.

Equipment

- One ball per game (twelve players)
- Cones to mark playing spaces if not already marked
- Two sets of coloured bibs

Players

Two teams of six players (6 v. 6).

Aim/intent

To score goals by kicking the ball between two posts or cones at one end of the field.

Playing rules

- The game begins by tossing up the ball for two players to contest in the middle of the field.
- After completing three handballs the attacking team can handball and/or kick as it wishes in order to kick a goal.
- If there is an infringement of any kind the ball must be turned over, and if it goes out the opposing team restarts with a throw in from the point at which the ball went out.
- If the defence intercepts the ball they continue in possession.

Modifications

- *More challenging*:
  1. Increase the number of handballs needed before kicking.
  2. Allow the defence to hit the ball away from the team in possession.
- *Less challenging*:
  1. Decrease the number of handballs required before passing.
  2. Increase the size of the space.

Activity 4: modified Australian football

This unit culminates in a modified game of Australian football, as outlined at the beginning of the chapter, played by smaller sides. Approximately 8 players per team can play across half a soccer/rugby field (or equivalent) or 12–15 players per team on a full rugby/soccer field (using the rugby posts as goals if on a rugby field). The smaller-sided game will give more touches of the ball but the larger-sided game provides opportunities for longer kicks and the tactical considerations that arise from this.

Sample questions

By this stage of the unit and with this final version of Australian football there should be little need for the teacher to ask questions. Instead he/she should provide opportunities for team talks and discussions about tactics at appropriate times during the game.

Playing area/set-up

Across half a soccer/rugby field (around 10 v. 10) or using a full-size soccer/rugby field (about 12–15 v. 12–15).

Equipment

- Large cones to mark four goal posts for the smaller-sided game (or use rugby posts and cones outside as posts for 'behinds')
- Two sets of coloured bibs and one ball per game

Players

Approximately 10 v. 10 for a half field and 12–15 v. 12–15 for a full field.

Aim/intent

The primary aim of the game is to score as many goals as possible. Players score by kicking the ball into the goal, earning six points, with one point for a shot that misses the main goal but goes between the outer posts for a 'behind'.

Playing rules

- There are no limits on the number of handballs or kicks, and a player may run with the ball but must either bounce the ball or touch it to the ground every ten metres.
- Tackles are performed by placing two hands around the waist of the player in possession, after which the ball carrier must immediately stop and kick or handball the ball within three seconds.
- No holding or interfering with players off the ball.
- If the ball goes out, the opposition restarts with a throw from the sideline where it went out, and no opposition players can be within five metres of the thrower.
- Begin the game and restart after a goal by tossing the ball up between two players who jump for the ball as in basketball.
- The defence may attack possession by trying to take the ball, but can only grab the ball.
- If two opposing players have a firm hold on the ball, restart with a toss-up on the spot.

Modifications

- *More challenging*:

  1. Reduce the width of the goals.
  2. Increase the number of players.
  3. Restart after a goal with a kick from in front of the goal to speed up the game.

- *Less challenging*:

  1. Widen the width of the goals.
  2. Make the tackle a two-handed touch.

10

SOCCER

Introduction

Soccer is undoubtedly *the* world game and is easily the most popular team sport for children across the world. Even in countries such as the United States and Australia, where it has struggled to compete with established codes of football at the most elite levels, it dominates in terms of the numbers of children and young people participating in it. Despite its tactical complexity and the level of skill required at elite levels, it is easily accessible for children and youth in terms of the skill demands for participation at the introductory level. It requires little more than a ball and some space to get a game started. The tactical learning arising from taking a Game Sense approach to teaching soccer is easily transferred to other football codes such as rugby and Australian football, as well as to other invasion games such as basketball and field hockey.

Little, if any, special skill teaching is required for beginners to be involved in modified games from the first lesson, making soccer an ideal game for taking a Game Sense approach to teaching/coaching. This unit begins with a focus on developing some basic soccer skills within the context of very simple games, building the complexity of the game contexts used as understanding and skill develop. As is the case with the other units, time and opportunity should be provided for reflection and collaborative problem solving. Opportunities for the players/students to suggest modifications to the games used should also be encouraged. I have found through practice and our research on Game Sense that once players/students adapt to its pedagogy they are quick to take up opportunities to discuss, make plans and test them in response to tactical problems or challenges (see, for example, Light 2002; Light and Butler 2005; Light and Georgakis 2007). As the modified games used increase, the teacher/coach should provide more opportunities for students/players to discuss, develop and test strategies and tactics as an essential part of the learning process.

The first few activities are focused on developing skills such as dribbling and passing, but, unlike in technical approaches, learning is situated in an environment where perception and some decision-making are both required and developed. As the learning experiences become more complex the students/players move into modified games that are far more complex than the first one or two activities, yet build upon them, with the students/players scaffolding on knowledge as their understanding grows. These modified games offer opportunities for team discussions about tactics and for the formulation of ideas that can be tested in action and evaluated by the players, with the unit culminating in a simple small-sided game that can be an end in itself, used as a training game or built upon in complexity, leading to playing the full game.

How to play 4 v. 4 soccer

This unit comprises four relatively simple game-like activities or modified games focused on developing tactically informed skill and decision-making within game contexts. The activities used progressively increase in complexity, leading to playing 4 v. 4 modified soccer as the end game. This involves small-sided games of 4 v. 4 in a small space, with no goalkeeper and modified rules, including placing a limit of three metres on the distance any player can dribble and modifying the tackle rule for learning and safety reasons. This is explained in more detail at the end of the chapter (pp. 129–131).

Unit plan

Activity 1	*Dribbling in traffic*
Focus	Dribbling and perception (seeing and moving into space)
Activity 2	*Multi-goal game*
Focus	Accurate passing, communication with partner, vision and anticipation
Activity 3	*Pass and run five*
Focus	Accurate and fast passing, leading teammate into space, positioning after passing, communication and anticipation, perception and decision-making
Activity 4	*Four passes*
Focus	Finding space off the ball, making effective passes, dribbling, using available space
Activity 5	*4 v. 3 soccer*
Focus	Using an extra player in attack and beating the goalkeeper
Activity 6	*4 v. 4 triangle soccer*
Focus	Quick focusing on and organizing an attack, continuity of play
Activity 7	*4 v. 4 soccer*
Focus	Developing passing and controlling skills in more complex contexts that require higher-level decision-making and the development of strategy and tactics

The unit moves through a series of three game-like activities focused on particular skills performed in contexts that are similar to games. Learning is then shifted to the modified game of four passes then into the final modified game of 4 v. 4 soccer. This involves a process through which learning contexts become progressively more complex.

Activity 1: dribbling in traffic

Players have a ball each and dribble in a defined space covering as much of the space as possible. They should focus their vision ahead of the ball and develop their peripheral vision to avoid making contact with the other players working within the same space, yet while moving about the entire space.

Sample questions

What can you do to avoid bumping into others in the grid? Where is the best point to focus your vision so that you can control the ball yet be aware of the spaces in your peripheral vision? What parts of your feet can you use to change the direction of the ball quickly? What can you do to stay in control of the ball so you can change direction quickly?

Playing area/set-up

Set up 20 × 20 metre spaces.

Equipment

* One soccer ball per player
* Large cones to mark lines in the spaces

Players

The number of players placed in each grid depends upon their experience and skill as well as how difficult the teacher/coach wants to make the game. The more crowded it is the more difficult it is to avoid contact and find space.

Aim/intent

The aim of the activity is for each player to cover as much of the playing space as possible and maintain constant movement without making contact with others.

Playing rules

All players should avoid making contact with others, maintain continuous movement and cover as much of the playing space as possible.

Modifications

Making this activity more or less challenging is achieved by manipulating the size of the space and/or the number of players working in the space.

Activity 2: multi-goal game

(This game has been taken from the Victorian Soccer Federation's (now called Football Federation Victoria) *GoalKick Training Manual*.)

This is a simple game that is easy to play, involving manipulation of the ball, decision-making, anticipation and communication. Players form pairs working in a defined space at the same time as other pairs do, creating a dynamic environment that develops perception and decision-making. A number of goals are set up with cones, with the aim being for each pair to score a goal by the partner in possession kicking the ball between the cones and the other stopping and controlling the ball on the other side to score a point. The receiving player then proceeds to another goal, where the other partner becomes the receiver, who must stop and control the ball as it is pushed between the cones to score. The players must negotiate the traffic in the playing area and cannot kick a goal when another pair is at the same goal. If the ball touches another ball when passing through the cones it is not a goal. This gives the students/players more things to think about and to perceive while moving about the space. Teachers should have students swap partners regularly to help develop relationships within the group/class and to develop the students' or players' ability to adapt to a new partner.

Sample questions

In what ways do you have to work together to get a good score? What strategies did you adopt to get the highest number of goals in thirty seconds? What sort of communication is needed to get a good score? What type of pass do you need to make sure the ball passes through the goals but can be stopped and controlled by your partner? Should you pass from a long way out or from close to the cones? Why?

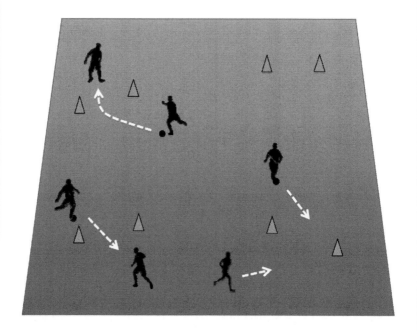

FIGURE 10.1   Multi-goal game

Playing area/set-up

Set up a number of goals with large cones in a playing area of about 20 × 20 metres and vary the size of the goal mouths to provide more tactical complexity.

Equipment

- One soccer ball per pair of players
- Cones to set up goals

Players

Players work in pairs but should change partners regularly, with between five and ten pairs in the 20 × 20 metre space.

Aim/intent

The primary aim of the game is for each pair of players to score as many goals as possible in the time decided on by the teacher.

Playing rules

- A goal is scored when one player passes the ball between the cones and his/her partner can stop and control it.
- Players cannot shoot at goal if someone else is shooting at goal; if the ball makes contact with another ball passing between the cones it does not count as a goal.
- No players can run between the cones.
- If enough goals are set up pairs cannot use the goals immediately beside the one in which they just scored.

Modifications

- *More challenging*:
    1. Ask the players to use alternate feet when shooting at goal.
    2. Reduce the size of the goal mouths.
    3. Reduce the width between the goals.
    4. Reduce the number of goals.
    5. Increase the number of pairs in the playing space.

- *Less challenging*:
    1. Increase the size of the goal mouths.
    2. Increase the number of goals.
    3. Reduce the numbers of pairs in the playing space.

Activity 3: pass and run five

The activity begins with players holding the ball in their hands and performing a two-handed bounce pass (the ball is bounced to help players see open channels for the pass). After passing, the passer must immediately run five metres to a space where he/she can receive a pass from his/her partner, but without contacting other players working in the space. He/she must also not be within five metres of his/her partner. Once the class adjusts to the dynamic environment the teacher asks them to now place the ball on the ground and use their feet, suggesting they keep looking for the same channels between the student/player in possession and the receiver. Depending upon the skill of the class or team this might be preceded by a little technical instruction on passing and stopping the ball. Players count the number of passes they make and try to improve on their scores through class/ team discussions as a group and in pairs to formulate ideas that they test in practice. The teacher or coach should also encourage them to communicate verbally and with gestures. Once the class or team understands the game the teacher/coach should provide some time out for the pairs to discuss tactics they can use to improve their score, with the teacher/coach noting improvements in scores.

Sample questions

When receiving a pass, where do you want the ball to go in relation to the direction in which you are running? What makes it easier or more difficult to receive and control the ball? When your partner is running into space where should you place your pass? How do you know where your partner is when you receive the ball and are looking to pass quickly? In what ways can you communicate? When you have the ball but don't have a clear passing channel, what can you do? What can your partner do?

Playing area/set-up

If it is large, the class can be split into two groups, or it can be kept as one group if it is not too large. The space used depends upon the ability of the class and the challenge the teacher wants to provide, with less space making the activity more difficult.

Equipment

- One soccer ball per pair
- Cones to mark out a field
- Taller cones to set up goals that can be adjusted in width

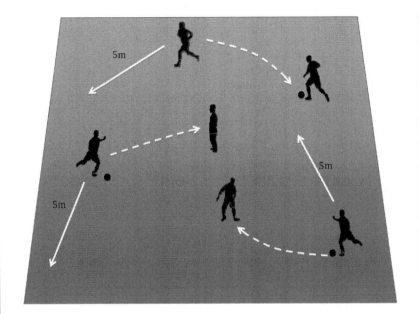

FIGURE 10.2   Pass and run five

Players

Form pairs, with one ball per pair, and rotate players regularly.

Aim/intent

The aim of this activity is to make as many passes as possible in the allotted time while meeting the requirement that after passing the passer must run five metres to space and pass at least a distance of five metres. The time would normally be thirty seconds.

Playing rules

- After passing, the player must run five metres but not toward the receiver. This distance can be modified to suit player abilities.
- All players must avoid body contact as much as they can.
- Players cannot interfere in any way with the ball of other pairs or with other players.

Modifications

- *More challenging*:

  1. Change the distance the player has to run. For example, have the players run ten metres to make it more challenging and make ten metres the minimum distance the ball must be passed.
  2. Ask more skilful players to use a one-touch technique in which, instead of stopping the ball then passing it, they just redirect the ball in one motion of the foot (this really increases the speed of movement).
  3. Use a smaller space.

- *Less challenging*:

  1. Make the space bigger.
  2. Use fewer players.

Activity 4: four passes

The aim of this game is for the team of players to make four successful passes that are cleanly controlled by the receiver on each occasion. When this is done the team receives one point and turns over possession to the other team. When there is an infringement, such as putting the ball out or excessive contact, the ball is turned over. If the opposition intercepts the ball, play continues with them now in possession and attempting to complete four clean passes. Younger, less skilful players should only be allowed to intercept passes, but if tackling is allowed it should only be attempted from directly in front of the player with the ball and not from the side. This is to make it easier to maintain possession and to reduce the danger of injury.

Sample questions

If you are off the ball, what can you do to make yourself able to accept a pass? If you are free of defenders and have space, how can you let the player in possession know? If the defence is tight and closing up open spaces when the receivers find space, what can the player with the ball do to help? What did you learn from previous games that you could apply here about passing to a moving receiver?

Playing area/set-up

Set up 4 v. 4 mini-games in a space about 25 × 25 metres.

Equipment

- One ball per game
- Cones to mark playing spaces
- Larger cones to set up goals or portable goals
- Sets of coloured bibs for each team

Players

Form two even teams of about four players. Depending upon the size of the class and their fitness, one or two 'bench' players can be used to rotate with the four on the field.

Aim/intent

In a 4 v. 4 team game the aim is to score as many points as possible, with one point being scored when one team makes four consecutive passes.

Playing rules

- One team starts in possession and attempts to make four consecutive passes.
- Once a team completes four passes and scores a point it must turn the ball over to the opposing team.
- If the ball goes out or there is an infringement of any kind the ball must be turned over.
- Players are allowed to dribble.
- If the defence intercepts the ball they continue in possession.
- There is no goalkeeper.

Modifications

- *Neutral*: do not allow dribbling, to force more passing and movement off the ball.
- *More challenging*:
    1. Change the ratio of players to favour the team defending, for example having 5 v. 3.
    2. Introduce a minimum number of one-touch passes.
    3. Use a smaller space.

- *Less challenging*:
  1. Favour the side in possession with a 5 v. 3 set-up.
  2. Use a larger space.

Activity 5: 4 v. 3 soccer

This game involves two teams of four, with both aiming to score goals, but the team in defence has to have one player operating as goalie, thus giving the attacking team a 4 v. 3 advantage in play but also presenting them with the challenge of beating the goalie.

Sample questions

To the attacking team: *how can you best take advantage of having an extra player in attack? How does having a goalie defending the goal affect the tactics you use to score? What are some ways in which you can speed up your attack once the ball is turned over?*

To the defending team: *if you lose possession in attack what tactics can you use to get a goalie in place as quickly as possible? In terms of field position and where your players are, what situations are particularly dangerous when you turn over possession and have to switch from attack to defence? How can you best respond to this situation? Is there any way you could avoid this happening or reduce its threat?*

Playing area/set-up

Set up games in a space about 25 metres long by 15 metres wide, with a goal at either end that is five metres wide.

Equipment

- One ball per game
- Cones to mark playing spaces
- Larger cones to set up goals or portable goals
- Sets of coloured bibs for each team

Players

Two teams of four players contest the game. In defence one player must drop back to be goalie, giving the opposition a 4 v. 3 advantage in play. The goalie should be rotated regularly to give all players equal experience in the position.

Aim/intent

The aim is to score more points than the opposing team, with one point awarded for each goal scored.

Playing rules

- One team starts in possession from their end of the field.
- If the ball goes out or there is an infringement of any kind the ball must be turned over.
- After a shot at goal, the defending team restarts play from the back line.
- If the defence intercepts the ball they continue in possession.
- The defending team must drop one player back to be goalie.
- If the attacking team loses possession the team that won possession must back pass to their goalie before attacking. During this time one player from the team that was attacking must drop back to be goalie (the opposition cannot intercept this back pass).

Modifications

- *More challenging*:

  1. Have a three metre dribble limit.
  2. Introduce a minimum number of passes before being able to shoot.
  3. Introduce the offside rule.

- *Less challenging* (in attack):

  1. Have a larger goal mouth.
  2. Allow immediate attack when the ball is turned over.

Activity 6: 4 v. 4 triangle soccer

(This game has been taken from the Victorian Soccer Federation's (now called Football Federation Victoria) *GoalKick Training Manual*.)

This game maintains the 4 v. 4 player format but introduces direction and the purpose of attacking toward a goal, and is played using a triangular space to provide the extra mental challenge of adapting to an unusual space and the need to quickly change the focus of attack. Three goals are set up in a triangular pattern twenty metres apart. The teacher randomly decides which team begins in possession in the middle of the triangle created by the three goals, with that team aiming to pass the ball through the goal to score, but instead of stopping, play continues and the scoring team are allowed to keep possession of the ball if they can. They can also score from either side of the three goals, and if they can maintain possession after the ball passes through a goal they continue attacking until dispossessed of the ball by the opposition, but they cannot score using the same goal. This means that they must immediately regroup to attack one of the other two goals. This is a very fast-paced game and players will tire quickly so teachers or coaches will need to have reserves on hand to rotate through the teams.

Sample questions

When in possession and attacking the goal, what things could you do as a team to anticipate and prepare for maintaining possession and trying to score the next goal? As there is no offside rule in this game, how can you or did you distribute players in attack? After scoring and maintaining possession, how can you or did you decide which goal to attack next? When defending, did you only think about stopping the opposition scoring the immediate goal or did you consider how to gain possession after they had shot for goal? How can you anticipate where the opposition will attack if they score and maintain possession?

Playing area/set-up

Set up three goals at the corners of an imaginary triangle with sides of 20 metres.

Equipment

- One ball per game
- Six large cones to mark three goals
- Sets of coloured bibs for each team

Players

Form two even teams of four players, with a 'bench' of players who can be rotated with the four on the field as they tire.

FIGURE 10.3   4 v. 4 triangle soccer

Aim/intent

The aim is to score as many points as possible, with one point being scored when the ball is passed through any of the three goals from either direction.

Playing rules

- The teacher or coach decides which team begins the game in possession of the ball, starting from the mid-point between the three goals (in the middle of the triangle).
- Tackles can only be attempted from in front of the player in possession and not from behind or beside the player in possession.
- No body contact, holding or interfering with players.
- No dribbling more than three metres.

Modifications

None suggested.

Activity 7: 4 v. 4 soccer

This game should be played in a space that is more like a full soccer/rugby field in terms of relative width and length, for example 15 × 20 metres. The game follows standard soccer rules, including the offside rule, where at least one opposition player must be in front of the person passing at the time of the pass. For younger students/players it is usually better to maintain the tackling rules from the previous game that stop the tackler coming in from the side.

Depending upon the progress of the students/players this game could begin by requiring the completion of four passes before the team is allowed to shoot for goal. This then builds on the knowledge developed in the four passes game, further developed in the 4 v. 4 triangle soccer game. From a constructivist perspective it scaffolds on prior knowledge and experience to construct new understandings in a process of adaptation (for a discussion of this, see Carpendale 1997). Small-sided games such as this offer more engagement for all players through increased touches of the ball as a core principle of TGfU and Game Sense. As this game is tactically complex allow for, and encourage, breaks for team meetings and tactical discussions to formulate and test ideas on attack and defence, as is normal practice in Game Sense as one of its core pedagogical features.

With a number of these games in progress at the same time, the teacher or coach has to move about the field monitoring the progress of each game and being prepared to intervene when necessary to ask questions or offer quick tips on technique. As suggested in Chapter 9, Activity 7, this could be organized as a mini-tournament or celebration, such as in Sport Education to finish off a physical education unit or to make a fun training session in youth sport. This would involve games of short duration, such as for five to ten minutes, with teams planning and even practising in anticipation of the next team they will play.

Sample questions

We practised passing and running to space immediately after passing in the pass and run five activity. In this game, where would you run to after passing? What options do you have for positioning your players in attack and defence? Which do you think would work better: one-on-one defence or a zone defence? Why?

Playing area/set-up

Same set-up as for the four passes game.

Equipment

Same as for the previous game.

Players

Same as for the previous game.

Aim/intent

The primary aim of the game is to score as many goals as possible. Players score by kicking the ball into the goal.

Playing rules

- Tackles can only be attempted from in front of the player in possession and not from behind or beside the player in possession.
- No body contact, holding or interfering with players.
- If the ball goes out, the opposition restart with a throw from the sideline where it went out and no opposition players can be within five metres of the thrower.
- After a goal, play is restarted by a defender from in front of the goal.
- No dribbling more than three metres.

Modifications

- *Neutral*: allow the students to suggest changes when and if any problems with the rules emerge, with the teacher facilitating decision-making.
- *More challenging*:

  1. Reduce the width of the goals.
  2. Add a goalie.

- *Less challenging*:

  1. Increase the width of the goals.
  2. Don't allow tackling, only intercepting.

11

FIELD HOCKEY

Introduction

Field hockey is the name used for this sport in countries where other forms of hockey, and ice hockey in particular, are popular, but in countries such as Australia, the United Kingdom and New Zealand it is just known as hockey. It is widely played in countries that have strong systems of community-based club sport at junior and senior levels, and boasts the third largest number of participants for a field team sport in the world, behind Association football (soccer) and cricket. It is also commonly included in the physical education curriculum in countries such as the United Kingdom, Germany and Australia, where it is a popular club sport. However, it does not enjoy a high profile as a professional/ spectator sport even in countries where it is popular as a participant sport.

Governed by the International Hockey Federation, hockey is an Olympic and a Commonwealth Games sport. It has a men's and a women's World Cup and a junior World Cup played every four years, as well as the annual Champions Trophy as a prestigious event contested by the best six national teams in the world. It was set up by Pakistan's Air Vice Marshall, Nur Khan, for men in 1980, with a women's version introduced in 1987. In the men's competition Australia, Germany, the Netherlands and Pakistan have been the most successful national teams and in the women's event the Netherlands, Australia and Argentina have been the most successful.

Hockey is a global sport with very high participation rates across the world and is tactically very similar to soccer although the skills involved in manipulating the ball are very different. The skill demands to begin playing even modified games also present a little more of a challenge than is the case for soccer. For this reason, after a warm-up game this unit of work begins with a focus on using the hockey stick that specifically involves dribbling, passing, trapping and tackling but within contexts that require and improve perception, some decision-making and the execution of appropriate skill in context. It then moves up in complexity into modified games that are, in turn, progressively made more complex.

Some of the activities in this unit have been used elsewhere in this section of the book but adapted to the specifics of hockey. This reinforces the tactical similarities between invasion games (particularly between soccer and hockey) and the variety of ways in which the games or activities used can be applied to different sports within the same game category. This is very evident in the very useful set of games cards published by the Australian Sports Commission as part of the Game Sense resources developed in the late 1990s, where all games are organized only in game categories. With the exception of some activities used in touch rugby and oztag, most modified games used for invasion games in this book are transferable across sports within that category, and can be modified by teachers, coaches and students/players to suit particular contexts, learning objectives and learners.

How to play half-field hockey

Half-field hockey is played on one half of a regular hockey field or soccer/rugby field between two teams of seven players, with one being the goalie. The goalie must have all safety equipment, including pads, helmet, chest protector, kickers, pelvis protectors and gloves. The game is played over two twenty-minute halves, with a five-minute break. There is no offside rule and tackles can only be attempted from directly in front of the player in possession. It uses most of the rules of minkey hockey, with the differences in playing rules outlined in detail at the end of this chapter. Penalties are awarded against players for dangerous play and for ridiculing or criticizing other players or the umpire.

Unit plan

Activity 1	*Handball hockey*
Focus	Dribbling and perception (seeing and moving into space)
Activity 2	*Dribbling and protecting the ball in traffic (stages 1 and 2)*
Focus	Dribbling and controlling the ball, vision and anticipation, responding to pressure from defence, maintaining possession
Activity 3	*5 v. 3 keepings off (stages 1, 2 and 3)*
Focus	Movement of the ball, accurate and fast passing, leading teammate into space, positioning after passing, communication and anticipation, perception and decision-making, maintaining possession and finding support under pressure
Activity 4	*Four hits and shoot*
Focus	Finding space off the ball, making effective passes, dribbling, tackling, using available space, accuracy in shooting for goal
Activity 5	*Minkey hockey*

Focus	Developing passing and controlling skills in more complex contexts that require higher-level decision-making, development of strategy and tactics
Activity 6	*Half-field hockey*
Focus	All aspects of hockey game play

This unit begins with a warm-up game that does not involve hockey sticks but does engage in hockey's tactical aspects. It then moves into game-like activities that are focused on developing skill in context, before moving into modified games from Activity 4 and finishing with the final modified game of half-field hockey.

Activity 1: handball hockey

This game is a warm-up game for mind and body. It is played across half a hockey field, or it can be played inside on a basketball court using portable hockey goals or goals marked with cones and a soft ball but no sticks. The ball used should be appropriate to the age and experience of the players, considering size and hardness. It is played using similar rules to hockey but the ball is rolled by hand instead of being struck with a hockey stick. Players must keep a low body position (the ball cannot bounce) and may run up to five metres with the ball but must roll the ball immediately if touched using a two-handed touch on the upper body. The game is played using two teams of between five and seven players. Players other than the goalie cannot touch the ball with their feet or legs but can intercept the ball with their hands.

Sample questions

What are you looking for when you want to roll the ball? In attack, once you have passed the ball what should you do? What are you doing when attacking but not in possession of the ball?

Playing area/set-up

Play across one-quarter of a hockey pitch, with goals set up at either end and a goal circle set up within which only the goalie can enter.

Equipment

- One ball per player, with the type of ball depending upon age and experience of players
- Large cones to mark the goals or portable goals
- Small soft cones to mark a goal circle five metres out from the goal

Players

The number of players placed in each grid depends upon their experience and skill, but normally this would involve five to seven players on each team.

Aim/intent

The aim of the game is to score as many goals as possible by rolling the ball into the goal from outside the goal circle.

Playing rules

- No excessive contact.
- Players must maintain a low body position.
- If the ball goes out the opposition team restart from where it went out.
- If the ball goes over the back of the court, the defending side restarts with a player rolling the ball out, and no other player can be within five metres of him/her.
- The ball cannot be thrown and must only be rolled.
- A tackle is performed by executing a two-handed touch, after which the player must roll the ball immediately.

Modifications

Vary the size and hardness of the ball used.

Activity 2: dribbling and protecting the ball in traffic

This activity is presented in two stages based upon the assumption that the players or students need to experience stage 1 to be able to participate successfully in stage 2, but the teacher/coach can decide where to start based on the players' or students' abilities.

STAGE 1

All players have a hockey stick and work in pairs, one with the ball and the other shadowing her/him. The player with the ball covers as much of the space as possible while avoiding other players. She/he should focus her/his vision ahead of the ball and develop their peripheral vision to avoid making contact with the other players working within the same space, yet while moving about the entire space. The shadowing player follows the dribbling player, moving around to the side of her/him as if to threaten the ball. The dribbling player must then move away from the shadow while keeping the ball close to the stick and under control.

Sample questions

What can you do to avoid bumping into others in the grid? What were you focusing your vision on? What were you thinking about? Where were you focusing your vision so that you could control the ball yet look for spaces? What can you do to stay in control of the ball so you can change direction quickly?

STAGE 2

The purpose here is to avoid a tackle. This activity builds the pressure on the player in possession by allowing the shadow to execute a tackle, but a tackle modified to provide enough opportunity for the player in possession to succeed and for safety reasons. The tackler must come at the player in possession from directly in front and cannot put her/his stick across the path of the player with the ball. If the shadow dispossesses the player in possession, she/he returns the ball and they restart.

Sample questions

How did introducing a tackle change the game? What tactics can you use to protect the ball from the tackler? What difference was there between the tackler coming from your left and from your right side? Which direction of tackle was easier to move away from and why? What can you do to protect the ball when a tackle is attempted from the left side (or right side if left-handed)?

Playing area/set-up

Play using one-eighth of a hockey pitch. If it follows from the previous game just divide the playing space in half.

Equipment

- One ball per player, with the type of ball depending upon the age and experience of the players

- One hockey stick for each player

Players

The players form pairs, with a total of five or six pairs in each space (10–12 players).

Aim/intent

The aim of the activity is to explore as much space as possible while dribbling, avoiding other players and responding to the threat of the shadow player. When tackling is introduced this adds the extra aim of keeping possession while still moving about the whole space.

Playing rules

- No body contact.
- The players and the ball must stay within the playing space.
- When tackling is introduced, the tackle must come from directly in front of the player in possession.
- Players cannot use the back of the stick.

Modifications

- *More challenging*: reduce the size of the playing space or increase the number of players in it.
- *Less challenging*:
  1. If some players are unable to deal with the pressure of the tackle, the teacher/coach could be open to allowing the tackler to approach from in front but not attack the ball.
  2. Enlarge the playing space or reduce the number of players in it.

Activity 3: 5 v. 3 keepings off

Play a game of keepings off in half of the space used in the previous game, splitting the teams, so if a 7 v. 7 was played across one-quarter of the pitch, then halve that area, with seven working in each space, which would be one-eighth of a full field. Divide the players to give uneven teams according to the skill and experience of the class or team. For example, this might start with a 5 v. 2 (five in attack) but change to 6 v. 1 if the skill level is low or to 4 v. 3 with skilled players. The aim is for the team in possession to make as many passes as possible in thirty seconds while the defending team attempts to intercept (but cannot tackle in the first stage of the game). Begin the game with only passing allowed, then introduce dribbling, with a three metre limit to take the game up a notch in complexity and skill demand. Finally, to step up again, in stage 3 introduce the tackling used in the previous activity (tackle from the front only).

STAGE 1

No dribbling or tackling is allowed, with a focus on moving off the ball, passing and trapping.

Sample questions

To the team in possession: *how can the receivers create maximum space for their team and make it most difficult for the defenders to mark all players? What can the player in possession do to help the receivers? As a receiver, how can you best position yourself in relation to a defender and the player in possession? For the player in possession, can you provide examples of how the type of pass you make has to match the situation?*

FIGURE 11.1 Expanded keepings off

To defenders: *can you suggest any strategies for defending? Should you pressure the player in possession or the receivers?*

STAGE 2

Introduce dribbling, but with a three metre limit to prevent the more skilled players dominating and to encourage team play.

Sample questions

To all: *how did bringing in dribbling change the game and your tactics?*

To the team in possession: *whose role was most affected by being able to dribble? With dribbling, how can the player in possession help the receivers find or get into space? Did it make being the player in possession easier or more difficult, and why?*

STAGE 3

Finally, introduce tackling, but as in the previous activity, with the tackler only being allowed to approach from directly in front of the player in possession.

Sample questions

To all: *how was it different when we introduced tackling for both sides? Which side did it help more? Why? How does that compare to the stage 1 game with no dribbling or tackling? How did it change the pressure that could be placed upon the player in possession?*

Playing area/set-up

Play across one-eighth of a hockey pitch.

Equipment

- One ball per game, with the type of ball depending upon the age and experience of the players
- One hockey stick for each player
- Two sets of coloured bibs
- Small soft marker cones to divide the previous quarter-pitch in two

Players

The number of players placed in each grid depends upon their experience and skill, but normally this would involve seven players. Decide the ratio of attacking to defensive players according to the skill level, ranging from low-skilled players using 6 v. 1 to high-skilled players using 4 v. 3.

Aim/intent

The aim of the game is to make as many completed passes (trapped and controlled) as possible in thirty seconds.

Playing rules

- No body contact.
- If the ball goes out or is intercepted by the defending team, the pass tally stops and has to begin again from zero.
- The ball must be trapped and controlled by the receiver to count as a completed pass.
- When tackling is introduced, the tackle can only be executed from directly in front of the player in possession.

Modifications

- *More challenging*: reduce space or increase the number of defenders.
- *Less challenging*: increase space, reduce the number of defenders or increase the number of attackers.

Activity 4: four hits and shoot

This game builds on the previous game at stage 3 with tackling and dribbling but gives the play direction and a focus on attacking the goal. Played by eight players in a 4 v. 4 configuration, it uses one-quarter of the hockey pitch and is played cross-field with a goal at either end of the playing space. Once a team has possession they must make four completed passes that are trapped under control, after which they can shoot for goal. Once they have completed four passes there is no limit on how many more passes they must make before shooting for goal. The game begins from the centre of the field with a push, and is restarted from the end line after a goal is scored or if the attacking team puts the ball over the end line. There is no goalie and shots for goal must be made from outside a goal circle but not from beyond the halfway line.

In this game let the students/players play and adapt to it, but once they appear to be developing an understanding of it provide opportunities for the two teams to have 'team talks' where they discuss tactical ideas (the debate of ideas), formulate plans and attempt to enact them in the game. At this stage the teacher/coach should be able to step back from structuring thinking through questions to the whole group and allow the students/players to begin asking their own questions. This requires the teacher/coach to move between teams to listen and only offer very brief comments or ask quick questions *if there seems to be a need*. If the teacher/coach has focused his/her thinking in the earlier games and activities he/she should be able to provide more autonomy for them and leave the questioning until the end of this game.

Sample questions

What ideas or tactics did you develop as a team and try out? Did they work? Why/why not? Did you adjust these ideas or tactics at all? How did that work? Did you discuss skill execution at all? What were the biggest two challenges or problems you had to deal with? How did you deal with them? Did this work? Why/why not? Did you draw on what we learnt in the earlier activities or games in this game? Can you see any of the experiences of earlier games in this game?

Playing area/set-up

Play on one-quarter of a hockey pitch, playing cross-field (55 × 23 metres) with a halfway line marked out and a semi-circular shooting circle seven metres from the goal. Set up a goal at either end with large cones and adjust the width according to skill level and how the game develops. A narrow goal usually forces players to get closer before shooting.

Equipment

- One ball per game, with the type of ball depending upon the age and experience of the players
- One hockey stick for each player
- Two sets of coloured bibs
- Small soft marker cones to divide the previous quarter-pitch in two
- Four large marker cones to set up goals

Players

This normally involves 4 v. 4 but could be increased up to 6 v. 6 depending upon the age, experience and skill level of the students/players.

Aim/intent

The aim of the game is to score as many goals as possible.

Playing rules

- No body contact.
- If the ball goes out, a player from the team that did not put it out restarts play from the point where it went out. At this time no other player may be within five metres of the player restarting.
- Play the ball only with the flat side (face) of the stick.
- No power hits.
- The stick cannot be raised beyond 45 degrees in back lift or follow through.
- The ball must be trapped and controlled by the receiver to count as a completed pass.
- When tackling is introduced, the tackle can only be executed from directly in front of the player in possession.

Modifications

- *More challenging*:

   1. Increase the number of defenders.
   2. Make the goals narrower.

- *Less challenging*: reduce the number of defenders (no fewer than three per team) or increase the width of the goals.

Activity 5: minkey hockey

Minkey hockey is a modified game played in Australia, with similar versions in other countries. It is played with six players on either team on one-quarter of a hockey pitch over two halves of fifteen minutes each with a five-minute break between. The version suggested here is slightly modified from the Aussie Sports (Curran 1991) version.

Sample questions

In this game, rather than ask questions of the class, the teacher/coach should provide opportunities for team discussions and for the formulation of ideas and tactics that are tested in the game.

Playing area/set-up

Play using one-quarter of a hockey pitch and playing cross-field, with a halfway line marked out and a line ten metres out from the goal. Set up a goal at either end with large cones 3.6 metres apart.

Equipment

- One ball per game, with the type of ball depending upon the age and experience of the players; primary school-aged players should use a minkey hockey ball or a softball
- One hockey stick for each player on the field; if available, use minkey hockey sticks for primary school-aged players
- Two sets of coloured bibs
- Small soft marker cones to divide the previous quarter-pitch in two
- Four large marker cones to set up goals

Players

Set up teams of ten, with six on the field, and rotate players regularly (6 v. 6). Alternatively, play three teams in rotation with a smaller 'bench'.

Aim/intent

The aim of the game is to score as many goals as possible.

Playing rules

- Begin with a push backwards from the centre of the field.
- At every start and restart all players must be on their side of the halfway line.
- There is no offside rule.

- There is no goalie.
- If the ball goes out a player from the team that did not put it out restarts play from the point where it went out with a push, and no other player may be within five metres of him/her.
- Tackles can only be executed from directly in front of the player in possession.
- For the following infringements a free hit is awarded to the opposition on the spot:

  - Power hits
  - Raising the stick above the knees on the backswing or follow through
  - Using the back of the stick
  - Playing the ball with hands or feet
  - Raising the ball
  - Criticizing or ridiculing players or the umpire
  - Obstructing opposition players with the body or stick
  - Striking an opposition player with the stick
  - Rough or dangerous play.

- If a rule is broken within ten metres of the goal (inside the ten metre line) by the defending team the attacking team gets a penalty push from five metres out from either goal post on the goal line. All attackers must stay behind the ten metre line and all defenders must stay behind the goal line until the ball is pushed.
- If the ball goes over the backline off an attacker's stick, play restarts with a free hit from the ten metre line by a defending player.

Modifications

No suggestions for modifications to the game, but teachers/coaches should consider letting students/players act as umpire to get a better understanding of the game and to foster consideration of officials and valuing fair play.

Activity 6: half-field hockey

This game is played on half a hockey field, with an extra player added as the goalie (7 v. 7) and using most of the rules of minkey but with a few changes. In this game the teacher should let primary school-aged children and perhaps the younger classes in secondary school continue to use minkey sticks (if available) and minkey balls or similar soft balls such as a kanga cricket ball. The goalie must have all safety equipment, including pads, helmet, chest protector, kickers, pelvis protectors, gloves. Normally three play forward, with two halves behind and a full back, but the importance of positioning and knowing roles might be something learnt from playing this game.

Sample questions

How does having a goalie change tactics in this game? How can or did you position the six players other than the goalie? In soccer and hockey there are forwards, midfield and defensive players. Would that be useful in this game? Why/why not? If all the attacking players are close to the opposition goal and the ball is turned over, what can happen? How can you prevent this?

As with minkey, provide opportunities for team talks, particularly at tactically important stages.

Playing area/set-up

Play across half of a normal hockey pitch, with goals as in minkey but with ten metre shooting (semi-)circle and a line 16 metres from the goal line at either end.

Equipment

Use standard hockey sticks but make the choice of type of ball dependent on the age and experience of the players and use standard protective equipment for the goalie.

Players

Play with teams of ten, with seven on the field, and rotate players regularly (7 v. 7). Alternatively, play three teams in rotation, with a smaller 'bench' playing one 'half' then rotating.

Aim/intent

The aim of the game is to score as many goals as possible.

Playing rules

As per minkey, with the following changes:

- Played over two twenty-minute halves with a five-minute break.
- If a rule is broken inside the shooting circle by the defending team, the attacking team gets a penalty push from ten metres out from either goal post on the goal line. All attacking players must remain outside the shooting circle and all defenders behind the goal line until the ball is pushed, with the exception of the goalie.
- If the ball goes over the backline off an attacker's stick, play restarts with a free hit from the 16 metre line by a defending player.

Modifications

None suggested.

12

BASKETBALL

Introduction

Basketball was first developed in 1891 by physical education teacher James Naismith to keep his college's American football team fit when winter weather prevented them training. It is played across the globe, is a valuable media sport and an Olympic sport but, at its most basic level, requires little equipment or space to get some sort of a game going. It is also widely played in schools in most countries around the world.

This unit presents five basic activities that progress from simple to more complex, culminating in playing a slightly modified version of the full game on a full court. It begins with what could be seen as a physical and mental warm-up game of tag ball that sharpens passing and catching skills while developing powers of anticipation, communication, decision-making and tactical knowledge. Both tag ball and keepings off have been around a long time and are commonly used by coaches and teachers but, as is the case with so much of what I suggest in Part II, the use of Game Sense pedagogy gets the maximum value from these games in terms of learning and enjoyment. Early in the unit the emphasis is placed on passing, catching and working off the ball, but midway through tally ball it introduces dribbling as an important skill in this game. I recognize that, with younger children in particular, it is likely that they may not have enough technical mastery of this skill to use it meaningfully in the game. In this case the teacher/coach might choose to pull out of the game for a short time to do some more focused work on dribbling, and I offer suggestions here for how this might be done without reverting to a decontextualized skill drill.

In Game Sense skills are learnt within modified games, but if a lack of skill is holding up the game the teacher/coach can do a little skill work to *enable* the game to continue. The teacher/coach should not, however, lose the focus on the game and get sidetracked into wanting to have the skill 'right' before going back to the game. As Thorpe makes very clear in the Australian Sports Commission (1997) Game Sense video, just do a little 'tweaking' of skill when it's needed individually and let the players develop it further within the context of a game.

Even when some specific skill work is needed out of the context of games it should not be done in complete isolation from the conditions of the game. For this reason I suggest working on the skill in an environment that is in some way similar to the dynamic context of game play, as outlined in Activity 3.1. My suggestion here for a little work on dribbling is not intended to be prescriptive in any way and any one of the activities suggested could be used depending on which one is most appropriate.

How to play modified basketball

Normally two teams of six players play on a full-size court, but with younger players you might be able to squeeze seven or eight in each team, with a bench that rotates regularly to allow more players more time on court. The aim of the game is to score more baskets than the other team by moving the ball down the court toward the hoop that the team is attacking. Movement can be achieved by passing or by dribbling the ball. Once the player dribbling the ball stops moving he/she cannot start again but must pass the ball. While there can be some reasonably heavy body contact in senior-level basketball, the form played here does not allow contact as this can discourage and even intimidate the less confident players. In a club sport setting the coach may choose to allow different degrees of contact depending upon the age, experience and competitive level of the players.

The other main modification in this game is the three-bounce limit on dribbling designed to prevent some players dominating and marginalizing the less confident/experienced players. From a positive perspective, it also forces the more confident and experienced players to think tactically by asking them what they should do after passing and encouraging them to interact with all players in their team. This is likely to be more important in a physical education class (see Chapter 4) but can also be important in many club sport settings. Apart from any equity and inclusion considerations, it does encourage all players to think about movement off the ball and their engagement in the game after passing.

The unit plan offers progressively more complex training/learning games but Activity 3.1 (dribbling practice) is included to provide an example of activities that can be used to improve a skill that might hold up the progression of games. Unlike the Tactical Games approach, this is not necessarily predetermined because if the students' or players' dribbling skills are good enough to enable the games to progress, then it would not need this activity. However, if some work on dribbling is needed it should be done within game-like contexts that require and improve perception, decision-making and flexible skill execution.

Unit plan

Activity 1	*Tag ball*
Focus	Accurate passing, catching, anticipation and leading the receiver
Activity 2	*Keepings off*
Focus	Working off the ball, appropriate passing, communication and anticipation
Activity 3	*Tally ball*
Focus	Accurate passing, communication with a partner, vision and anticipation, creating space
Activity 3.1	*Dribbling practice*
Focus	Basic dribbling, perception and evasion while dribbling
Activity 4	*Keyball*
Focus	Accurate and fast passing, leading a teammate into space, positioning after passing, communication and anticipation, perception and decision-making
Activity 5	*Modified half-court basketball*
Focus	Further developing skills, decision-making and tactical understanding from previous activities
Activity 6	*Modified basketball*
Focus	Further development of skills and knowledge focused on in previous activities

Activity 1: tag ball

This is an excellent warm-up game for ball-handling games such as basketball, netball and rugby. Like many other games presented in Part II it is commonly used in training sessions, but the key to getting the most out of it for learning and increasing performance lies in the use of Game Sense pedagogy. At its most basic level it is a simple game in which two even teams use a determined playing space, with the team in possession of the ball eliminating opposition players by tagging them with the ball. One problem with elimination games is that they leave many players (and often always the same players) sitting out the game after being eliminated early. To get around this, I suggest asking the team in possession to see how many they can tag in thirty seconds and then turning the ball over.

The size of the playing area is critical in this game, with a smaller area making it easier for the team in possession to tag the opposition and a larger area making it more challenging. Tags must be made with control of the ball and players cannot run with the ball in hand, making it a passing and catching game. From my experience of using this game, I invariably see very rapid improvement as players become accustomed to the game and improve their passing, catching and anticipation skills. Using the same two teams per playing area, the point score for eliminating opposition players can be accumulated over several rounds, with the teacher/coach focusing questions on appropriate technique, such as the type of pass needed to get the ball to players in a position to tag in time to complete a tag.

Sample questions

What tactics can you use to tag opposition players? Where in the playing space is the best place to move the opposition players (in the centre or in corners?), and why? When the opposition player you want to tag is being shadowed by a teammate and is moving quickly, where should you pass the ball? As you don't have much time, what type of pass do you need to throw? How can the ball carrier know where teammates in a position to tag are?

Playing area/set-up

Use a defined area that provides the appropriate amount of space to facilitate tagging, yet make it challenging. You can use some of the existing markings on a court (basketball, badminton, tennis, etc.) or mark a space out with soft marker cones.

Equipment

- Two sets of coloured bibs for each game
- A basketball for each game

Players

Two equal teams of six to eight players.

Aim/intent

The aim is for the team in possession to tag as many opposition players as possible in thirty seconds.

Playing rules

- No body contact.
- Players in the team being chased cannot leave the playing space. If they do, they are counted as being tagged.
- The ball must be under control to complete a tag.
- The tagging team cannot hold the opposition players.

Modifications

- *More challenging*: make the space larger or use two balls at once.
- *Less challenging*: use a smaller space.

Activity 2: keepings off

This is also a commonly used game in training for many invasion sports but it really requires the use of Game Sense (or similar) pedagogy to get the most learning from it. Often also called 'piggy in the middle', the game involves two players in possession trying to make as many passes as possible in thirty seconds, with a single defender attempting to intercept the ball or to slow down the number of passes made. Just setting out the game and letting the learners play typically results in a static game of merely lobbing the ball between the players in possession, with the defender moving very little. This is where the questioning used in Game Sense is important in bringing the game to life and promoting learning. Through appropriate questioning the teacher/coach can encourage far more movement on the part of the two players in possession and, consequently, more movement on the part of the defender. Through the stimulation of good questioning that encourages the players to move into the best positions to receive a pass and for the ball carrier to move with the ball this can become a very dynamic game that requires and develops high levels of skill and tactical under-standing. It also develops game-specific fitness and agility. The teacher/coach will need to be active in asking questions to stimulate the players to explore space, be creative and 'think outside the box' in moving to facilitate passing and catching. Initially it is only a passing game, but as skill and understanding improve, dribbling can be introduced to allow the ball carrier to move to facilitate clean passing by dribbling.

Sample questions

To the players in possession: *where is the best place that the player off the ball can move to receive a pass and to exclude the defender? Where can the receiver move to cut out the defender? If the players in possession are taller than the defender, what type of pass might be good? If the defender is taller than the two in possession, what pass might be best to use?*

To the defenders: *which player should you pressure, and why? What sort of body posture or stance can you use to prevent the ball carrier from passing? Should you pressure the ball carrier or the receiver? Why?*

Playing area/set-up

Any area with enough room for the three players to move freely.

Equipment

- Coloured bibs (two of one colour and one of another colour)
- A basketball for each game

Players

Three players, two in possession and a defender. Ensure roles are regularly changed.

Aim/intent

The aim is for the two in possession to make as many passes as possible in thirty seconds.

Playing rules

- No body contact.
- The defender cannot attempt to dispossess the ball carrier.
- If the ball is intercepted the count ends and the two in possession restart.
- Players in possession must be at least one metre apart.

Modifications

- *More challenging*:
  1. Allow the ball carrier to dribble (in this case you might discuss the purpose of dribbling).
  2. Expand to a 3 v. 2 game.
- *Less challenging*:
  1. Play 3 v. 1.
  2. Use a bigger space.

Activity 3: tally ball

Tally ball is often used in basketball training to develop passing and catching, but when a Game Sense approach is adopted it enables the development of these basic skills within a tactical context while also developing tactical knowledge, decision-making ability and enhancing relationships within the team/class. I also suggest introducing dribbling once the passing, catching and movement off the ball have developed enough to build the game in complexity.

In a half-court and a 6 v. 6 set-up the team in possession attempt to make six clean passes to score a point, with defenders only able to intercept the ball. The aim is to score more points than the opposing team and the game builds on the knowledge developed in keepings off, with receivers striving to find space and take a reception, and ball carriers helping get the pass away by moving through dribbling. I suggest starting with no dribbling, using only passing and introducing dribbling once the players have settled into the game. This helps them understand when and why to dribble and how it fits into the game of basketball.

Dribbling is a more demanding skill than catching and passing and may require a little direct instruction during the game if a lack of skill in dribbling is impeding the development of the game. If it is necessary to spend some time dribbling I suggest contextualizing the practice and developing perceptual ability as outlined in Activity 3.1.

Sample questions

To the team in possession: *which teammates should you pass to and why? What techniques can you use to get away from the defender to be open to receive a pass? How can you communicate between open receivers and the ball carrier? In what situations would you use a lob pass and a bounce pass? If the receiver is moving quickly, where should the pass go? When and why should the ball carrier dribble?*

To the defending team: *what are the differences between a one-on-one defensive pattern and a zone defence? Which do you think would be better in this game, and why?*

Playing area/set-up

Play on half a basketball court.

Equipment

- Two sets of coloured bibs
- One basketball

Players

Play with two teams of six players (6 v. 6).

Aim/intent

The aim is for the team in possession to score more points than the opposition by making as many sets of six passes as possible and limiting the opposition's completion of sets of six passes.

Playing rules

- No body contact.
- Defenders cannot dispossess the ball carrier.
- If the ball is intercepted the pass tally ends and the team in possession restarts.
- Players in possession must be at least one metre apart.

Modifications

- *More challenging*:
    1. Introduce dribbling but with a limit on the number of bounces (in this case you might discuss the purpose of dribbling).
    2. Allow defenders to dispossess the ball carrier and/or interfere with the ball.
    3. Reduce the playing space.
- *Less challenging*:
    1. Enlarge the playing space.
    2. Have uneven teams, with one more in the attacking team, but when the ball is turned over one player moves into the team now in possession.
    3. Have fewer passes required to score a point.

Activity 3.1: dribbling practice

Step 1

Work in a defined playing space. Form pairs, with one dribbling and moving about the playing area and the other shadowing from behind as the dribbler explores all the space in the area, and regularly change directions. This involves perception of the shadowing player, developing control of the ball while dribbling and changing direction, and lower-level decision-making.

Step 2

The shadowing player now applies mild pressure by moving to the side of the player dribbling and can even say something to provide auditory information for the player in possession, such as 'Here', if the dribbler does not respond to this movement. When the shadow moves to the side the dribbler must move away from him/her. For example, if the shadow moves to the dribbler's right the dribbler needs to immediately move to the left. This is occurring within a space where other pairs are doing the same thing, providing a moving environment that has to be negotiated as spaces open and close. As with all other activities, the teacher/coach needs to adjust the space and numbers of pairs to suit the learners and provide the right balance between challenge and success for all.

Step 3

To 'take it up a notch', the 'defender' can move in front of the dribbler, who moves away while maintaining control of the ball (but does not attack the ball), while the player in possession continues dribbling and trying to block the 'defender' with his/her body. Finally, more pressure can be placed on the player in possession by allowing the shadow to attempt to dispossess the ball carrier, but only from directly in front and not from the side. Of course, with advanced players who have the necessary skill, normal basketball rules with regard to dispossessing can be applied.

Sample questions

When dribbling, what are you looking for? What things do you need to be aware of and think about? Where do you or should you focus your gaze, and why? What decisions do you need to make? What things do you need to think about when making decisions? Did you or do you think you can improve your awareness of what is happening around you? What senses do you use to know about or be aware of spaces and movement of people around you? What cues can or did you respond to?

Playing area/set-up

A defined space of an appropriate size.

Equipment

- One coloured bib for each pair
- A ball for each pair

Players

Work in pairs, swapping roles regularly and swapping partners within each playing space.

Aim/intent

The aim is for the player with the ball to avoid defensive pressure while dribbling and controlling the ball.

Playing rules

- No body contact.
- When the defender is allowed to dispossess and is successful, he/she returns the ball to his/her partner.

Modifications

See the steps outlined above. It is not always necessary to move through all the steps or to start at the most simple task. This should be decided by the teacher/coach after consideration of factors such as the ability of learners, their interests and prior experience.

Activity 4: keyball

This game moves on from tally ball to further develop the same skills, tactical understanding and decision-making but giving the game direction and introducing a little simple shooting. Played on a full court by between six and eight players, the game is constructed around getting the ball to a shooter who stands in the key at the end the team is attacking toward. No one else can enter the key, so when the player in the key gets the ball he/she gets a free shot. The team must make four clean passes (similar to the previous game) before being able to pass to the shooter. Standard basketball rules apply, except that dribbling is restricted to three bounces. This stops particular players dominating and forces them to think more tactically. Once they pass, where do they move to, and why? It also engages more players in the game, making it more inclusive and a better learning experience for all players, skilled and less skilled (see Light 2002).

While this is typically more of a problem in physical education classes than in sports clubs, where there is usually less variation in skill, confidence and physical capacity, it can still occur in clubs. Letting strong players dominate by dribbling from one end of the court to the other benefits no one. It can intimidate and exclude the less confident, detracts from it being a team game and does not improve the play of the dominant player(s). Having a rule that limits dribbling to three bounces includes more players in the game, makes it a team game and gets the more experienced players thinking tactically.

Sample questions

Continue the use of the same questions from the previous game but include questions on defending such as: *what defensive strategies can you use to stop the shooter getting the ball? What options do you have open to you for stopping the opposition getting the ball to their shooter?*

Playing area/set-up

Use a full basketball court.

Equipment

- Two sets of coloured bibs
- A basketball

Players

Two teams of six to eight players.

Aim/intent

The aim is for the team in possession to make four passes then get the ball to the shooter in the key, who aims to score a goal. The team with the greater number of goals wins.

Playing rules

- No body contact.
- Defenders cannot attempt to dispossess the ball carrier (this can be changed to suit the level of the players).
- Put a three-bounce limit on dribbling when it is introduced.

Modifications

Allow the defence to dispossess the ball carrier.

Activity 5: modified half-court basketball

This game is played by two teams of three or four players each, using half a basketball court. The game is played using standard basketball rules, except for the previously introduced three-bounce limit on dribbling, the no-contact rule and the requirement for a compulsory three passes before shooting for a basket. If there is a shortage of space, extra players can be rotated into the game as others are asked to have a rest. The attacking team starts from the halfway line and when the ball is turned over the team now in possession restart from the halfway line. This is a fast and dynamic game and the players should be given ample opportunity to stop, discuss tactics, formulate ideas or plans and test them in the game. This can also serve to let them catch their breath.

The questions might be asked by the teacher or coach on the run or using the 'freeze play' (Turner 2005) strategy of calling, 'Freeze!' to stop the game and asking one or two questions that direct the players toward thinking about any particular aspect of the game that the teacher/coach thinks is important enough to stop the game. All the tactical and technical points addressed in Activities 1–3 should be reinforced in this game.

Sample questions

Questions should focus on aspects of play that the teacher feels need to be improved or that are holding up the progress of the game. At this stage most questions will link to previous questions and activities in the unit, but might include: *once you have passed successfully what should you do/where should you move to? If the defence is tight, what sort of pass do you need to throw when the receiver makes a little space? What tactics can you use to get past a tall defender? When and why would the ball carrier dribble?*

Playing area/set-up

Use half a basketball court.

Equipment

- Two sets of coloured bibs
- A basketball

Players

Two teams of three or four players. (You can include a bench for rotation.)

Aim/intent

The aim is to shoot more baskets than the other team.

Playing rules

Standard basketball rules, with the following differences:

- No body contact.
- A three-bounce limit on dribbling when it is introduced.
- When there is an infringement the ball is turned over and the team with the ball starts from the halfway line.

Modifications

Adjust the number of players to change the amount of pressure through playing uneven teams, such as 5 v. 3 or 4 v. 2.

Activity 6: modified basketball

The unit culminates in playing the full version of basketball but with a few of the rule modifications already introduced in earlier games maintained. These rules are put in place to make the game more enjoyable and to enhance learning for all players. Using a full basketball court, form teams of six to eight players, with a rotating bench of a few players if space is a problem.

Sample questions

At this stage of the unit and with this tactically complex game, questioning would typically be restricted to facilitating team discussions that the teacher/coach calls at appropriate times and to drawing attention to any major issues or problems that arise during the game.

Playing area/set-up

Use a full basketball court.

Equipment

- Two sets of coloured bibs
- A basketball

Players

Two teams of six to eight players. (You can include a bench of two or three for rotation.)

Aim/intent

The aim is to shoot more baskets than the other team.

Playing rules

Standard basketball rules, with the following differences:

- No body contact.
- A three-bounce limit on dribbling when it is introduced.

Modifications

In a physical education setting with a large class and use of only one basketball court I suggest setting up some kind of round robin type competition with games of short duration, for example ten to fifteen minutes each. The non-playing team or teams could thus be watching their next opponents and discussing team strategies and tactics and/or practising if space is available. With a class of around thirty or so students there would likely be three teams, which should give plenty of game time for all of them. By this stage of the unit, and particularly if the teacher has been using a Game Sense or similar approach for a while, the students should be tuned into thinking about and solving tactical problems as a team (for example, see Light and Butler 2005). This means that they are likely to pay attention to the game in progress when not playing, particularly if they know which team they are going to play.

13

NETBALL

Introduction

Netball is derived from basketball and was developed in England in the 1890s to be more suitable for women at a time when vigorous exercise was seen to be inappropriate for them. It was initially called women's basketball. By the 1960s international playing rules had been developed and a national governing body formed. In 2011 the International Federation of Netball Associations (IFNA) comprised over seventy national teams organized across five world regions.

Mixed netball is commonly played in countries where netball is popular at a social level but it is predominantly played by girls and women in countries that are members of the Commonwealth Nations, with more than twenty million players across eighty nations participating. The Netball Superleague in Great Britain and the ANZ Championships played in Australia and New Zealand are the main two annual international competitions. The World Netball Championships are played every four years and it is a major team sport at the Commonwealth Games (also played every four years). The World Netball series is played annually and has been recognized by the IOC since 1995.

Netball is a passing game that emphasizes movement off the ball because no dribbling or running with the ball is allowed. Contact is also strictly controlled and goals are scored by shooting the ball up into a raised goal ring at either end, but there is no backboard behind the ring and interference with the shooter is strictly limited. Some of the basketball games or activities in this book that focus on passing and off-the-ball movement are interchangeable but basketball players would typically not be able to stop as quickly as netballers can. This unit has a modified version of netball as the end game that is called netta netball.

How to play netta netball

Netta netball is played by the same number of players as netball (seven) and played on a standard netball court with the raised rings at either end, with the main difference being the rules governing player movement. As with netball, play begins with three players in the attack zone, three in the defence zone and one in the centre. For the team beginning play, their player must be wholly within the centre circle and pass to a teammate who comes into the centre as soon as play begins but not before. The rules on foot movement are more lenient, players have six seconds in possession before they have to pass (instead of three) and defenders cannot be any closer to the ball carrier than 1.2 metres (four feet, rather than three feet). The game is described in more detail at the end of this unit.

In England the All England Netball Association use a similar modified game for children aged nine to eleven called high five netball, with only five positions. It also has regular rotations so that all children experience all positions, but included in this rotation is the expectation that when a player is not on the court she/he is assisting in another way, for example as a timekeeper or scorekeeper, and this could be a useful addition to netta.

Unit plan

Activity 1	*Tag ball*
Focus	Accurate passing, catching, anticipation and leading the receiver
Activity 2	*5 v. 3 keepings off*
Focus	Working off the ball, appropriate passing, communication and anticipation
Activity 3	*Three passes and shoot*
Focus	Accurate passing, communication with a partner, vision and anticipation, creating space, goal shooting
Activity 4	*End ball*
Focus	Quick movement down the court and creating space for receivers
Activity 5	*Zone netball*
Focus	Strategic positioning of players, responding to constraints of movement rules, responding to increased tactical complexity
Activity 6	*Netta netball*
Focus	Further developing skills, decision-making and tactical understanding from previous activities/games as performed in a game very close to full netball

Activity 1: tag ball

This is an excellent warm-up game for ball-handling games for the mind and the body and was used in the basketball unit in this book (pp. 149–163). Indeed, it is commonly used in many other sports, but the key to getting the most out of it for learning lies in the use of Game Sense pedagogy. It is a simple game in which two even teams use a determined playing space, with the team in possession of the ball eliminating opposition players by tagging them with the ball. One problem with elimination games is that they leave many players (and usually the same players) sitting out the game after being eliminated early. To get around this I suggest asking the team in possession to see how many they can tag in thirty seconds and then turning the ball over.

The size of the playing area is critical in this game, with a smaller area making it easier for the team in possession to tag the opposition and a larger area making it more challenging. Tags must be made with control of the ball and players cannot run with the ball in hand, making it a passing and catching game. From my experience of using this game, I invariably see very rapid improvement as players become accustomed to the game and improve their passing, catching and anticipation skills. Using the same two teams per playing area, the point score for eliminating opposition players can be accumulated over several rounds, with the teacher/coach focusing questions on appropriate technique, such as the type of pass needed to get the ball to players in a position to tag in time to complete a tag.

Sample questions

What tactics can you use to tag opposition players? Where in the playing space is the best place to move the opposition players (in the centre or in corners), and why? When the opposition player you want to tag is being shadowed by a team-mate and is moving quickly, where should you pass the ball? As you don't have much time, what type of pass do you need to throw? How can the ball carrier know where the teammates are who are in a position to tag?

Playing area/set-up

A defined area that provides the appropriate amount of space to facilitate tagging yet making it challenging. You can use some of the existing markings on a court (basketball, badminton, tennis, etc.) or mark out the area with soft marker cones.

Equipment

- Two sets of netball bibs for each game
- A netball for each game

Players

Two equal teams of six to eight players.

Aim/intent

The aim is for the team in possession to tag as many opposition players as possible in thirty seconds.

Playing rules

- No body contact.
- Players in the team being chased cannot leave the playing space. If they do they are counted as being tagged.
- The ball must be controlled to complete a tag.
- The tagging team cannot hold the opposition players.

Modifications

- *More challenging*:

  1. Use a larger space.
  2. Use two balls at once.

- *Less challenging*:

  1. Use a smaller space.
  2. Use a softer ball.

Activity 2: 5 v. 3 keepings off

This game is also recommended in the basketball unit but is made a little more complex by playing 5 v. 3 instead of 2 v. 1. It involves three players in possession trying to make as many passes as possible in thirty seconds, with two defenders attempting to intercept the ball or to slow down the number of passes made. It is played in half a netball court but could be played in one-quarter of a netball court to make it more challenging. Any forms of keepings off are quite simple and need the questioning used in Game Sense to bring the game to life and promote learning. Through appropriate questioning the teacher/coach can encourage far more movement on the part of the two players in possession and, consequently, more movement on the part of the defender. Through the stimulation of good questioning that encourages the players to move into the best positions to receive a pass and the ball carrier to move with the ball, this can become a very dynamic game that requires and develops high levels of skill and tactical understanding while placing demands on fitness and agility. The teacher/coach will need to be active in asking questions to stimulate the players to explore space, be creative and 'think outside the box' in moving to facilitate passing and catching.

Sample questions

To players in possession: *where is the best place that the player off the ball can move to receive a pass and to exclude the defender? Where can the receiver move to cut out the defender? If the players in possession are taller than the defender, what type of pass might be good? If the defender is taller than the two in possession, what pass might be best to use?*

To defenders: *whom should you pressure, the ball carrier or the receiver, and why?*

Playing area/set-up

On half a netball court.

Equipment

- Two sets of netball bibs for each game
- A netball for each game

Players

Five players, three in possession and two defenders, with roles regularly changed.

Aim/intent

The aim is for the two in possession to make as many passes as possible in thirty seconds.

Playing rules

- No body contact.
- The defender cannot attempt to dispossess the ball carrier.
- If the ball is intercepted the count ends and the two in possession restart.
- Players in possession must be at least one metre apart.

Modifications

- *More challenging*: increase the number of players to 6 v. 4 or 5 v. 4.
- *Less challenging*: play 5 v. 2.

Activity 3: three passes and shoot

This game is played in half a netball court with a 4 v. 4 set-up and builds on 5 v. 3 keepings off by giving the game direction. The team in possession attempts to make four clean passes, after which it can attempt to shoot a goal. Players on the defending team cannot attempt to dispossess the ball carrier but can gain possession by intercepting the ball when passed or picking up a loose ball. Once the team has completed four passes there is no limit to the number of passes before shooting for goal, but the team only gets one shot at goal. The aim is to score more goals than the opposing team, and the game builds on the knowledge developed in the 5 v. 3 keepings off game.

Sample questions

When attacking: *which teammates should you pass to, and why? What techniques can you use to get away from the defender to be open to receive a pass? How can you communicate between open receivers and the ball carrier? In what situations would you use a lob pass and a bounce pass? If the receiver is moving quickly where should the pass go? When and why should the ball carrier dribble?*

When defending: *which passes are the easiest to intercept, and why? Which are the hardest, and why? How could/did you organize your defence? How did it work?*

Playing area/set-up

Use half a netball court.

Equipment

- Two sets of four netball bibs
- A netball

Players

Two teams of four players each.

Aim/intent

The aim is for the team in possession to score more points than the opposition by scoring more goals.

Playing rules

- No body contact.
- Defenders cannot attempt to dispossess the ball carrier.
- If the ball is intercepted the pass count ends and the team in possession restarts from the halfway line.
- Players in possession must be at least one metre apart.

Modifications

- *More challenging*:
    1. Increase the number of players in the same space.
    2. Reduce the space to one-quarter of a court.
    3. Allow only five passes, with the person receiving the fifth pass having to shoot from where she/he receives the ball.

- *Less challenging*:
    1. Play 3 v. 3 in the same space.
    2. Require three passes before a player can shoot for goal.

Activity 4: end ball

This game begins a shift into using the full court if possible, and thus requires and develops more depth and width of perception and the thinking and adaptation of tactics required by this change. End ball is another commonly used warm-up game in coaching invasion games that develops tactical understanding, which is very relevant to netball. If space is available it should be played on a full netball court but if this is not possible it could be played in two smaller games across the court using half the court for each game. The game is explained here assuming use of a full court.

The aim of the game is to have a player in the attacking team catch the ball in the end zone at the end of the court when passed by one of her or his teammates. The court is divided into three even zones and the ball cannot be passed over more than one line dividing the zones, and there must be at least one pass *within* each zone. There is no running with the ball and only one step is allowed after catching the ball. Players are free to move about the court but only one player from the attacking team can cross into the end zone at a time and no players from the defending team can enter the end zone, which should be only one metre in depth to make it more challenging to get the ball to the player in the end zone.

Sample questions

In addition to asking questions of the class/team, the teacher/coach should provide time for team talks to discuss tactics for attack and defence. The role of the teacher or coach during these team talks is to facilitate discussions with questions if dialogue is not developing and bring in those who might be reluctant to speak. If dialogue is developing and all team members seem to be engaging, then the teacher/coach should not interfere and should limit comments to general, positive ones.

When attacking: *where should the receivers go to take a pass? How can the ball carrier know where his/her teammates are? What tactics did/could you use to make the one pass required by the rules in each zone yet get the ball quickly down the court?*

When defending: *what defensive patterns do you think might be good for this game? Should you pressure the ball carrier or the receivers? What things would you have to consider if thinking about concentrating defenders close to the end zone the opposition are attacking to stop them scoring?*

FIGURE 13.1   Endball

Playing area/set-up

Use a full netball court or play two games across half the court, with the court divided into three zones.

Equipment

- Netball bibs
- A ball for each game
- Marker cones to mark the end zone

Players

Two teams of four to eight players each when using a full court and two teams of three to four each when using a half-court.

Aim/intent

The aim is for one player from the attacking team to take a clean catch in the end zone.

Playing rules

- No body contact.
- Players can only take one step after receiving a catch.
- The ball cannot be passed across two zones and at least one pass must be completed within each zone.
- If the team in possession takes the ball out of play the game restarts from a throw by the opposite team at the point where it went out.
- Play begins from the end of the court in the direction that the team in possession is attacking.
- When a point is scored, play is restarted by the team that was scored against from the end of the court where the point was scored.

Modifications

- *Less challenging*: make the end zone wider (more than one metre).

Activity 5: zone netball

As with netball, this game is played on a full netball court and involves two teams of 10–12 players, with seven players on court at any one time (between three and five on the bench). It brings in restrictions (restraints) that require tactical negotiation and thus intellectual engagement. The court is divided into the normal three zones used in netball. They comprise a defensive, centre and attacking zone, with two players in the defensive and attacking zones and three in the centre zone. One player is nominated from each team as a mobile player who can move into the next zone but no further. This means that (1) the mobile player in the defensive zone can enter the centre but not the attacking third of the field, (2) the mobile player in the defensive zone can only enter the centre but (3) the mobile player in the centre can move into either the attacking or defensive third of the court.

Sample questions

Employ appropriate breaks for team talks as in the previous game.

When attacking: *it would be possible to put five players in your defensive or attacking zone. What advantages and disadvantages would there be in doing this? What factors would you consider when deciding where and when you move your mobile players?*

When defending: *would you/did you use a zone defence or a one-on-one defence? Why?*

Playing area/set-up

Use a full netball court.

Equipment

- Two sets of coloured bibs
- A netball

Players

Two teams of 10–12 players, with seven on the court and the remainder as substitutes.

Aim/intent

The aim is for the team in possession to move the ball down to their goal circle and shoot a goal.

Playing rules

- Play begins with a pass from the centre by one side and at this time no one must be within three metres of this player.
- When the ball goes out or is taken out, the team not responsible restarts play with a throw in from the point at which the ball went out.
- Players may hold the ball for up to six seconds but lose possession if they exceed this time limit.
- The ball carrier can only take one step after receiving the ball but may shuffle a little to gain balance.
- The ball cannot be passed across two zone lines and at least one pass must be completed within the zone when received before a player is allowed to pass into the next zone.
- Once the player receives the ball in the goal circle no defence is allowed.
- Defenders cannot be any closer to the ball carrier than 1.2 metres (four feet).
- No obstruction is allowed.
- When there is an infringement, the opposition is awarded a free pass that any player can take, but cannot use it to shoot for goal.
- Unlimited replacements at quarter, half and three-quarter time.
- The game is played over four five-minute quarters, with enough time allowed for team discussions between quarters.
- All players must play at least two quarters.
- Players should be rotated around the court and experience being a fixed and a mobile player.
- Two points are scored for a goal and one point for a miss that touches the ring.

Modifications

- *More challenging*: reduce the time limit for holding onto the ball from six seconds to three seconds.
- *Less challenging*:
    1. Allow a longer break at half-time for a more in-depth team discussion.
    2. Allow players to use a smaller ball (size 4).

Activity 6: netta netball

This is a modified version of netball and the details of the game are available on the Netball Australia website. Although netball Australia recommends not scoring in this game, I suggest that this is necessary to keep the players focused and directed. As long as there are equally balanced teams and effort and improvement are emphasized over results, students/players can all enjoy this modified game. They should all be given equal playing time and be able to experience the different positions on the court through the teacher or coach rotating the players at the end of each quarter. I also suggest giving teams ample time between quarters to discuss team tactics that the teacher or coach should encourage.

The game builds on zone netball by using the same numbers of players and playing on a full netball court, with the main difference being the rules governing player movement. It would make sense to use the correct netball names for positions, but in countries where netball is not widely played this is not necessary. Play begins with three players in the attack zone, three in the defence zone and one in the centre. For the team beginning play, their player must be wholly within the centre circle and pass to a teammate who comes into the centre as soon as play begins.

The following table shows the general responsibilities of positions and the court areas that they can use. The positions are Goal Shooter (GS), Goal Attack (GA), Wing Attack (WA), Wing Defence (WD), Centre (C), Goal Defence (GD) and Goal Keeper (GK). The court areas referred to are (1) goal circle, (2) attack zone, (3) centre, (4) defence zone and (5) defence goal circle.

Position	Position responsibilities	Court areas
GS	Shoot goals and work with GA in attack	1, 2
GA	Work with GS to score goals and shoot goals	1, 2, 3
WA	To feed the ball to the attacking players (GS and GA)	2, 3
C	Take centre pass to begin and link defence and attack	2, 3, 4
WD	Make interceptions and stop opposition WA feeding GS and GA	3, 4
GD	Win ball and reduce effectiveness of opposition attack	3, 4, 5
GK	Work with GD to prevent opposition GS from scoring	4, 5

The questions might be asked by the teacher or coach on the run or using the 'freeze' strategy of calling, 'Freeze!' (Turner 2005) to have the game stop and ask one or two questions to direct the players toward thinking about any particular aspect of the game that the teacher/coach thinks is important enough to stop the game. The knowledge and understanding developed in the previous activities/games should be drawn on in this game, with the teacher/coach encouraging players to think back to what they have learnt previously and apply it here.

Sample questions

For this game, provide ample opportunities for team talks at tactically critical moments.

Playing area/set-up

Use a standard netball court.

Equipment

- Two sets of netball bibs
- A netball

Players

Two teams of 10–12 players, with seven on the court.

Aim/intent

The aim is to move the ball toward the goal circle by passing and to score goals.

Playing rules

The rules used for zone netball are used in this game, but using the changes in player movement restrictions from netball and with the addition of the following rules:

- Only the two designated 'attack' players (GS, GA) can score goals.
- The game is played over four ten-minute quarters.

Modifications

None suggested.

14

CRICKET (KANGA)

Introduction

Cricket is widely played in England and the former British colonies, such as Australia, South Africa, New Zealand, the West Indies and India, where it has an enormous following. It is a sport in the Commonwealth Games, has World Cups in fifty- and twenty-over versions of the game and a world ranking system for the five-day test matches. During the 1980s the Australian Sports Commission (ASC) developed a range of modified versions of major sports to make them more accessible and appealing to children and young people. Among these modified games, kanga cricket was developed as a simple form of cricket that is inclusive and non-threatening. Using plastic equipment and a soft ball, it can be played indoors or outdoors and offers an ideal introduction to the game of cricket. It enhances existing skills, develops new ones and contributes to developing a conceptual understanding of striking games in general.

Many of the skills, such as throwing and catching, required for playing cricket are similar to softball and baseball, yet other skills, such as bowling and batting, are distinctly different. The core tactical concepts are, however, the same. The batting side attempts to create time to run, while the fielding side seeks to reduce this time. I taught cricket to study-abroad students from the United States and Canada in Australia for five years, to masters students in France and to undergraduate students in Asia, where I learnt that emphasizing this basic tactical understanding of the game is helpful in facilitating learning. In countries such as England, India and Australia, where cricket is a major sport, all children bring some knowledge of cricket to PE lessons, but in settings such as the United States, France and Japan, where cricket is not well known, this unit might require some more specific, technical practice. In particular, bowling and batting are skills that are very specific to cricket. The same would likely apply to much of North America.

This chapter begins with a simple modified game that requires only basic skills and which allows players to begin developing game understanding from the beginning of the unit. The games progressively increase in complexity and in the level of the skills required while allowing for collaborative problem solving. Teachers/ coaches should provide ample opportunity for students to discuss, develop and test strategies and tactics as an essential part of the learning process. The teacher can facilitate learning this way by asking for team discussions at strategic or tactically critical moments in the game. Research I conducted on the implementation of this unit with a year six primary school class in Australia confirms the positive influence that opportunities for interaction and dialogue can have on enjoyment and learning when adopting Game Sense pedagogy (Light 2008b).

How to play kanga cricket

The rules of kanga cricket are explained more fully at the end of this chapter (Activity 4), but a brief outline is offered here. In kanga the batters bat in pairs for a number of 'overs' (sets of six balls bowled) determined before the game. They score runs by hitting the ball to give them enough time to run from one end of the pitch to the other (giving one run) or back and forth. They cross over but can be 'run out' if the ball hits the wicket before the batter makes the crease (the line at the wicket he/she is running toward). Batters can also score by hitting the ball past a predetermined boundary to get an automatic score of four runs without running, or six runs if the ball travels over the boundary on the full (the ball travels over the boundary without hitting the ground).

Batters get 'out' by being caught in the field, run out (as above) or bowled, where the ball strikes the wicket (set of three stumps). However, in kanga the batters do not actually have to leave the wicket. They stay in, regardless of how many times they get out, until their agreed number of overs is finished. When they get out, the out is recorded against their runs scored and at the end of their innings the total number of runs is divided by the number of outs to give a final score. In normal cricket the less able get less time to improve because they get out quickly but in kanga all players get to face the same number of overs.

Unit plan

Activity 1	*Around the cone*
Focus	Game understanding, ball placement for batters, teamwork in fielding
Activity 2	*Run the cones*
Focus	Tactically informed risk taking for batters, bowling skill and tactics, batting skill, setting and bowling to a field
Activity 3	*Zone cricket*
Focus	Batters finding space and keeping the ball on the ground, forward drive in batting, fielders attacking the ball and backing up each other
Activity 4	*Kanga cricket*
Focus	All tactical knowledge, decision-making and skills required for this game

Activity 1: around the cone

This is a very simple game that is easy to play, allowing the teachers to help the students focus on the core concepts and tactical decision-making as a team. It also introduces students to the skill of batting in cricket, with a vertical bat striking the ball placed upon a batting tee. The aim is to strike the ball to provide as much time as possible to run to a cone and back to the wicket as many times as possible.

Sample questions

To the batting side: *what are some of the ways you were able to score runs? How can you best create time to run as many times as possible? What are you looking for when you step to hit the ball? What things do you consider when deciding where to hit the ball? Did any of you try to deceive the fielding side at all?*

To the fielding side: *what did you think about when deciding where the fielders should stand? Did you change positions according to who was batting? Did you anticipate where and how hard the batters would hit the ball? How can you support the fielder near you when he/she is moving to stop a well-hit ball? If you gave the batters a lot of extra time through over-throws, how can you work as a team to prevent this or reduce it?*

FIGURE 14.1 Around the cone

Playing area/set-up

This game can be played indoors (for example on an indoor basketball court) or outside in a space of any shape. As batters in cricket can strike the ball anywhere in a 360-degree radius, the batting tee should be placed toward the centre of the space to allow batters to strike the ball backward. The cone the batters run to would normally be set 10–15 metres to one side of where the batter stands. Two more cones should be used, with one marking where the bowler has to stand and one where the batter stands, which is also where s/he must touch his/her bat on a return run.

Equipment

- A plastic cricket bat
- At least one kanga ball or a tennis ball
- Three cones
- A kanga cricket batting tee

Players

Form two even teams of about six to twelve players depending upon the space available and the size of the class/group. The students should discuss and decide on the batting order and where players should be positioned in the field. The bowler should be rotated during the innings, particularly if the teams are reasonably large.

Aim/intent

The primary aim of the game is for the batters to create time to allow them to score as many runs as possible. This would typically involve hitting the ball into space and away from the bowler, because the batter must stop running as soon as the bowler catches the ball, holds it up and calls 'Stop!' The primary aim of the fielding side is to get the ball to the bowler as quickly as possible, which requires skill and the use of tactics.

Playing rules

- One team bats and the other fields.
- The batter hits the ball off a batting tee and runs to a cone set an appropriate distance to the left or right of the batting tee and back to the wicket as many times as is possible before the bowler holds the ball above his/her head and shouts 'Stop!'
- A run is scored when the batter touches the bat on the ground past the cone and again when the bat is touched past the wicket.

- The batter must not drop the bat – no runs can be scored without the bat.
- The fielding side must return the ball to the bowler as quickly as possible but cannot run with the ball.
- The bowler does not actually bowl in this game but stands 15–20 metres in front of the batter. When the bowler catches the ball he/she holds it above his/her head and calls 'Stop!' At this point the batter must stop running, with his/her completed runs added to the team's tally.
- The fielding team must get all the batting team out and then it is their turn to bat. There should be two innings to provide the opportunity to engage in developing strategies and tactics, which become particularly important in the second innings of the team which bats second.
- Batters are out only when the ball is caught before hitting the ground, but this is unusual when hitting the ball from a kanga cricket tee.
- Each team bats twice. If time does not permit this the teacher should keep a record of the players and scores to continue next time.

Modifications

As this is a very simple game there is little scope for modification, but the distance from the wicket to the cone could be changed to make it easier or more difficult and the shape and/or size of the space used could be changed.

Activity 2: run the cones

This game builds on the previous game, around the cone, to make it more complex by introducing bowling and by forcing batters to make instant decisions about taking runs that involve considering how much risk is appropriate for the situation. It introduces bowling and the need to bowl tactically to a field. With experienced players you can ask them to bowl overarm (with no run-up) but if they are inexperienced you can ask the bowlers to bowl underarm. The teacher/coach should also ask the bowlers to bowl gently to enable the game to progress and ensure that the bowling is suitable for the batter. There is no out by bowling, so the aim of the bowling is to enable a hit but to make it difficult to hit to space.

As this is a more tactically interesting and complex game than the previous game the teacher/coach should provide opportunities for team discussions on tactics at critical times. For example, if one team is twenty runs behind with only four batters remaining you could stop and ask both teams to discuss what tactics they should adopt at this point in the game.

Sample questions

Use many of the same questions used in the previous game but add questions that focus on batting and bowling (to batters and bowlers) and the amount of risk that is appropriate for the game situation as an important tactical dimension of cricket, for example: *what things did you or should you consider when deciding which cone to run for? As the game progressed and you found your team well behind the other team with only a few batters left, how did this affect the decisions you made about taking risks?*

Playing area/set-up

This game can be played indoors (for example on an indoor basketball court) or outside in a space of any shape. Set up a wicket for the batter to defend and mark a point 5–20 metres from the wicket as the point from which the bowler must bowl. The distance depends upon the age and abilities of the players. For this game set up a line of six cones spaced one to three metres apart at a 45-degree angle from the batter. The space between the cones will depend upon the age and ability of the players.

Equipment

- A plastic cricket bat
- At least one kanga ball or a tennis ball
- Six cones
- A kanga cricket wicket (three plastic stumps)

Players

Form two even teams of about six to twelve players depending upon the space available and the size of the class. The students should discuss and decide on the batting order and where players should be positioned in the field. The bowler should be rotated during the innings, particularly if the teams are reasonably large.

Aim/intent

As with the previous game, the primary aim is for the batters to create time to allow them to score as many runs as possible. A run is scored by reaching a cone and touching the bat beside it and getting back to the wicket before the bowler strikes it. The number of runs is decided by how far the batter runs – as measured by the cones – and is able to get back to his/her wicket. For example, if the batter reaches the fifth cone and gets home safely he/she gets five runs. However, he/she can only run once. This means that he/she must decide how far to run immediately after striking the ball.

Playing rules

- One team bats and the other fields.
- A bowler stands in the same position as in the previous game but bowls the ball. The ball must be bowled with a straight arm but can be delivered underarm or overarm. If he/she bowls overarm the bowler cannot run up but must take no more than one step (this is to reduce the pace of the bowl). The ball should also bounce before being struck and be considered a fair ball by the class. A fair ball is one that the batter has a reasonable chance of hitting.
- If the batter hits the ball in the air and is caught he/she is out.
- If the bowler hits the stumps the batter is out.
- The batter must run when he/she strikes the ball no matter how far it travels. He/she then decides which of the five cones lined up to run to. The batter must ground the bat next to the cone then run back to the wicket.
- Once the batter has hit the ball and run, the fielding team must get the ball back to the bowler. Once the bowler has the ball he/she can bowl at the wicket (but cannot throw it). If the ball hits the wicket before the batter is home, the batter is out and does not get any runs. If the bowler misses, the fielding team can return the ball for him/her to have another bowl before the batter gets home.
- The batter may hit the ball with the bat to prevent it hitting the wicket as he/she approaches it on the return run.
- The runs scored are calculated according to the cone the batter ran to and was able to safely return from (for example, if he/she gets to the fifth cone and back he/she gets five runs). If the batter drops the bat as in baseball/softball, no runs can be scored.

Modifications

- *More challenging*: introduce a high-risk option for a game-winning score. This could be a cone set a very long way away earning a score of ten or more or could even involve negotiating an obstacle to make it more playful.
- *Less challenging*: instead of the batter being out when caught or bowled, give one run to the bowling side.

Activity 3: zone cricket

In this game there is no running, with the emphasis on placing the ball forward of the wicket and on fielding technique and tactics. The playing space is divided into three zones forward of the wicket, with more points scored for the zones the ball travels through after being hit by the batter. A predetermined number of balls are bowled for each batter and if he/she gets out due to being caught or bowled, the batter stays at the wicket but does not get a score.

Sample questions

To batters: *what did/do you consider when deciding on where to try to score (which zone to attack)? What could you do if the field is concentrated close to the batter to reduce the runs scored?*

To fielders: *what do you consider when setting the field? What could you do with a 'big hitter' batting to best limit the runs scored? What can you do as a team to reduce the score from a good hit when it gets past the first fielder? Where should you stand in the zone to be able to attack the ball? How do you set your field in relation to the game situation? What technique is important in stopping the ball as early as possible?*

Playing area/set-up

Set up in the same way as for the previous game but without the cones and place the wicket at one end of the space. Divide the area in front of the batter into zones that are clearly marked.

Equipment

- A plastic cricket bat
- At least one kanga ball or a tennis ball
- Six cones
- A kanga cricket wicket (three stumps)

Players

Form two even teams of about six to twelve players depending upon the space available and the size of the class/group. The students should discuss the batting order and where players should be positioned in the field.

Aim/intent

The batters aim to hit the ball as far as possible forward without being caught out. Points/runs are earnt according to the zone in which the ball is stopped by the fielding side. For example, if there are three zones and the ball is stopped in zone 2 the batter scores two runs. Each batter faces six balls (which must be fair balls). If a ball is bowled that is not fair, the batting side get one run and the bowler must bowl another ball. The score is the tally for each over of six balls faced for each batter. The team's tally is calculated by adding up all the batters' scores. If the batter is caught on the full or bowled by the ball hitting the wicket, he/she is not out – he/she just does not score a run.

Playing rules

- One team bats and the other fields.
- The bowlers bowl an over of six balls and change after each over so that all players in the team bowl. They must bowl with a straight arm and the ball can be delivered underarm or overarm. If he/she bowls overarm the bowler must take no more than one step to reduce the pace of the ball. The ball should also bounce before being struck and be considered a fair ball by the class – one that the batter has a reasonable chance of hitting.
- If the batter hits the ball in the air and is caught, he/she is not out but does not score any runs.
- If the bowler hits the stumps with the ball, the batter is not out but scores no runs for that ball.

Modifications

Introduce high-risk and high-reward possibilities for scoring to provide a challenge for the better batters. For example, if playing indoors score four runs if the ball hits the back wall in any way and six if it hits it on the full, but with the score being zero if the ball is caught off the wall. The teacher could also place a large plastic bin or target somewhere for the batter to hit or strike the ball so it drops into the bin for a large bonus score.

To develop batting strokes to the side or behind the pitch, set up different spaces. For example, to develop a square cut, play in a shorter, wider space with the zones and bonus targets set up square of the batter.

Allow more capable classes/teams to bowl with a run-up and use more complex tactics and strategies.

Activity 4: kanga cricket

Batters score a run when the ball is struck and the two batters cross to touch bats over the line at the end of the pitch at the opposite end to where they were standing. They can score up to six runs in this manner. They can also score without running if the ball is struck and reaches the boundary set-up. If the ball goes over the boundary on the full the batter scores six runs and cannot be caught out beyond the boundary. Each time the batter gets out it is recorded, but he/she stays on the pitch so that all players face the same number of overs. At the end of the innings the team's total number of runs is divided by its total number of outs to give its score for the innings.

Batters get out when:

1. The ball bowled strikes the wicket.
2. The ball hit by the batter is caught before it hits the ground by anyone in the fielding team.
3. The wicket that either of the two batters is running toward to score a run is hit by the ball before the batter touches the bat over the 'crease' (a line about one metre in front of the wicket at either end). This can be achieved by a direct throw from a fielder or by one of them throwing the ball to the wicket keeper or to the bowler, who hits the wicket with the ball in hand.
4. The ball bowled hits the batter's leg and the umpire is *certain* that the ball bowled would have hit the wicket. In this case the batter is given out LBW (leg before wicket) and this is typically a contentious decision at any level of cricket.

Sample questions

Questioning for this game and at this stage of the unit should be limited to facilitating team debates and discussions about tactics unless the teacher/ coach sees a major problem or issue that both teams need to discuss and reflect upon as a group, during the game and/or after it.

Playing area/set-up

Kanga cricket can be played indoors (for example on an indoor basketball court) or outside in a space of any shape. It can also be played on a normal concrete cricket pitch. The pitch is set up in the middle of the playing space and the ball can be hit anywhere in a 360-degree radius. As with standard cricket two batters play, with one at the 'striking end' facing the bowler and the other at the 'non-striking' end of the pitch (the bowler's end).

Equipment

- Two plastic cricket bats
- Kanga balls or a tennis balls
- Two sets of plastic kanga cricket wickets
- A reasonably firm and flat surface on which the ball will bounce evenly
- A means of identifying a boundary for scoring four or six runs

Players

Form two even teams of about six to twelve players depending upon the space available and the size of the class/group. The students should discuss and decide on the batting order and where players should be positioned in the field. The bowler must be changed every over (a set of six bowls). Bowling should be shared evenly among all players, but choosing which bowler bowls to which batter is an important strategic decision that has to be made by the teams.

Aim/intent

The primary aim of the game is for the batting side to score as many runs as possible by actually running between wickets or hitting a four or six and to get as few outs as possible. The fielding side aims to get as many outs as possible and to prevent the opposition scoring.

Playing rules

- One team bats and the other fields, and there should be two innings.
- Bowlers bowl six-ball overs then change.
- Bowlers change ends after each over.
- Bowlers must deliver the ball with a straight arm.
- A ball that is too wide to hit is called a wide, giving the batting side a run, and must be bowled again.
- Batters bat in pairs and face an agreed number of overs (for example three overs – eighteen balls).
- All players on the batting side must bat, and bat in pairs. The innings is finished when every pair has faced the decided number of overs.
- No batters actually get out. Even though they get out they remain on the pitch, but the out is recorded on the score sheet.
- Batters get out through being bowled, caught, run out or LBW as explained on p. 186.

- When there is an out the batters change ends.
- A run is scored when the batter strikes the ball, runs and touches the bat on the ground beyond the wicket.
- Four runs are scored if the ball is hit and reaches the boundary and six runs if it goes over the boundary on the full.

Modifications

The scoring system for kanga cricket is a fair way of determining the winning team but makes it difficult for teams to keep track of their comparative progress, which is important for team decision-making on tactics. A simpler scoring system – such as, for example, deducting five runs for an out – could possibly be incorporated to allow teams to better keep track of their progress.

15
SOFTBALL

Introduction

The similarities between softball and baseball are obvious but softball is an easier game to play because it is played on a much smaller diamond and the ball is larger than a baseball. However, despite the game being called softball the ball used is not any softer than a baseball. The game is well over 100 years old, with its rules first published in 1895, but it was not actually called 'softball' until 1926. In 1996 fast-pitch softball was introduced into the summer Olympic Games but it has since been removed. It is widely played in schools around the world as a major striking game that is accessible for most children and young people at an introductory level. There have been variations in its development that include different size balls of varying hardness and variations in the size of the diamond, and these offer options for teachers and coaches to modify the game to suit the needs of the learners.

The approach I have suggested in this book for taking up Game Sense allows for flexibility in how teachers interpret it and implement it, and this is reflected in variations in the design of lessons/sessions. For example, the unit on soccer included some activities that were quite focused on skill development within game-like contexts, while other units follow a pattern of beginning with simple games and building complexity into them. The approach taken here with softball is to begin with a simple modified game that requires only basic skills and allows players to begin developing game awareness and understanding from the beginning of the unit, and to progressively increase the complexity and the level of skill required while allowing for collaborative problem solving. Teachers/coaches should provide ample opportunities for students/players to discuss, develop and test strategies and tactics as an essential part of the learning process, facilitated by asking for team discussions at strategic or tactically critical moments in the game.

This chapter uses two of the same basic games suggested for teaching cricket, reinforcing how easily most of the modified games used in this book can be adapted for learning in other sports within the same game category. Many of the skills required for playing softball, such as throwing and catching, are the same as those required for baseball and cricket, yet many other skills, such as pitching and batting (compared to cricket), are distinctly different. While little, if any, positive skill transfer can be expected, tactical knowledge transfer does occur because games within the same game category share tactical concepts and problems that arise when playing them. Research suggests how this can occur between net games (Mitchell and Oslin 1999) and, more specifically, between cricket and softball (Light 2008b).

How to play modified softball

This modified game is very close to the full game of softball. It is played on a diamond using all standard softball equipment. It is presented here in two forms: one simple and one more complex. In the simple form there are no strikes (no three-strikes-and-you're-out rule), all players bat and the pitcher is expected to pitch a 'fair ball' (slow) to get the game going. The more complex form introduces the strike zone, the three-strikes-and-you're-out rule and the three-out-all-out rule, so that all players on the batting team might not get to bat. This make it very close to the full game, but teachers should feel free to make decisions (perhaps in consultation with students) about whether or not to introduce all these changes at once. Alternatively, they could be introduced in subsequent lessons if this is possible. When the three-strikes-and-you're-out rule is introduced, three new players should be introduced in subsequent innings and enough innings should be played to enable all players to have a bat.

Unit plan

Activity 1 Around the cone
Focus   Game understanding, ball placement for batters, teamwork in fielding
Activity 2 Run the bases
Focus   Tactically informed risk taking for batters, pitching skill and tactics, batting skill, setting and pitching to a field
Activity 3 Modified softball (simple version)
Focus   Decision-making for fielding side and batting side
Activity 4 Modified softball (more complex version)
Focus   All tactical knowledge, decision-making and skills required for this game

---

Activity 1: around the cone

This is a simple game that is easy to play, with the aim for the batters being to strike the ball to provide as much time as possible to run. Their aim is to reach first base to earn three points, but they can score fewer points by reaching cones set up between home base and first base. Two cones are set at one-third and two-thirds of the way from the batting tee to first base, with the batter earning one point for reaching the first cone and two for reaching the second cone. The batter must stop running when the ball is returned to the 'pitcher', who stands in the position where a pitcher would normally stand. When the pitcher catches the ball, he/she stands to attention with the ball held up to shout 'Stop!' and the batter must stop running.

The focus for the batting team is to create as much time as possible by, for example, hitting the ball away from the pitcher and/or into space. The focus for the fielding team is to field the ball and return it to the pitcher using a *catchable* throw as quickly as possible. This requires backing up in the field to support the player fielding the ball and the pitcher when the ball is thrown to him/her. This teamwork in the field requires anticipation, which the students learn by playing this game (doing) and reflecting upon action in the game, stimulated by teacher questioning.

Once the class or team gets a feel for the game, provide a few breaks for them to discuss and formulate tactics that they can test in the game.

Sample questions

To the batting side: *what are some ways you were able to score runs? Should you hit the ball toward the pitcher or away from him/her? Why? How can you best create time to run as many times as possible? What are you looking for when you step up to hit the ball? What things do you consider when deciding where to hit the ball? Did any of you try to deceive the fielding side at all?*

To the fielding side: *what did you think about when deciding where the fielders should stand? Did you change positions according to who was batting? Did you anticipate where and how hard the batters would hit the ball? How can you support the fielder near you when he/she is moving to stop a well-hit ball? If you gave the batters a lot of extra time through over-throws, how can you work as a team to prevent this or reduce it? When a ball is hit hard and you think that your teammate might miss it, what should you do to help? What makes a good throw?*

Playing area/set-up

Set up a T-ball batting tee with first base only and cones marking out points one-third and two-thirds of the way from home base to first base. Students/players should be encouraged to be creative, so there should be no limits on where the players/students can hit the ball at this stage. I normally, intentionally, do not make this clear, but students (particularly younger ones) invariably ask whether or not they can do this, or just do it anyway. Opportunities for this type of creative thinking should be provided by ensuring that there is some room behind the batting tee. The teacher should set up a base where first base would be, with two cones marking out one-third of the distance from home base to first and a second cone marking the point two-thirds from home base to first base. Another cone or plate should mark where the bowler has to stand.

Equipment

- A T-ball batting tee
- A softball bat
- Home base, one base for first base and a pitching plate
- A softball
- Two small soft marker cones

Players

Players should be divided into two even teams or, if space and equipment allows it, into two separate games requiring four teams in total when the class or squad/team is large. The pitcher should be rotated regularly.

Aim/intent

The primary aim of the game is for the batters to create time to allow them to run to first base and score three points. This would typically involve hitting the ball into space and away from the pitcher, because the batter must stop running as soon as the pitcher catches the ball, stands up straight holding up the ball and calls 'Stop!' The primary aim of the fielding side is to get the ball to the pitcher as quickly as possible, which requires skill, anticipation, thinking, communication and tactics.

Playing rules

- One team bats and the other fields.
- The batter hits the ball off a T-ball batting tee and tries to run to first base before the pitcher shouts 'Stop!'
- Three points are scored when the batter reaches first base, one point for making the first cone and two points for making the second cone.

- The batter must drop (but not throw) the bat.
- The fielding side must return the ball to the pitcher as quickly as possible, but the fielder cannot run with the ball.
- The pitcher stands 10–20 metres in front of the batter. When the pitcher catches the ball he/she holds it above his/her head and calls 'Stop!' At this point the batter must stop running.
- The fielding team must get all the batting team out (not just three of them) and then it is their turn to bat. There should be two innings so that the students have the opportunity to engage in developing strategies and tactics, which become particularly important in the second innings of the team which bats second.
- Batters are out only when the ball is caught before hitting the ground and no points can be scored.

Modifications

As this is a very simple game there is little scope for modification, but the distance from the wicket to first base could be changed to make it easier or more difficult and the shape and/or size of the space used could be changed.

Activity 2: run the bases

This game builds on the previous game, around the cone, to make it more complex by introducing underarm pitching and by forcing batters to make instant decisions about taking runs that involve considering risk. It also begins to use the softball diamond to relate learning to the context within which the full game is played. In introducing pitching the teacher should encourage students to pitch tactically to a field. The teacher/coach should also ask the pitcher to pitch at a speed appropriate to the skill of the batter to enable the game to progress. As I have stressed elsewhere in the book (for example, in Chapter 17 on volleyball), this is to ensure that it is a good game that does not break down because some batters are not skilled or confident enough to get bat to ball. This typically requires some agreement among the class or team about what a fair ball is, and this agreement will be easier to reach in a class that has developed a supportive culture through using the Game Sense approach. There is no way of getting the batter out by pitching because there is no three-strikes-and-you're-out rule, so the aim of the bowling is to enable a hit but to make it difficult to hit to space and to entice the batter to hit where more fielders are.

The game is played using a diamond, with bases and marker cones placed halfway between bases and with the batters scoring two points for every base they reach and one point for making the halfway cone. As with softball the ball must not go outside first or second base, otherwise it is a foul ball. As with the previous game, the ball must be returned to the pitcher, who stands upright holding the ball up to shout 'Stop!' At this point, if the batter has run beyond the halfway point between cone and base or base and cone but has not reached the next base, he/she is out and no points are scored. If she or he is safe, he/she scores points. For example, if he/she is on the cone between first base and second base the batter scores three points.

Once the batters strike the ball they have to decide which base or mid-point cone to run to after hitting the ball because they can't turn back. As this is a more tactically interesting and complex game than the previous one, the teacher/coach should provide opportunities for team discussions on tactics at critical times. For example, if one team is twenty runs behind with only four batters remaining you could stop and ask both teams to discuss what tactics they should adopt at this point in the game. At least two innings should be played to provide for situations that require strategic and tactical decisions to be agreed on.

Sample questions

Use many of the same questions used in the previous game but add questions that focus on batting and pitching and the amount of risk that is appropriate for the game situation as an important tactical dimension of softball, for example: *what things did you, or should you, consider when deciding which base or cone to run for? As the game progressed and you found your team well behind the other team with only a few batters left, how did this affect the decisions you made about taking risks?*

Playing area/set-up

This game is played outside on a diamond, with the size of the diamond dependent upon the age of the students/players. For this game, set up bases and a cone halfway between the bases.

Equipment

- A softball bat
- At least one softball
- Three bases, two plates and three marker cones
- Softball gloves and a catcher's mitt for the catcher and the required protective clothing/equipment to ensure player safety

Players

Form two even teams of about eight to twelve players depending upon the space available and the size of the class. The students should discuss and decide on the batting order and where players should be positioned in the field. The pitcher should be rotated regularly during the innings.

Aim/intent

The primary aim for the batting side is for the batters to create time to allow them to score as many points as possible by running as far as possible around the diamond. Two points are scored for reaching a base and one for reaching a cone. This is cumulative (for example, if the batter reaches second base he/she scores six points (two for each base plus one for each cone).

The fielding side aims to reduce the time the batters have to run around the diamond by fielding the ball and returning it to the pitcher as quickly as possible. As with the previous game, this requires developing some skills in catching, throwing and backing up that the teacher can comment on and offer tips on. These skills should have begun to be developed in the previous game and should be built upon in this game.

Playing rules

- One team bats and the other fields.
- A pitcher stands in the same position as in the previous game but pitches the ball underarm. The distance the pitcher stands from the batter can be adjusted to suit different abilities of the pitcher and the batter. Again the emphasis is on pitching a fair ball. A fair ball is one that the batter has a reasonable chance of hitting.
- If the batter hits the ball in the air and is caught, then he/she is out.
- The batter must run when he/she strikes the ball no matter how far it travels, unless it is a foul. After a fair hit, he/she decides how far to run.
- Once the batter has hit the ball and runs, the fielding team must get the ball back to the pitcher. Once the pitcher has the ball he/she stands up and calls 'Stop!'
- The points scored are accumulated according to the bases and cones the batter ran to (two per base and one per cone).
- The batter must drop the bat as in baseball/softball, as no runs can be scored.

Modifications

Modifications can apply to all players or just some players to provide more challenge where needed and less challenge where needed.

- *More challenging*:

    1. Remove the cones between bases or don't allow the better players to stop on them.
    2. (For the fielding side) Make the fielding team perform a minimum number of throws (for example two or three).

- *Less challenging*: use more cones or have shorter distances between bases.

Activity 3: modified softball (simple version)

This game is set up in the same way as Activity 2 but introduces a number of modifications that move it closer to the full game of softball. The game begins the same way, with the pitcher pitching underarm to the batter while attempting to deliver a 'fair ball' that the batter strikes. However, the cones between bases are removed and to get the batter out the ball must now be caught by a fielder standing on the base that the batter is running toward before the batter arrives at the base. The only way to score is by making the journey around the three bases and getting home safely to score a home run. All players bat and there is still no three-strikes-and-you're-out rule, meaning batters only get out by being caught or run out by not making the base they are running to. There can only be one batter on each base, which brings in many tactical considerations of softball, such as dealing with what to do when the bases are loaded. No base stealing is allowed. (The base runner must stay on the base until the ball leaves the pitcher's hand but once it has she/he can try to run to the next base and if she/he is successful this is called stealing a base.)

This game is far more complex than run the bases. It is more challenging for the batting side because batters have to run further to get to the base and make enough time to do so. They also have to discuss tactical decisions *as a team* to get a batter home and decide what the batter at the plate can do to help this happen. There is also more complexity now for the fielding side and a significant increase in the tactical problems they have to find solutions for. For example, they must consider where they position the fielders who are to take the catch on the base and who is going to have that responsibility at each base. In some cases, teachers or coaches might decide to rotate players on the bases to ensure that all players have a chance to experience this role. This would probably also be the case with the pitcher and backstop.

Although this game takes a step up in tactical complexity it is still very inclusive. There is no three-strikes-and-you're-out rule and no three-out-all-out rule, meaning that all players on the batting team get to bat and stay at the plate until they have hit a fair ball. Rotating the pitcher, catcher and players on the bases will also ensure inclusion and make sure that fielders experience different roles and the understanding that will arise from this. In this game much of the questioning should be specific to the tactical problems or issues that arise within the game. This would involve the teacher or coach stopping play (only briefly) to ask questions about a play that has just been completed or to identify a tactical issue and give the two teams a few minutes to discuss it before returning to the game to try out their solutions.

Sample questions

To batters: *what could you do if the field is concentrated close to the batter to reduce the number of runs scored? Where would you try to hit the ball to help get a runner home from third base, and why?*

To fielders: *what can you do as a team to reduce the score from a good hit when it gets past the first fielder? Where should you stand in the zone to be able to attack the ball? How do you set your field in relation to the game situation? What technique is important in stopping the ball as early as possible?*

Playing area/set-up

The same as for the previous game but without the cones.

Equipment

As for the previous game.

Players

As for the previous game.

Aim/intent

The batting team aims to get runners home without getting out, as in normal softball, scoring one run for every player who makes it home.

Playing rules

The rules are the same as for the previous game but with the following changes:

- Runners are out when a fielding player catches the ball while standing on the base the runner is running toward before the runner makes contact with the base.
- A run is scored when the runner is able to run to and make contact with home base from third base before any player from the fielding team is able to catch the ball while standing on home base.

Modifications

None suggested.

Activity 4: modified softball (more complex version)

This game is the same as the previous game but adds the strike zone, three-strikes-and-you're-out and three-out-all-out rules. This makes it very close to the full game (no tagging is required), but teachers should feel free to make decisions (perhaps in consultation with students) about whether or not to introduce all these changes at once. Alternatively, they could be introduced in subsequent lessons if this is possible, one change at a time, which would offer a good opportunity for players/students to appreciate the tactical significance of these rules. When the three-out-all-out rule is introduced enough innings should be played to ensure all players have a bat.

Sample questions

Questioning for this game and at this stage of the unit should be limited to facilitating team debates and discussions about tactics unless the teacher/coach sees a major problem or issue that both teams need to discuss and reflect upon as a group, during the game and/or after it.

Playing area/set-up

As for the previous game.

Equipment

As for the previous game.

Players

As for the previous game.

Aim/intent

As for the previous game.

Playing rules

As for the previous game but for the following changes:

- If a batter strikes at the ball and misses or if it is delivered between the knees and shoulders (whether struck at or not) three times, then he/she is out.
- When three batters are out the batting innings is over and the teams change.

Modifications

As suggested above, the game complexity could be developed by adding the three-strikes-and-you're-out rule and three-out-all-out in two stages.

16

ULTIMATE FRISBEE

With Christina Curry

Introduction

Ultimate frisbee is a high-energy game, which involves a range of generic skills such as running, jumping, throwing and catching, and trying to out-think the opposition. Perhaps the most appealing aspect of ultimate frisbee is its dynamic spirit of sportsmanship and its emphasis on fair play and enjoyment. This makes it a particularly good game to include in a physical education programme and this is what sets it apart most from the other games in this book. A rapidly growing non-contact sport played with a frisbee (also called a disc), ultimate frisbee was invented in 1968 by some American high school students who started playing frisbee football in their school car park. They called it 'ultimate' because they enjoyed it so much. Today it's played in over fifty countries by hundreds of thousands of people and has developed to the point where it has national championships and world championships.

Ultimate frisbee combines elements of basketball, soccer and gridiron into a fast-paced, athletic sport. Competitions usually have co-ed teams, where men and women or boys and girls play together. The spirit of sportsmanship, which places the responsibility for fair play on the player, is fundamental to the game and is representative of the tradition it grew out of. It is also unique because the sport is self-refereed, which is reflective of this 'spirit' where players are responsible for adhering to and overseeing the rules themselves. Although 'ultimate' is highly competitive, the bond of mutual respect between players and adherence to the agreed upon rules of the game are never compromised, thus resulting in a basic joy of play which underpins the popularity and growth of this unique game. Protection of these vital elements serves to eliminate adverse conduct from the ultimate field. Such actions as taunting opposing players, dangerous or aggressive behaviour, intentional fouling, or other 'win at all costs' behaviours are contrary to the spirit of the game and are not tolerated at any level.

Ultimate was traditionally based on American university campuses and in 1970 a number of clubs were formed. This was quickly followed by the advent of a players' association and in 1984 the World Flying Disc Federation was formed as the international governing body for disc sports. Ultimate has become extremely popular at all levels and as its popularity grew so have the number of competitions. There are Hat tournaments (where players join as individuals), which have an emphasis on having fun, socializing and meeting other players. Leagues continue to grow and cater for men, women and youth. In some countries it has been offered as part of the PDHPE/PE curriculum, and competitive school sport and leagues have been formed in high schools and colleges in the United States.

There is a range of worldwide tournaments, including the world games, world championships and European championships, with some countries such as India and Malaysia holding open tournaments. Just like volleyball, ultimate has developed a strong beach-based game, which is played in teams of four or five players on small fields of sand and has developed rapidly to include beach tournaments. One of the most remarkable features of this game is that it can be played on almost any surface, both indoors or outdoors. Indoor ultimate has become very popular in Northern Europe during the winter due to the cold and wet weather conditions. It has even been played on ice! It is simple to learn, fun to play, affordable and is imbued with the spirit of fair play and having fun.

How to play ultimate frisbee

Ultimate games are contested between two teams of seven players on a large rectangular pitch. As is the case with games like cricket and Australian football, there is no predetermined size for the pitch/field, meaning that the size can be determined by what space is available. A line is drawn across the pitch at either end to create two 'end zones', which are the goal-scoring areas. The basic aim of the game is for the team with the disc to pass it up the field to others on their team without dropping it and finally to catch it in their end zone to score a point. This is very similar to the training game of end zone used in other chapters, for example in Chapter 13, on netball, and involves similar tactical problems and capabilities. The person in possession of the disc in the attacking team cannot run with the disc, making it a passing/throwing game like netball. The defensive team contests possession by trying to intercept or knock the disc down while it is in the air. If they succeed, they get a turnover of possession and can move the disc toward the end they are attacking and attempt to score. The disc can be thrown in any direction, but once a player has the disc they are not allowed to run with it and they have ten seconds to throw it.

Ultimate is a non-contact sport, with any contact declared a foul. The players themselves decide on whether or not a foul has been committed, relying upon the *Spirit of the Game* code of conduct as there are no referees. The responsibility for fair play is thus shared between all players. If there are any disagreements regarding incidents, the disc returns to the player who made the last pass and the game resumes. The Spirit of the Game award is a prestigious and highly sought after accolade that is coveted at all tournaments.

Unit plan

Activity 1	*Throw/catch introductory games*
Focus	Basic pass and catch skills in contexts that require some thinking and decision-making related to the game
Activity 1.1	*Hot potato*
Focus	Familiarization with the disc
Activity 1.2	*Throw–catch tally*
Focus	Throwing and catching the disc under mild pressure
Activity 1.3	*Frisbee mobile archery*
Focus	Accurate throwing and low-level decision-making
Activity 2	*Throw and run five*
Focus	Throwing and catching skills in dynamic contexts, anticipation, tactical thinking and decision-making
Activity 3	*Piggy in the middle*
Focus	Working off the disc, cutting out the defence, communication and making space
Activity 4	*Frisbee soccer*
Focus	Maintaining possession (avoiding interception), attacking and defending
Activity 5	*Indoor end zone*
Focus	Applying all skills and tactical understandings developed in previous activities
Activity 6	*Game of ultimate frisbee*
Focus	Applying all skills and understandings in the full game

Activity 1: throw/catch introductory games

Owing to the fact that throwing and catching a disc may be a new skill for the learners, this unit begins with a focus on developing these skills within game contexts using a number of simple games.

Activity 1.1: Hot potato

This is an activity used to familiarize players with the disc. It is an individual activity where players hold the disc with one hand, toss it into the air and catch it with the other hand, then toss it again and catch it with the original hand. Students should practise catching the disc above and below the waist and with both hands as well.

Sample questions

What makes it more difficult to catch with one hand, and why? What can you do to make it easier to catch? What difference does it make when you toss the frisbee high in the air? Where is it easier to catch, below the waist or above the waist, and why?

Playing area/set-up

Play with 1–2 square metres of space per player.

Equipment

- One disc per player

Aim/intent

To successfully transfer the disc from one hand to the other.

Playing rules

None.

Activity 1.2: throw–catch tally

This activity introduces catching and throwing a disc under a little pressure and is played with twelve players split up into pairs. Players stand ten metres apart and all pairs commence throwing at the same time, aiming to complete as many throws and catches as possible in thirty seconds. Mark ten metres and five metres with cones and offer the pairs the option of throwing from ten metres to score two points for a catch or from five metres for one point. If the disc has to be retrieved, then the receiver must return to their original position before the return throw. Rotate players and adjust the distance between the catchers according to skill level.

Sample questions

What can you do to make it as easy as possible for the receiver to catch the frisbee? What technique can you use to make an accurate throw? What do you think is the best angle of release and how does this affect the distance thrown? Where did you decide to throw from (five metres or ten metres), and why? What factors would you think about when deciding whether to pass from five metres or ten metres?

Playing area/set-up

The playing space should allow pairs to be ten metres apart and to be free from interference by other pairs.

Equipment

- One disc per pair of players

Players

Work in pairs.

Aim/intent

For pairs to successfully throw the disc to each other and catch it over a distance of at least five metres as many times as possible in thirty seconds.

Playing rules

As above.

Activity 1.3: frisbee mobile archery

This is also a simple activity used to develop the skill of throwing the disc in a context where it requires a little low-evel decision-making and adjustment. Groups of threes move about a defined space, with one 'target' holding the hoop and two either side of it but five metres away. One of these players tries to throw the frisbee through the hoop for the one on the other side of the hoop to catch it. The team of three scores one point for a throw that goes through the hoop plus a bonus point if it is caught (a total of two). The target moves by walking slowly but making the hoop available and can assist by moving it. Work between three and five teams of three in an area about 20 × 20 metres according to skill level. Having more teams makes it more challenging. Teams work together to score as many points as possible in thirty seconds, rotating roles after each thirty seconds. The target must change directions after each throw (turning 90 degrees left or right). The target cannot stop and the thrower/catcher pairs can move freely to align with the hoop but must stay five metres from the hoop.

Sample questions

What tactics did you use to get a high score (throwing/catching technique and movement)? How did you anticipate and adjust to the target's change in direction?

Playing area/set-up

Work in an area about 20 × 20 metres, with the number of teams depending upon the skill level (three to five).

Equipment

- One disc per team of three

Players

Have three to five teams of three in an area about 20 × 20 metres according to their skill level, with one holding the hoop and the other two working either side of the hoop to throw and catch.

Aim/intent

To successfully throw the disc to the other catcher over a distance of at least five metres, with it passing through the hoop as many times as possible in thirty seconds.

Playing rules

- No interference with other teams is allowed.
- The player holding the hoop can move it to assist his teammates but must always hold it in two hands.
- The thrower must be at least five metres from the hoop to score a point.

Activity 2: throw and run five

Used elsewhere in this book, this game steps up the complexity of the game and the skill demands. It is played in pairs with the aim of making as many catches as possible in thirty seconds, but the player who throws must immediately run to a point that is five metres away from the player now in possession before receiving a throw. Pairs aim to cooperate to score as many points as possible, with one point scored per catch. This game is much more complex than the previous game because a number of pairs play in the same space at the same time. This means that players have to develop perceptual ability to see and anticipate spaces that they can run into or lead their partner into and make constant decisions about when and how to throw. The size of the space and the number of players will depend upon the age, experience and skill levels of the players or students, and forms a central mechanism for adjusting the levels of challenge and opportunities for success to suit the learners' needs and abilities.

Sample questions

What strategies did you use to score as many points as possible? Do you think the receiver needs to find space for the thrower to pass to, or should the thrower lead into space? How can the thrower anticipate the receiver's movement? What type of throw is needed when there is a lot of traffic and spaces close down quickly? How can you communicate?

Playing area/set-up

The space requirement varies according to the number of players, their age, skill and experience, but can usually work in a space of about fifteen square metres.

Equipment

* One disc per pair of players

Players

Work in pairs, beginning with four pairs (eight players) working in a space of fifteen square metres.

Aim/intent

To successfully throw the disc to the other catcher over a distance of at least five metres as many times as possible in thirty seconds.

Playing rules

- No intentional body contact.
- Must stay within defined space.
- There is no score if the frisbee is dropped.
- A throw must travel at least five metres to score a point.

Modifications

- *More challenging*: use more players or less space.
- *Less challenging*:

    1. Use fewer players or more space.
    2. Throw only three metres to score a point.

Activity 3: piggy in the middle

This game is widely used in game-based teaching such as in Game Sense and TGfU because it is such a simple yet effective game. In this book it is also used in Chapter 11, on field hockey, Chapter 12, on basketball, and Chapter 13, on netball. It allows players to engage in tactical decision-making, improve their defending and attacking skills and practise skills in context. In groups of three, have the thrower and receiver stand ten metres apart with the piggy in between them. The aim is to connect passes without the piggy getting the disc. The thrower must throw inside-out or outside-in throws by altering the outside angle of the disc. Once the class/team have familiarized themselves with the game, introduce the idea of scoring a point for each catch and challenge pairs to score as many points as possible in thirty seconds. The defender should be rotated regularly and this could extend to changing the make-up of the three people in each game as well.

The throwers can move about anywhere they like to improve their scores, as can the defender in trying to shut down their scoring. Typically this begins as a static game and the teacher will have to ask questions to help engage the students intellectually for them to explore all possibilities for moving and cooperating to improve their scores.

Sample questions

To the attackers: *how can you get the disc around the piggy? What types of throws could you use? If the defender is blocking your channel to the receiver, where can you move to open it up? The time the disc spends in the air when thrown is longer than with a ball. How does this affect your throwing? If the receiver is moving quickly, where would you throw the disc? If the time the disc spends in the air allows the defender to intercept it, how can you adjust your passing?*

To the defender: *where is the best place to position yourself? What defensive strategies can you use? How can you anticipate which way the pass will go? Should you pressure the receiver or the thrower?*

Playing area/set-up

This is best played in open space with about ten square metres of space per game.

Equipment

* One disc per game

Players

Three players per game.

Aim/intent

To successfully throw the disc to the other catcher without it being intercepted by the piggy as many times as possible in thirty seconds.

Playing rules

* No body contact.
* The defender cannot attack the disc when it is held.
* The defender can only gain possession by intercepting.
* When the disc is intercepted, the defender returns the disc to the opposing pair.
* The pair in possession must be at least three metres apart to score a point.

Modifications

- *More challenging*: add another player so there are two players in the middle or make it a 3 v. 2 game.
- *Less challenging*: use foam discs for younger players.

Activity 4: frisbee soccer

Frisbee soccer is played on a soccer pitch using soccer goals, with a goal being scored by throwing the disc into the goal. The disc is moved down the field by passing. Players are not allowed to run with the disc, but the disc is allowed to touch the ground or roll along the ground. This means that players in possession can roll the disc along the ground, follow it and pick it up (as the equivalent of dribbling in soccer or basketball). When the disc is on the ground, players from either team may pick it up, while still maintaining the non-contact rules. If two players attempt to pick up the disc simultaneously, then the team that was in possession before the disc went to ground retains possession. Frisbee soccer can be played on a full field with 10–15 players per team or alternatively played cross-field on a half-field using large cones to mark out the goals with between five and ten players on each team.

Play begins with either team on their side of the halfway line. Once the whistle blows the attacking team players run into the opposition half for the player with the disc to throw it to. After this there is no offside. After a goal is scored play is restarted in this way by the team that was scored against. If the disc goes out, play restarts from the point where it went out with a throw from the non-offending team.

Sample questions

To the attacking team: *when play is started or restarted from halfway, where should the players from the attacking team run to? How can the attacking team spread the field to make more space available? In attack, if the defending team is crowded around the player in possession, where would the opportunities be to move the disc forward? What are the disadvantages of using a long throw to a teammate? What can you do to make yourself available to receive a pass and create a scoring opportunity? How can you best maintain possession while still moving the disc toward the opponent's goal?*

To defenders: *which attacker should you pressure? Where should you position yourself? How can you force the ball carrier to pass early? How can you make it harder for your opponents to score? How can you reduce the attacking team's time and space?*

Playing area/set-up

Use a full or half soccer/rugby pitch.

Equipment

- One disc per game
- Coloured bibs (not sashes)
- Soccer goals or large cones to mark out goals

Players

For a full field, have teams of 10–15 players. For half a field, have teams of 5–10 players.

Aim/intent

To score more goals than the opposition. A goal is scored by throwing the disc in the goal.

Playing rules

- Players cannot run with the disc but may roll the disc, chase it and pick it up (dribbling).
- Players defending must be at least one metre away from the thrower.
- Infringements on field during play result in turnover, and all opposition players must be at least five metres away from the player restarting.
- The game restarts in the following instances:

  1. When the disc goes out the non-offending team restarts with a throw from the point where it went out and no players can be within five metres of the thrower (for all restart throws).
  2. When the disc goes over the goal line the non-offending team throws in from the point where the disc went out. After a goal is scored, begin from halfway, with the team scored against restarting.

Modifications

- *More challenging*:
    1. Introduce a rule that the disc cannot be passed backwards.
    2. Make it so that every player on the team must touch the disc before a shot at goal is allowed.
    3. Limit the number of throws per team.
    4. Have a limit on the minimum number of throws before shooting for a goal.
    5. Have a team member in the end zone who has to catch the disc in order to score.

- *Less challenging*: increase the goal size.

Activity 5: indoor end zone

Indoor end zone is played on a netball or basketball court. The end zone is the goal circle (netball) or keyhole (basketball). Each team has between four and six players, and after catching the disc in the end zone to score a goal, players touch the disc to the ground and start again, by attacking the goal at the opposite end of the court. Each team has two substitutes, with substitution able to happen at any time by tagging the player on the sideline. A game is usually played for fifteen minutes.

Sample questions

To attackers: *how can you vary the height of throws to avoid intercepts? Which type of throw is most effective? When would you use a short throw and when would you use long throws? How can you best position yourself to move toward the opposition goal and score? Which throws work the best? How do you decide where you can run to be in a position to score? Once a goal is scored what do you need to do if you are not the one who caught the disc?*

To defenders: *which attacker should you pressure? Where should you position yourself? How can you force the ball carrier to pass early? If you want to catch the disc, how can you deceive your defender and get 'open'? What do you need to do if the opposition scores against you?*

To all: *what rules can be added to improve the game?*

Playing area/set-up

Use a basketball court with two end zones 2.5 metres deep (or a netball semi-circle can be used).

Equipment

- One disc per game
- Marker cones to define the playing area and end zones (if needed)
- Different coloured bibs for each team

Players

Four to six players per side.

Aim/intent

To score more goals than the opposition.

Playing rules

- Play is continuous. After a goal is scored, the scoring team taps the disc on the ground and immediately plays on, attempting to score at the other end zone.
- If a pass is intercepted, knocked to the ground or dropped, the opposing team gets possession of the disc and may restart immediately. Opposition players must retreat three metres away from the restarting player.
- No contact is allowed.
- A team scores one goal when it completes a pass to a player in the end zone it is attacking.
- The first team to score fifteen goals wins or you could play to a time cap.

Modifications

- *More challenging*:
    1. Vary the field size according to the number of players and their ability.
    2. Play in a smaller area to increase the development of passing and catching skills.
    3. Introduce zones for defensive and offensive/attacking players.
    4. Only change possession when the disc is intercepted with a successful catch.
    5. Allow for two uncompleted passes before possession changes.
    6. For a faster game, reduce the time allowed to hold the disc to five seconds.

7. Add zones and rotate players through the 'bench'.
8. Use a catcher situated inside a square.

- *Less challenging*: players can score around the back of the end zone.

Activity 6: game of ultimate frisbee

This is where students/players combine all the skills they have learnt through the modified games into one full game of ultimate frisbee. The whole class or team could play on a soccer/rugby field or two smaller games could be set up and played at the same time using two half-fields and playing cross-field. This could then become a round robin competition where games are played for approximately ten minutes before they rotate. In co-ed classes a good variation is to implement the following rules to ensure fair gender play: (1) girls/women get two points for scoring; (2) the disc must be passed to two girls/women before an attempt to score is made.

At this stage, instead of asking questions the teacher/coach should provide opportunities for team talks at strategically and tactically critical stages of the game. He/she can move between teams to listen and stimulate interaction through a little questioning if needed but not feel obliged to interfere if this is not needed. He/she can also stop the whole game or 'freeze play' (Turner 2005) if there is something important enough to justify this intervention and ask one or two big questions of the whole group. More focused and specific questions can be used at the end of the game as a reflection on the game and the unit.

Sample questions

How can you work together to get the team into a good scoring position? What strategies did your team decide to use to score more points? What tactics did you decide on using and how did they work in the game? Which ones did not work, and why?

Playing area/set-up

Use a full soccer/rugby pitch or play cross-field on half a soccer/rugby pitch.

Equipment

- One disc per game
- Two sets of different coloured bibs
- Large cones to mark out goals if needed

Players

Eight to twelve players per team on a full field and six to nine players on a half-field.

Aim/intent

To score more goals than the opposition.

Playing rules

- No running with the disc.
- Throwing in any direction (forwards, backwards, sideways) is allowed.
- A team scores by a player from the attacking team catching the disc in the end zone.
- A turnover occurs when the disc is dropped or hits the ground, goes out of bounds or is knocked down by a defensive player.
- At a turnover, the other team picks the disc up where it was last dropped to resume play.
- The marker must be at least one metre away from the thrower.
- All other players must be at least three metres away from the thrower.
- No contact is allowed.

Modifications

None suggested.

17
VOLLEYBALL

Introduction

Volleyball is another game played across the globe that is both an Olympic sport and a sport widely taught in physical education programmes. This alone justifies including it in a book on Game Sense, but it is also a good example of a net/wall game, with the approach taken here able to inform ideas on teaching other net/wall games such as tennis and badminton. Indeed, as the first training game used in this unit, volleyball tennis could be used for learning tactical lessons in a unit on tennis. Unlike most other sports presented in this book, such as soccer and Australian football, volleyball is a technique-intensive game. In most invasion games the skill required to just get a game going allow even the most inexperienced and 'unskilled' players to make a start, but this is not the case in volleyball.

The skills required to enable volleyball to be played are quite demanding and can make it more challenging to adopt a Game Sense approach than with invasion games because of the need for a degree of technical competence to be able to play the game. This is probably most noticeable with the skill of digging, which is so difficult to perform for most novices yet necessary for receiving the ball to get an attack going. This then presents a challenge for the Game Sense teacher/coach that requires a little adjustment in the normal approach taken but without losing sight of the need to focus on the game and not the skill or technique. However, this does not mean reverting to a lesson drilling each of the four core skills of serve, dig, set and spike before moving on to play the game, as I remember doing when a high school PE teacher. I also remember the futility of this approach as it was never possible to develop an engaging game because of a lack of tactical understanding, game awareness and the impossible challenge of actually improving these techniques over the short duration of a physical education unit.

To address this problem of dealing with the need for technical proficiency I offer the approach I have used with undergraduate PETE students and in teaching senior primary school students and junior high school students. This involves focusing on developing tactical understanding while gradually introducing volleyball skills as tactical complexity builds up, but keeping the focus on *the game*. In this approach I try to hold back the introduction of all the specific volleyball skills to emphasize tactical learning over skill learning early in the unit. This is not to suggest that you should neglect skill by focusing on tactics because the skills are developed as the activities progress in complexity. However, there is likely to be good justification for some specific teaching focused on technique. However, this should still be located within a game-like activity in which there is a need for perception, some decision-making and the adaptation of skill/technique to context. As I have stressed throughout this book, this is only an example of an approach that has worked for me and is in no way intended to be prescriptive.

How to play volleyball

This unit culminates in a game of volleyball using the standard rules but with modifications if necessary. The final game of volleyball is developed from a game of volley-stars in which the difficulty of executing the skills of digging, setting and spiking is reduced by allowing players to first catch the ball, toss it up and then perform the skill. This development involves removing the option of catching beginning with the spike, and then with the set and, finally, the dig. However, not all players will progress at the same pace and it may be prudent for teachers to consider allowing the option of a ball catch first for the dig because it is so demanding. This could be on a whole-class basis or offered as an option on an individual basis to prevent the game breaking down. This is very likely to be necessary for primary school children, and allows them to understand the game and develop tactical knowledge before they are able to competently perform all the skills.

Unit plan

Activity 1	*Volleyball tennis*
Focus	Tactical decision-making, creating space, angles of attack
Activity 2	*Newcombe ball*
Focus	Tactics for serving, discovering the best point of attack
Activity 3	*Volley-stars volleyball*
Focus	Using possession to construct an attack, developing perception (where are the spaces?) and deciding on the best point of attack
Activity 3.1	*Introducing the spike*
Focus	Constructing an attack for a spike and where to set the ball for the spiker

Activity 3.2	*Introducing the set*
Focus	The relationship between the 'dig' and set and between the set and the spike in constructing attacks
Activity 3.3	*Introducing the dig and specific skill practise*
Focus	Performing the dig and providing good possession
Activity 3.4	*Introducing the serve*
Focus	Placing the ball at the back of the opposition court
Activity 4	*Modified volleyball*
Focus	Developing team strategies for constructing a point and defending

Activity 1: volleyball tennis

This game helps develop game understanding and introduces learners to the basic tactical aspects of volleyball and any other net/wall game such as tennis, squash or badminton. In most gyms and basketball courts there are badminton courts marked out, and these are ideal for this game. It is a very good game for younger players, such as those of primary school age, and can be used to develop tactical knowledge of any net/wall game. In India it is widely played as a stand-alone game.

As a warm-up game for learning to play volleyball I suggest the game be played in a 2 v. 2 format using a volleyball that is thrown with two hands, using tennis rules. If enough space is available a 1 v. 1 can also be used. If pushed for space perhaps a 3 v. 3 game could even be used. Players can only use a two-handed throw as the power and ball speed generated in a one-handed throw make it too easy to score. The players explore ways to score using angles and creating space by moving the opposition about the court. The teacher/ coach stops the games from time to time to ask questions that lead the players to discover tactical considerations such as pushing the opponents back on the court to make it difficult for them to score and learning from experience where it is easier to score from (close to the line dividing the two sides), and therefore where they can make it as difficult as possible for the opposition to score.

Sample questions

The questioning should focus on discovering how it is easier to score from close to the 'net', and why, while focusing on manipulating time and space and angles, for example: *what tactics did you use to score points? From where was it easiest to score, and why? Where was it most difficult to score from, and why? If it is easier to score from close to the 'net', how can you get to that position? How can you prevent the opponent(s) from being able to attack from close to the 'net'? What are you looking for when you catch the ball?*

Playing area/set-up

Use the badminton court markings.

Equipment

* One volleyball per game

Players

Two players in each team (2 v. 2 per court).

Aim/intent

The aim of the activity is to score more points than the opposition using tennis rules.

Playing rules

* Players must use a two-handed throw.
* Players must catch the ball then throw (no hits are allowed).
* The ball is out if it is caught when any part of either foot is outside the side or back line.

Modifications

* *More challenging*:

  1. Introduce the use of a low bench to act as a 'net'.
  2. Allow one-handed throws.

* *Less challenging*: use a soft ball for younger students/players.

Activity 2: Newcombe ball

In this game use a standard volleyball court, net and volleyball, with six players on either team. Players score in the same way as in volleyball, trying to hit the floor with the ball on the opposition's side of the court. After each change of service, have players rotate one position on the court.

Unlike volleyball, the ball is caught and thrown and only one throw is allowed, meaning that players can only score from the point where they catch the ball. Start with the net a little lower than normal for volleyball, allowing for faster throws that put pressure on the team receiving the ball. This will also ensure that any player who intercepts the opposition's throw close to the net has a good chance of scoring. This reinforces some learning from volleyball tennis, in which players came to understand that it is easier to score from close to the net than from the back of the court.

Next, raise the net to normal volleyball height and allow two throws per team on the side of the net where they receive the ball. Teams will soon, if not immediately, get the ball to a player on the net, who will jump up to execute a powerful throw at a space on the floor in the opposition's half of the court to score a point. The teams can be asked how to defend against this attack and if they place more players close to the net the attacking team should be encouraged to look for the spaces further from the net that this opens up. Defending players should also be allowed to block the 'spike'.

Sample questions

Where are the spaces on the other side of the net? Can you see the spaces on the other side of the net when you are playing? If the attacking team attacks close to the net and from a high point, how can you defend against this? If the defending team is anticipating your point of attack and blocking it or catching the ball, how can you vary your tactics?

Playing area/set-up

Use a volleyball court with a net that can be adjusted for height.

Equipment

- One volleyball per game

Players

Have six players in each team. If you have extra players, rotate them in and out of the team after every change of service.

Aim/intent

The aim of the activity is to score more points than the opposition by having the ball hit the floor on the opposition's side of the net or by forcing them to make an error.

Playing rules

- Players must catch the ball then throw it (no hits are allowed).
- Players cannot move with the ball in hand.
- The ball is out if it is caught when any part of either foot is outside the side or back line.
- A point is scored when the ball hits the floor inside the court on the opposition's side of the net.
- No rebounds off the net are allowed.

Modifications

- *More challenging*: have more players.
- *Less challenging*:
    1. Have fewer players if the teams are finding it difficult to score.
    2. Make the scoring shot a two-handed throw (this is less challenging to defend against).

Activity 3: volley-stars volleyball

This game is set up in the same way as volleyball, with the same number of players in each team (six) and a maximum of three transfers of the ball allowed on one side of the net. The difference between this game and volleyball is that for each transfer of the ball it is caught first then tossed up to be dug, set or spiked. Unless the class or group is very young they can begin with a standard volleyball underarm serve. Allow younger children two or three attempts at the serve, with the understanding that this is needed to get a game going. This is done to maintain the development of tactical learning without the pressure of learning difficult technical skills at the same time, yet while slowly introducing volleyball skills as the unit progresses.

Sample questions

When attacking: *when you see a space on the opposition's side of the court, what do you think is important in trying to take advantage of it to score? If you try to score from the back of the court, what makes it difficult? Where is the easiest place to score from in attack? Why? How do you get the ball to that place and position on the court? Are there any ways you think you could trick the opposition so they don't know where you will attack from?*

When defending: *can you anticipate where the opposition will attack from and where the attack will be? If they attack from the back of the court, where should you move in defence? If they attack from close to the net, where should you move? Which shots are easier to defend against? Which are the most difficult? Why? What does this tell you about tactics for attack?*

Playing area/set-up

Use a volleyball court and net.

Equipment

• One volleyball per game

Players

Have six players in each team, rotating extra players after each change of service.

Aim/intent

The aim of the activity is to score more points than the opposition, as in normal volleyball.

Playing rules

Play with the same rules as volleyball, but players must catch the ball first then pop it up to perform dig/set/spike.

Modifications

From here, introduce the volleyball skills of serving, digging, setting and spiking into the volley-stars game and in doing so gradually move the game toward volleyball, or at least a modified form of it.

Activity 3.1: introducing the serve

Once the class/group is able to play this game competently the volley-stars techniques are slowly replaced with full volleyball techniques. This begins with the serve because it is the easiest skill to perform. As the students/players know the shape of the game they could be taken out of it briefly to be shown the basic techniques involved in the serve and practise in pairs serving to a partner who tries to catch the ball without having to move from where he/she is standing. After this the students/players would return to the volley-stars game to introduce the serve to start the game. Allow less able children to serve from closer to the net by providing lines from which they can choose to serve if they have trouble serving from where they would normally serve. This allows the game to proceed and is in the best interests of all players/students.

Sample questions

Thinking back to the lead-up games you have played, where do you want to place the ball, and why? How high does the ball need to go, and why? Where is it easier to score from for the opposition and what does this suggest to you about the serve?

Activity 3.2: introducing the spike

After introducing the serve the teacher/coach should then introduce the spike, because the prior learning has been focused on structuring an attack through the spike and tactically this is what the focus should be on. Each team has three transfers of the ball to get the ball in the best position possible for an attacking shot close to the net and from a high point. In this first step the players catch the serve, pop it up and dig it to a setter, who catches it with hands above his/her head (as would be the position for a normal set). He/she then pops the ball up with hands still above his/her head for the ball to be spiked, as in normal volleyball. At this stage of the game teachers/coaches should focus on structuring the point and setting the ball where the spiker wants it. This could involve some brief meetings and discussions within teams for players to arrive at the best position for the ball to be set for the spiker, and should involve learning from the perspective of the spiker and the setter. Opportunities should also be provided for players to be creative with the team's attacking plays, including dummy spikes.

Sample questions

Where are the spaces? When you are setting up an attack are you aware of where the spaces are? When you spike, how can you take away the time the defence has to counter? What tactics can you use to stop the opposition players blocking your spiker? When you are spiking, where do you want the ball and what sort of pass do you want?

Activity 3.3: introducing the set

Building upon the previous game, where the spike was introduced, now intro- duce the volleyball set. There is nothing wrong with focusing on some of the technical details of setting, such as having knees flexed, eyes on the ball and elbows and fingers in what would normally be the correct position. It could also be first introduced briefly through some skill-focused activities, such as standing in a circle to see how many times the team/group can set the ball, with the teacher/coach emphasizing keeping the knees bent and eyes on the ball while moving to adjust to the ball's movement. This approach to working on skill outside the game after having discovered its relevance and place in the game is similar to the Tactical Games approach and its pattern of game–skill work–game. Indeed, in skill-intensive sports such as volleyball I adopt the same approach.

However, the teacher/coach should not spend too much time working on skill before going back to the game being developed. At this stage of the developing game I would introduce the set. This means that the volley-stars dig is still used (catch–toss–dig) but that the ball must then be set as per normal volleyball rules and received from a volley-stars type dig. At this point students/players need to be thinking about the relationships between the dig and the set and between the set and the spike. This might involve asking the setter how he/she likes to receive the ball to best facilitate setting from the digger and asking the spiker the same question. When students/players are rotated they can develop an understanding of the inter-relationship between skills while also developing some tactical understanding and perceptual ability, such as seeing the gaps and spaces that they can attack.

Once the set and spike can be performed reasonably well teams can be given time to develop some predetermined tactical plays. This could involve allowing the attacking team to begin one, two or three attacks that begin with the 'digger' being allowed to just toss the ball to the setter instead of receiving it from an opposition serve. This provides a good opportunity for team debate, formulating ideas/tactics, testing them and evaluating them, which is a key means of learning through Game Sense.

Sample questions

When you are setting the ball where is it best for you to receive the ball? How can you provide some options for the setter? How can you move the defence to create a space to score? Where should you face when you are the setter, and why?

Activity 3.4: introducing the dig and specific skill practise

This is the most difficult skill to introduce into the developing game and it can often present real problems in keeping the game going and building in tactical complexity. It is also unlikely that all students/players will be able to dig well enough for the game to develop. While I have focused on introducing skills into the progressively developed modified game, I still suggest not losing sight of the Game Sense focus on the whole game instead of the discrete skills seen to be necessary to play it. This means that I cannot let the technical difficulty of the dig stop the game progressing. I have memories of teaching volleyball at high school, teaching each of the four discrete skills for four weeks, then playing the game in week five to find that none of the skills I had taught were put into practice, and with games invariably being chaotic and frustrating for me and for the students. That is to say that even when the teacher or coach spends a lot of time drilling skills such as digging, it invariably makes little if any contribution to good game play.

With this in mind I suggest considering bypassing the onerous task of teaching students or young people how to dig well for the sake of getting a good game going and enhancing the learning that arises from it. This could be achieved by offering students/players the option of using the dig or using the volley-stars version of it to allow the game to proceed, because the focus should be on the game and not on learning discrete skills. If you have been able to develop a class or team culture of fair play and a focus on having an enjoyable game, these types of adaptations should not present a problem.

Much TGfU literature suggests that if the game is being held up by a lack of skill, teachers/coaches might consider stopping the game briefly to practise the skill then return to the game. Indeed the Tactical Games approach sets this up as a pattern to follow. In Game Sense my preference would normally be to change the game so that learning can be kept within games as much as possible, but in the case of the dig in volleyball it is probably better to do some specific practise. This is not, however, to suggest reverting to drills out of context. As is evident elsewhere in the examples suggested for volleyball in this chapter and other games in this book, you can focus on skill but keep it contextualized to some extent (see Chapters 1, 3 and 5). The problem with decontextualized skill drills is that a skill learnt out of context has little use or purpose outside that setting, as Dewey (1916/97) suggests is the case with education more generally. Learning within games *situates* learning (Lave and Wenger 1991) in authentic physical contexts within which it is broad and deep, with much of it taking place unnoticed and in addition to the learning intended by the teacher/coach. Even when there is a need to practise a skill, it should be contextualized to some degree to involve the skill execution being informed by perception and some decision-making.

When teaching older or more capable students/players, digging can be further developed by practising it in *game-like* activities that require some perception, some decision-making, movement and a degree of competition. These games can be more focused on technique/skill but retain aspects of the game and build from simple to more complex, and I provide an example of this for improving the dig. There is little that is more likely to kill motivation, enjoyment and learning than placing unskilled children or young people under the gaze of the teacher/coach and their peers as they fail, time and time again, to be able to 'master' the difficult skill of performing the dig. With this in mind, I would suggest that (1) it is not that important for children and young people to master the dig because the focus of Game Sense is on the game (den Duyn 1997) and (2) any work on it should be conducted in game-like settings both to give it meaning and to allow the less skilled to be free of the critical gaze of others.

This practice involves dividing the court into three long, narrow courts of the normal depth but one-third of the normal width. Start with a player on one side of the net at the back of the court and two or three players on the other side. The player on one side throws to a digger at the back of the court on the other side of the net, his/her aim being to pop the ball up to a player standing where a setter would be likely to stand in a game, facing him/her, and aiming for the 'setter' to move as little as possible to catch the ball. This can be built upon by adding a third player on this side as the spiker and then a defender on the other side in a 3 v. 2 situation. The attacking team of three tries to score a point and the defending pair try to catch the ball, with the teacher/coach adjusting numbers to get the right balance of challenge and success. Here, a basic skill-focused activity is built into more of a modified game as the skill develops.

Sample questions

Is it easier to move backwards or forwards to dig the ball when served? When you are able to successfully dig the ball and control it, where should you place it? If you are under pressure and having trouble with the dig, where should you put the ball? If your dig pulls a setter back to cover it, where could you move to?

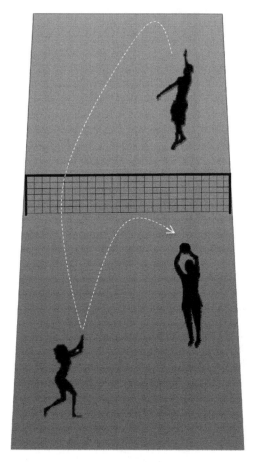

FIGURE 17.1 Skill-focused practise for the dig

Activity 4: playing modified volleyball

Student or player-centred approaches such as Game Sense are inherently inclusive due to their focus on the game and the pedagogy that they adopt. They are also enjoyable because they engage a wide range of learners regardless of their skill, experience and confidence. For teaching or coaching the students or young players that this unit on volleyball is pitched at, inclusion, enjoyment and keeping the game going should be the focus of the teacher or coach. To this end, the end game of modified volleyball should be designed to accommodate a range of skills and abilities by allowing players the option of performing the standard volleyball skills of serving, digging, setting and spiking to enable the game to proceed and allowing players to learn by playing the game. This requires the teacher or coach developing a culture in the class or team in which fair play is well understood, differences in ability and disposition are accepted and all rules and modifications are accepted because they make it a better and more enjoyable game for everyone.

The students or players can thus decide on the degree to which the game is modified on an individual level, but with consideration of all others in the game and the idea that making it a fair game makes it an enjoyable game. The discussions and collaboration involved in the Game Sense approach facilitate communication across the class or team and should sensitize students or players to the expectations of peers and the folly of using the rules to gain an unfair advantage over others. Teams that are experienced in this approach could also be trusted to identify weaknesses in their game and given time to design and implement training activities to address these weaknesses. Through all these strategies for keeping the game going in the face of the challenges of demanding techniques the students and players are learning how to play volleyball as a game and learning much about themselves at the same time.

Playing area/set-up

Use a volleyball court and net.

Equipment

- One volleyball per game

Players

Play with six players in each team, rotating extra players after each change of service.

Aim/intent

The aim of the activity is to score more points than the opposition.

Playing rules

Use the standard volleyball rules, but teachers should allow those players whose skills are stopping the game progressing to revert to the catch–toss–skill approach used in the previous game.

Modifications

- *Less challenging*:
  1. Be prepared to allow players to revert to the volley-stars rules where necessary on an individual and/or team basis.
  2. Teachers may also lower the net for younger players.
- *More challenging*: None suggested.

BIBLIOGRAPHY

Almond, L. and Launder, A. (2010) 'A critical dialogue between TGfU and Play Practice: Implications for practice and the research agenda', paper presented at the TGfU Seminar, AIESEP World Congress, La Coruña, Spain, 6 October.

Armour, K. M. (2004) 'Coaching pedagogy', in R. L. Jones, K. M. Armour and P. Potrac, *The Cultures of Coaching*, London: Longman.

Arnold, P. (1986) 'Moral aspects of an education in movement', *Proceedings for the 57th Annual Meeting of the American Academy of Physical Education*, Champaign, IL: Human Kinetics.

Australian Sports Commission (1991) *Sport for Young Australians: Widening the Gateways to Participation*, Canberra: Australian Sports Commission.

Australian Sports Commission (1997) *Game Sense: Developing Thinking Players* (video), Belconnen, Australia: Australian Sports Commission.

Bengoechea, E. G., Strean, W. B. and Williams, D. J. (2004) 'Understanding and promoting fun in youth sport: Coaches' perspectives', *Physical Education and Sport Pedagogy*, 9(2): 185–197.

Bourdieu, P. (1986) *Distinction: A Social Critique of the Judgement of Taste*, London: Routledge.

Breed, R. and Spittle, M. (2011) *Developing Game Sense through Tactical Learning: A Resource Book for Teachers and Coaches*, Melbourne: Cambridge University Press.

Brooker, R. and Abbott, R. (2001) 'Developing intelligent performers in sport: Should coaches be making more sense of game sense?', *Journal of Sport Pedagogy*, 7(2): 67–83.

Brooker, R., Kirk, D. and Braiuka, S. (2000) 'Implementing a game sense approach to teaching junior high school basketball in a naturalistic setting', *European Physical Education Review*, 6(1): 7–26.

Bruner, J. S. (1966) *Toward a Theory of Instruction*, Cambridge, MA: Belknap Press of Harvard University.

Bunker, D. and Thorpe, R. (1982) 'A model for the teaching of games in secondary school', *Bulletin of Physical Education*, 18: 5–8.

Bunker, D. and Thorpe, R. (1986) 'The curriculum model: Rethinking games teaching', Department of Physical Education and Sports Science, University of Technology, Loughborough, UK.

Butler, J. (1996) 'Teacher responses to Teaching Games for Understanding', *Journal of Physical Education, Recreation and Dance*, 67: 28–33.

Butler, J. (2005) 'TGfU pet-agogy: Old dogs, new tricks and puppy school', *Physical Education and Sport Pedagogy*, 10(3): 225–240.

Butler, J. and Griffin, L. L. (2010) *More Teaching Games for Understanding: Move Globally*, Champaign, IL: Human Kinetics.

Butler, J., Griffin, L., Lombardo, B. and Nastasi, R. (2003) *Teaching Games for Understanding in Physical Education and Sport*, Champaign, IL: Human Kinetics.

Carpendale, J. (1997) 'An explicitation of Piaget's constructivism: Implications for social cognitive development', in S. Hala (ed.) *The Development of Social Cognition*, Hove, UK: Psychology Press Ltd.

Cassidy, T., Jones, R. L. and Potrac, P. (2004) *Understanding Sports Coaching: The Social, Cultural and Pedagogical Foundations of Coaching Practice*, London: Routledge.

Charlesworth, R. (1993) Designer Games, Hockey Australia, Level 3 NCAS Course, Canberra, December, available at HTTP: http://www.sportsouthland.co.nz/files/docs/hs_designergames.pdf (accessed 30 December 2011).

Chen, Q. and Light, R. (2006) ' "I thought I'd hate cricket but I love it!": Year six students' responses to Game Sense pedagogy', *Change: Transformations in Education*, 9(1): 49–58.

Chen, W. and Rovegno, I. (2000) 'Examination of expert and novice teachers' constructivist-oriented teaching practices using a movement approach to elementary physical education', *Research Quarterly for Exercise & Sport*, 71(4): 357–372.

Coakley, J. (2001) *Sport in Society: Issues and Controversies*, 7th edn, Boston, MA: McGraw Hill.

Côté, J., Baker, J. and Abernathy, B. (2003) 'From play to practice: A development framework for the acquisition of expertise in team sport', in J. Starkes and K. A. Ericsson (eds) *Expert Performance in Sport: Advances in Research on Sport Expertise*, Champaign, IL: Human Kinetics.

Curran, D. (1991) *Lets Get into Minkey Hockey*, Surry Hills, Australia: Aussie Sports Books Pty Ltd.

Curry, C. and Light, R. (2007) 'Addressing the NSW Quality Teaching Framework in physical education: Is Game Sense the answer?', *Proceedings of the Asia Pacific Conference on Teaching Sport and Physical Education for Understanding*, available at HTTP: http://sydney.edu.au/education_social_work_work/professional_learning/resources/papers/proceedings_TGfU_06_AsiaPacioficSport.pdf ge7 (accessed 7 July 2010).

Cushion, C. J., Armour, K. M. and Jones, R. L. (2003) 'Coach education and continuing professional development: Experience and learning to coach', *Quest*, 55: 215–230.

Davis, B. and Sumara, D. (1997) 'Cognition, complexity and teacher education', *Harvard Educational Review*, 67(1): 105–125.

Davis, B. and Sumara, D. (2003) 'Why aren't they getting this? Working through the regressive myths of constructivist pedagogy', *Teaching Education*, 14(2): 123–140.

Davis, B., Sumara, D. and Luce-Kapler, R. (2000) *Engaging Minds: Learning and Teaching in a Complex World*, Mahwah, NJ: Lawrence Erlbaum Associates.

den Duyn, N. (1997) *Game Sense: Developing Thinking Players*, Canberra: Australian Sports Commission.

DeVries, R. and Zan, B. (1996) 'A constructivist perspective on the role of the sociomoral atmosphere in promoting children's development', in C. T. Fosnot (ed.) *Constructivism: Theory, Perspectives and Practice*, New York and London: Teachers College Press.

Dewey, J. (1916/97) *Democracy in Education*, New York: Free Press.

Dewey, J. (1938/97) *Experience and Education*, New York: Touchstone.

Dixon, M. (2010) 'Game Sense as a holistic approach to soccer coaching: Perceptions of premier league academy coaches', paper presented at the TGfU Seminar, AIESEP World Congress, La Coruña, Spain, 6 October.

Ennis, C. (1999) 'Creating a culturally relevant curriculum for disengaged girls', *Sport, Education and Society*, 4(1): 31–50.

Evans, J. R. (2011) 'Elite rugby coaches' interpretation and use of Game Sense in Australia and New Zealand: An examination of coaches' habitus, learning and development', unpublished thesis, University of Sydney.

Fosnot, C. (1996) *Constructivism: Theory, Perspectives, and Practice*, New York: Teachers College Press.

Fox, R. (2001) 'Constructivism examined', *Oxford Review of Education*, 27(1): 24–35.

Greener, I. (n.d.) *GoalKick Training Manual*, South Melbourne: Victorian Soccer Federation.

Gréhaigne, J.-F. and Godbout, P. (1995) 'Tactical knowledge in team sports from a constructivist and cognitivist perspective', *Quest*, 47: 490–505.

Gréhaigne, J.-F. and Godbout, P. (1998a) 'Formative assessment in team sports in a tactical approach context', *Journal of Physical Education, Recreation and Dance*, 69(1): 46–51.

Gréhaigne, J.-F. and Godbout, P. (1998b) 'Observation, critical thinking and transformation: Three key elements for a constructivist perspective of the learning process in team sports', in R. Feingold, R. Rees, G. Barette, I. Fiorentino, S. Virgilio and E. Kowalski (eds) *Education for Life*, New York: Adelphi University.

Gréhaigne, J.-F., Godbout, P. and Bouthier, D. (1997) 'Performance assessment in team sports', *Journal of Teaching in Physical Education*, 16: 500–516.

Gréhaigne, J.-F., Richard, J.-F. and Griffin, L. L. (2005) *Teaching and Learning Team Sports and Games*, London and New York: Routledge.

Griffin, L. L. and Butler, J. (2005) *Teaching Games for Understanding: Theory, Research, and Practice*, Champaign, IL: Human Kinetics.

Griffin, L. L. and Patton, K. (2005) 'Two decades of Teaching Games for Understanding: Looking at the past, present, and future', in L. L. Griffin and J. Butler (eds) *Teaching Games for Understanding: Theory, Research, and Practice*, Champaign, IL: Human Kinetics.

Griffin, L. L., Mitchell, S. A. and Oslin, J. L. (1997) *Teaching Sport Concepts and Skills: A Tactical Games Approach*, Champaign, IL: Human Kinetics.

Harrison, W. (2002) *Recognizing the Moment to Play: Anticipation, Imagination, Awareness*, Spring City, PA: Reedswain.

Heidegger, M. (1968) *What Is Called Thinking*, trans. J. Gray, London: Harper & Row.

Holt, N., Strean, W. and Bengoechea, E. G. (2002) 'Expanding the Teaching Games for Understanding model: New avenues for future research and practice', *Journal of Teaching in Physical Education*, 21(2): 162–177.

Hopper, T., Butler, J. I. and Storey, B. (eds) (2009) *TGfU . . . Simply Good Pedagogy: Understanding a Complex Challenge*, Ottowa: HPE Canada.

Howarth, K. (2000) 'Context as a factor in teachers' perceptions of the teaching of thinking skills in Physical Education', *Journal of Teaching in Physical Education*, 19(3): 270–286.

Jess, M., Atencio, M. and Thorburn, M. (2011) 'Complexity theory: Supporting curriculum and pedagogy developments in Scottish physical education', *Sport, Education and Society*, 16(2): 179–199.

Jin, A. (2011) 'Challenges facing Chinese PE curriculum reform', paper presented at the Australian Association of Research in Education, Hobart, Australia, 27 November–1 December.

Jones, R. (2002) 'Summer soccer camp enjoyment: Parent, coach and child perceptions', *Journal of Physical Education*, 7: 45–62.

Jones, R. L. (2006) 'How can educational concepts inform sports coaching?', in R. L. Jones (ed.) *The Sports Coach as Educator*, London and New York: Routledge.

Jones, R. L., Armour, K. M. and Potrac, P. (2004) *The Cultures of Coaching*, London: Longman.

Kidman, L. (2001) *Developing Decision Makers: An Empowerment Approach to Coaching*, Christchurch, New Zealand: Innovative Print Communications.

Kidman, L. (ed.) (2005) *Athlete-centred Coaching: Developing Inspired and Inspiring People*, Christchurch, New Zealand: Innovative Print Communication.

Kirk, D. (2004) 'Framing quality physical education: The elite sport model or Sport Education?', *Physical Education and Sport Pedagogy*, 9(2): 185–196.

Kirk, D. (2010) 'Towards a socio-pedagogy of sports coaching', in J. Lyle and C. Cushion (eds) *Sport Coaching: Professionalisation and Practice*, Edinburgh: Elsevier.

Kirk, D. and Macdonald, D. (1998) 'Situated learning in Physical Education', *Journal of Teaching in Physical Education*, 17: 376–387.

Kirk, D. and MacPhail, A. (2002) 'Teaching games for understanding and situated learning: Rethinking the Bunker–Thorpe model', *Journal of Teaching in Physical Education*, 21: 117–192.

Krtetchmar, S. (2005) 'Understanding and the delights of human activity', in L. Griffin and J. Butler (eds) *Teaching Games for Understanding: Theory Research and Practice*, Champaign, IL: Human Kinetics.

Launder, A. G. (2001) *Play Practice: The Games Approach to Teaching and Coaching Sports*, Champaign, IL: Human Kinetics.

Launder, A. and Piltz, W. (2006) 'Beyond understanding to skilful play, through Play Practice', *Journal of Physical Education New Zealand*, 39(1): 49–59.

Lave, J. and Wenger, E. (1991) *Situated Learning: Legitimate Peripheral Participation*, Cambridge: Cambridge University Press.

Light, R. (1999) 'Regimes of training and the construction of masculinity in Japanese university rugby', *International Sports Studies*, 21(2): 39–54.

Light, R. (2002) 'The social nature of games: Pre-service primary teachers' first experiences of TGfU', *European Physical Education Review*, 8(3): 291–310.

Light, R. (2003) 'The joy of learning: Emotion, cognition and learning in games through TGfU', *New Zealand Journal of Physical Education*, 36(1): 94–108.

Light, R. (2004) 'Australian coaches' experiences of Game Sense: Opportunities and challenges', *Physical Education and Sport Pedagogy*, 9(2): 115–132.

Light, R. (ed.) (2005a) 'An international perspective on Teaching Games for Understanding', special issue of *Physical Education and Sport Pedagogy*, 10(3).

Light, R. (2005b) 'Making sense of the chaos: Games Sense coaching in Australia', in L. Griffin and J. Butler (eds) *Examining a Teaching Games for Understanding Model*, Champaign, IL: Human Kinetics.

Light, R. (2005c) 'Introduction: An international perspective on Teaching Games for Understanding', *Physical Education and Sport Pedagogy*, 10(3): 211–212.

Light, R. (2006) 'Situated learning in an Australian surf club', *Sport, Education and Society*, 11(2): 155–172.

Light, R. (2008a) ' "Complex" learning theory in physical education: An examination of its epistemology and assumptions about how we learn', *Journal of Teaching in Physical Education*, 27(1): 21–37

Light, R. (2008b) *Sport in the Lives of Young Australians*, Sydney: Sydney University Press.

Light, R. (2009) 'Understanding and enhancing learning in TGfU through Complex Learning Theory', in T. Hopper, J. Butler and B. Storey (eds) *TGfU . . . Simply Good Pedagogy: Understanding a Complex Challenge*. Ottawa: HPE Canada.

Light, R. and Butler, J. (2005) 'A personal journey: TGfU teacher development in Australia and the USA', *Physical Education and Sport Pedagogy*, 10(3): 241–254.

Light, R. and Curry, C. (2009) 'Children's reasons for joining sport clubs and staying in them: A case study of a Sydney soccer club', *ACHPER Healthy Lifestyles Journal*, 56(1): 23–27.

Light, R. and Evans, J. (2010) 'Elite level rugby coaches' interpretation and use of Game Sense: A question of pedagogy', *Physical Education and Sport Pedagogy*, 15(2): 103–115.

Light, R. and Fawns, R. (2001) 'The thinking body: Constructivist approaches to games teaching in Physical Education', *Melbourne Studies in Education*, 42(2): 69–87.

Light, R. and Fawns, R. (2003) 'Knowing the game: Integrating speech and action through TGfU', *Quest*, 55: 161–177.

Light, R. and Georgakis, S. (2005a) 'Taking away the scary factor: Female pre-service primary school teachers' responses to game sense pedagogy in physical education', *Higher Education in a Changing World: Research and Development in Higher Education*, Volume 28. Annual International HERDSA conference proceedings, University of Sydney, (pp. 271–277).

Light, R. and Georgakis, S. (2005b) 'Integrating theory and practice in teacher education: The impact of a Games Sense unit on female pre-service primary teachers' attitudes toward teaching physical education', *Journal of Physical Education New Zealand*, 38(1): 67–80.

Light, R. and Georgakis, S. (2007) 'Preparing primary school pre-service teachers to teach physical education through a focus on pedagogy', *ACHPER Healthy Lifestyles Journal*, 54(1): 24–28.

Light, R. and Kentel, J. A. (2010) 'Soft pedagogy for a hard sport: Disrupting hegemonic masculinity in high school rugby through feminist-informed pedagogy', in M. Kehler and M. Atkinson (eds) *Boys' Bodies*, New York: Peter Lang Publishers.

Light, R. and Kirk, D. (2000) 'High school rugby, the body and the reproduction of hegemonic masculinity', *Sport, Education and Society*, 5(2): 163–176.

Light, R. and Nash, M. (2006) 'Learning and identity in overlapping communities of practice: Surf club, school and sports clubs', *Australian Educational Researcher*, 33(1): 145–162.

Light, R. and Wallian, N. (2008) 'A constructivist approach to teaching swimming', *Quest*, 60(3): 387–404.

Light, R., Swabey, K. and Brooker, R. (2003) *Proceedings of the 2nd International Conference: Teaching Sport and Physical Education for Understanding*, University of Melbourne Australia, available at HTTP: http://www.conferences.unimelb.edu.au/sport/proceedings/PROCEEDINGS.pdf ge=26 (accessed 11 June 2010).

Light, R. L., Curry, C. and Mooney, A. (in press) 'Game Sense as a model for developing quality physical education', *Asia-Pacific Journal of Health, Sport & Physical Education*.

Liu, R., Li, C. and Cruz, A. (eds) (2006) *Teaching Games for Understanding in the Asia-Pacific Region*, Hong Kong: Hong Kong Institute of Education.

McInerney, D. M. and McInerney, V. (1998) *Educational Psychology: Constructing Learning*, 2nd edn, Sydney: Prentice Hall.

McNeill, M., Fry, J., Wright, S., Tan, C., Tan, S. and Schempp, P. (2004) '"In the local context": Singaporean challenges to teaching games on practicum', *Sport, Education & Society*, 9(1): 3–32.

McNeill, M., Fry, J., Wright, S., Tan, C. and Rossi, T. (2008) 'Structuring time and questioning to achieve tactical awareness in games', *Physical Education and Sport Pedagogy*, 13(3): 231–249.

McNeill, M., Fry, J. and Wright, S. (2010) 'Children's perspectives on conceptual games teaching: A value added experience', *Physical Education and Sport Pedagogy*, 15(20): 139–158.

Mahlo, F. (1974) *Acte tactique en jeu* [Tactical action in play], Paris: Vigot.

Martens, R. (2004) *Successful Coaching*, 3rd edn, Champaign, IL: Human Kinetics.

Mauldon, E. and Redfern, H. B. (1969) *Games Teaching: A New Approach for the Primary School*, McDonald and Evans Ltd.

Memmert, D. and Harvey, S. (2008) 'The Game Performance Assessment Instrument (GPAI): Some concerns and solutions for further development', *Journal for Teaching in Physical Education* 27(2): 220–240.

Memmert, D. and Roth, K. (2007) 'The effects of specific and non-specific concepts on tactical creativity in team ball sports', *Journal of Sport Sciences*, 25: 1–10.

Mitchell, S. A. and Oslin, J. L. (1999) 'An investigation of tactical transfer in net games', *European Journal of Physical Education*, 4: 162–172.

Mitchell, S. A., Oslin, J. L. and Griffin, L. L. (1995) 'The effects of two instructional approaches on game performance', *Pedagogy in Practice – Teaching and Coaching in Physical Education and Sports*, 1: 36–48.

Moeran, B. (1986) 'Individual, group and *seishin:* Japan's internal cultural debate', in T. Sugiyama and W. P. Lebra (eds) *Japanese Culture and Behaviour*, Honolulu, HI: University of Hawaii Press.

Mosston, M. (1972) *From Command to Discovery*, Belmont, CA: Wadsworth.

Mosston, M. and Ashworth, S. (1986) *Teaching Physical Education*, 3rd edn, Columbus, OH: Merrill.

Oslin, J. L., Mitchell, S. A. and Griffin, L. L. (1998) 'The Game Performance Assessment Instrument (GPAI): Development and preliminary validation', *Journal of Teaching in Physical Education*, 17(2): 231–243.

Pearson, P., Webb, P. and McKeen, K. (2006) 'Linking Teaching Games for Understanding and quality teaching in NSW secondary schools', in R. Liu, C. Li and A. Cruz (eds) *Teaching Games for Understanding in the Asia-Pacific Region*, Hong Kong: Hong Kong Institute of Education.

Phillips, D. C. (1997) 'Coming to grips with radical social constructivism', *Science and Education*, 6: 85–104.

Pill, S. A. (2007) *Play with Purpose: A Resource to Prepare Teachers in the Implementation of the Game-centred Approach to Physical Education*, Hindmarsh, South Australia: ACHPER Australia.

Pope, C. (2005) 'Once more with feeling: Affect and playing with the TGfU model', *Physical Education and Sport Pedagogy*, 10(3): 271–286.

Richard, J.-F. and Godbout, P. (2000) 'Formative assessment as an integral part of the teaching–learning process', *Physical and Health Education Journal*, 66(3): 4–10.

Richard, J.-F., Godbout, P. and Gréhaigne, J.-F. (1998) 'The establishment of team-sport performance norms for grade 5 to 8 students', *Avante*, 4(2): 1–19.

Richard, J.-F., Godbout, P., Tousignant, M. and Gréhaigne, J.-F. (1999) 'The try-out of a team-sport assessment procedure in elementary and junior high school PE classes', *Journal of Teaching in Physical Education*, 18(3): 336–356.

Richard, J.-F., Godbout, P. and Gréhaigne, J.-F. (2000) 'Students' precision and reliability of team sport performance', *Research Quarterly for Exercise and Sport*, 71(1): 85–91.

Rink, J. (ed.) (1996) 'Tactical and skill approaches to teaching sport and games', special issue of *Journal of Teaching in Physical Education*, 15(4).

Rink, J. (2001) 'Investigating the assumptions of pedagogy', *Journal of Teaching in Physical Education*, 20: 112–128.

Roberts, J. (2011) 'Teaching Games for Understanding: The difficulties and challenges experienced by participation cricket coaches', *Physical Education and Sport Pedagogy*, 16(1): 33–48.

Rossi, T., Fry, J. M., McNeill, M. and Tan, C. W. K. (2007) 'The Games Concept Approach (GCA) as a mandated practice: views of Singaporean teachers', *Sport, Education and Society*, 12(1): 93–111.

Rovegno, I. and Dolly, J. P. (2006) 'Constructivist perspectives on learning', in D. Kirk, D. Macdonald and M. O'Sullivan (eds) *The Handbook of Physical Education*, London: Sage.

Rovegno, I. and Kirk, D. (1995) 'Articulations and silences in socially critical work on physical education: Toward a broader agenda', *Quest*, 47: 447–474.

Saito, A. (1996) 'Social origins of cognition: Bartlett, evolutionary perspective and embodied mind approach', *Journal for the Theory of Social Behaviour*, 26(4): 399–421.

Siedentop, D. (1994) *Sport Education: Quality PE through Positive Sport Experiences*, Champaign, IL: Human Kinetics.

Slade, D. (2010) *Transforming Play: Teaching Tactics and Game Sense*, Champaign, IL: Human Kinetics.

Strean, W. B. and Holt, N. L. (2000) 'Coaches', athletes' and parents' perceptions of fun in youth sports: Assumptions about learning and implications for practice', *Avante*, 6(3): 83–98.

Tan, S., Wright, S., McNeill, M., Fry, J. and Tan, C. (2002) 'Implementation of the games concept approach in Singapore schools: A preliminary report', *Review of Educational Research and Advances for Classroom Teachers*, 21(1): 77–84.

Thorpe, R. and Bunker, D. (2008) 'Teaching Games for Understanding – Do current developments reflect original intentions?', paper presented at the fourth Teaching Games for Understanding conference, Vancouver, BC, Canada, 14–17 May.

Thorpe, R., Bunker, D. and Almond, L. (eds) (1986) *Rethinking Games Teaching*, Loughborough: Loughborough University of Technology.

Turner, A. (2005) 'Teaching and learning games at the secondary level', in L. L. Griffin and L. I. Butler (eds) *Teaching Games for Understanding: Theory, Research and Practice*, Champaign, IL: Human Kinetics.

Varela, F. J., Thompson, E. and Rosch, E. (1991) *The Embodied Mind: Cognitive Science and Human Experience*, Cambridge, MA: MIT Press.

Vygotsky, L. S. (1978) *Mind in Society: The Development of Higher Psychological Processes*, Cambridge, MA: Harvard University Press.

Wade, A. (1967) *The F.A. Guide to Training and Coaching*, London: Heinemann.

Wall, M. and Côté, J. (2007) 'Developmental activities that lead to dropout and investment in sport', *Physical Education and Sport Pedagogy*, 12(1): 77–87.

Wallian, N. and Chang, C.-W. (2007) 'Language, thinking and action: Towards a semio-constructivist approach in physical education', *Physical Education and Sport Pedagogy*, 12(3): 289–311.

Webb, P., Pearson, P. and McKeen, K. (2006) 'A model for professional development of Teaching Games for Understanding in NSW', in R. Liu, P. Pearson and K. McKeen (eds) *Teaching Games for Understanding in the Asia Pacific Region*, Hong Kong: Hong Kong Institute of Education.

Wein, H. (2001) *Developing Youth Soccer Players*, Champaign, IL: Human Kinetics.

Weinberg, R., Tenenbaum, G., McKenzie, A., Jackson, S., Anshel, M., Grove, R. and Fogarty, G. (2000) 'Motivation for youth participation in sport and physical activity: Relationships to culture, self-reported activity levels, and gender', *International Journal of Sport Psychology*, 31: 321–346.

Weiss, M. R. (1995) 'Children in sport: An educational model', in S. M. Murphy (ed.) *Sport Psychology Interventions*, Champaign, IL: Human Kinetics.

Wiggins, G. P. (1993) *Assessing Student Behavior: Exploring the Purpose and Limits of Testing*, San Francisco: Jossey-Bass Publishers.

Wright, J. and Forrest, G. (2007) 'A social semiotic analysis of knowledge construction and games centred approaches to teaching', *Physical Education and Sport Pedagogy*, 12(3): 273–287.

Wright, S. C., McNeill, M. C. and Fry, J. M. (2009) 'The tactical approach to teaching games from a teaching, learning and mentoring perspective', *Sport, Education and Society*, 14(2): 223–244.

Zessoules, R. and Gardner, H. (1991) 'Authentic assessment: Beyond the buzzword and into the classroom', in V. Perrone (ed.) *Expanding Student Assessment*, Alexandria, VA: Association for Supervision and Curriculum Development.

INDEX